WITHDRAWN
From Bertrand Library

WOMEN IN CONTEMPORARY
INDIA AND SOUTH ASIA

Women in Contemporary India and South Asia

Edited by
ALFRED de SOUZA

MANOHAR
1980

© Indian Social Institute 1980
First Published November 1975
Reprinted March 1977
Second Revised Edition July 1980

Published by
Ramesh Jain
Manohar Publications
2, Ansari Road, Daryaganj
New Delhi-110002

Printed by
Ashokas Press
New Deihi-110005
at Rashtravani Printers
New Delhi-110064

*To the men and women who contributed
to the continuous publication
for 30 years, 1951-80
of*
SOCIAL ACTION

Acknowledgements

This revised second edition was possible because of the unstinted cooperation of several women and men scholars who have worked in the countries of South Asia but are located in Asia, the United States and Britain. This edition differs from the first in significant ways, not the least being its broader scope with regard to both theme and geographical coverage. Several papers in the first edition have been replaced by important papers on methodological issues in the study of women in South Asia, and on the changing social and economic situation of women in Pakistan and Bangladesh. Apart from the introductory paper, two papers focus on the methodological refinements required to eliminate sex-biases in census and research data; three papers discuss the complex question of female participation rates in the urban and rural labour force. The remaining seven papers focus on the social, cultural and legal variables which affect the overall status of women, particularly their social and occupaational mobility, patterns of marriage and family environment, freedom of movement and diversity of life styles.

It is a great pleasure to acknowledge my indebtedness to all the contributors who were always most cooperative. I am particularly grateful to Stan D'Souza for help and advice. I have also to thank Ms Loretta Saldanha, Aleyamma Mathews and vi *Acknowledgements*

Vimala Kuriakose for their assistance in preparing the manuscript. As always, it was a pleasure to work with Ramesh Jain, the publisher.

Alfred de Souza

Indian Social Institute
New Delhi

Contents

	Acknowledgements	v
	Women in India and South Asia: An Introduction *Alfred de Souza*	1
1.	The Data Base for Studies on Women: Sex Biases in National Data Systems *Stan D'Souza*	31
2.	The Study of Women in South Asia: Some Current Methodological and Research Issues *Andrea Menefee Singh*	61
3.	Trends and Structure of Female Labour Force Participation in Rural and Urban Pakistan *Nasra M. Shah and Makhdoom A. Shah*	95
4.	Family Status and Female Work Participation *Victor S. D'Souza*	125
5.	Women in Bangladesh: Food-for-Work and Socio-Economic Change *Marty Chen and Ruby Ghuznavi*	141
6.	Women and the Law: Constitutional Rights and Continuing Inequalities *Joseph Minattur*	165
7.	Women and Religion: The Status and Image of Women in Some Major Religious Traditions *Ursula King*	179

x   Contents

8. Muslim Women in Uttar Pradesh: Social Mobility and Directions of Chauge
Zarina Bhatty 199
9. Purdah and Public Space
Ursula M. Sharma 213
10. Etiquette among Women in Karnataka: Forms of Address in the Village and the Family
Helen E. Ullrich 241
11. Asian Women in Britain: Strategies of Adjustment of Indian and Pakistani Migrants
Verity Saifullah Khan 263
12. The Aging Woman in India: Self-Perceptions and Changing Roles
Sylvia Vatuk 287

Select Bibliography 311
Index 321

Contributors

Zarina Bhatty lectures in Sociology at the College of Jesus and Mary, New Delhi

Marty Chen is Executive Assistant, Women's Programme, Bangladesh Rural Advancement Committee, Dacca

Stan D'Sauza is Demographic Scientist at the International Centre for Diarrhoeal Disease Research, Dacca

Victor S. D'Souza is Head of Department of Sociology, Punjab University, Chandigarh

Ruby Ghuznavi is Bangladesh Delegate to Terre des Hommes (Switzerland)

Verity Saifullah Khan is Director, Linguistic Minorities Project at the Institute of Education, London University

Ursula King lectures in Comparative Religion at the Univsrsity of Leeds

Joseph Minattur is Professor of Law, Cochin University, Kerala

Nasra M. Shah is Senior Fellow, East-West Population Institute, Hawaii

Makhdoom A. Shah is Associate Specialist, School of Public Health, University of Hawaii

Ursula M. Sharma lectures in the Department of Sociology and Social Anthropology, University of Keele xii *Contributors*

Andrea Menefee Singh has been Consultant to the Population Council, UNICEF and other UN agencies

Alfred de Souza is Director, Indian Social Institute, New Delhi

Helen E. Ullrich is in the Department of Oriental and African Language and Literature, University of Texas at Austin

Sylvia Vatuk is Professor of Anthropology at the University of Illinois at Chicago Circle

Women in India and South Asia: An Introduction

Alfred de Souza

At the mid-point of the UN Decade for Women: Equality, Development and Peace, we are now in a position to see that the World Conference for the International Year of Women in Mexico, 1975, stimulated a world-wide movement which has steadily gained momentum. While progress in improving the quality of life of women throughout the world, particularly in the developing countries, has at times appeared to share the 'invisibility' that characterises women in the rural areas and the informal urban sector, some substantial progress has been achieved that could form the basis of more effective implementation of the major goals of the UN Decade for Women—to improve the overall status of women by eliminating inequalities between men and women in education, employment, nutrition and health, and participation in economic and political decision making, and to integrate them at every level in the process of national planning for development.

However much one may debate the extent or quality of improvement that has resulted in the situation of women because of the UN Decade for Women, there is no doubt that certain changes have taken place that are of permanent value in any strategy to change the conditions that continue to keep women in situations of inferiority, dependency and exploitation. There are four major areas in which substantial progress has been achieved in increasing our understanding of the social and cultural factors that affect the status of women.

First, there has been the growth of a critical approach to traditional data sources on women, particularly women belonging to the lower income groups. It is now generally recognised that census data require to be corrected for distortions brought about by the social and cultural stereotypes regarding the different facets of women's status in society. As a result of this critical examination of census data and micro-level research, more reliable information is likely to be made available that could form the basis of both national policy and programmes for women. As Stan D'Souza suggests, 'a basic understanding of women's status and role in her country as well as the particular stage of her family-life cycle are important prerequisites for the collection of quality data on women that can be utilised for planning purposes'.* Second, in view of the increasing recognition of the linkage between research, national policy and programmes oriented to women, greater stress is now placed on full and accurate statistics on women. Further, more and better data are sought not so much to provide a framework for marginal welfare services for women but rather to situate them firmly in economic planning and national development.

Third, the widely shared perception that women in any particular country constituted a homogeneous category is now being questioned since groups of women differ from each other not only in demographic characteristics but in distinctive patterns of behaviour that are determined by social and cultural factors such as caste, region and religion. Fourth, the preoccupation with quality data on women has also led to a deeper understanding of the structural factors that operate in maintaining the exploitation of women and the denial of equality of opportunities in education, employment and political participation.

Within this broad framework of continuity and change this paper will be concerned with introducing the reader to the major issues related to the status of women in the countries of South Asia, namely, education, employment, marriage and the family,

*The references given in the footnotes are to sources other than the papers in this volume.

the cultural context of women's life and work, migration, and the specific methodological problems involved in the study of women in the sex segregated societies of South Asia.

Methodological Issues

The Report of the Committee on the Status of Women in India noted the 'paucity of data' on important social and economic indicators related to women—occupation, education, economic conditions and participation in economic and political decision making.[1] This lack of full and accurate statistics on women is found not only in India but also in Pakistan, Bangladesh and Afghanistan. The main sources of data on women are the censuses, national surveys and micro-level research studies. The census data have often produced a distorted picture of women, particularly of their participation in the economy and the labour force, because of the biases introduced by sex based stereotypes and also by the assumption, as Stan D'Souza observes, that 'data collection methods applicable for men will automatically suit women'. For example, cultural and social stereotypes regarding the concept of head of household has given rise to unreliable data and serious under-reporting of the economic contribution of women in agriculture and in the informal urban sector. Singh reports that in a recent study of self-employed women in the resettlement colonies of Delhi a very small proportion of women were considered primary earners although 81 per cent of them stated that they worked to provide basic support to their families. Thus, she points out, the dependency assumption that a woman cannot be a primary earner as long as there is an adult male in the household tends to make household surveys underestimate the economic contribution of women to the household.

The study of rural women in Bangladesh who were participating in the food-for-work programme reveals that 50 per cent of these women were the chief income earners in their families

---

1. *Towards Equality: Report of the Committee on the Status of Women in India* (New Delhi: Department of Social Welfare, Government of India, 1974).

and some of them supported the whole family—in one case, her father and siblings and, in another, an invalid husband and children for several years. Apart from under-reporting the economic activity of women in the rural areas and in the informal urban sector, planning for social welfare services tends to overlook the fact that household heads, particularly in developing countries, are often widows who may have institutional support but often find themselves, as Stan D'Souza notes, 'in tragic circumstances even if theoretically they should be held in high respect'. Further, divorced and separated women, lack institutional support and social acceptance and yet, as we see from the study of rural women in Bangladesh by Chen and Ghuznavi, they are often heads of households and solely responsible for the maintenance of the family.

Migration data in South Asia for rural-rural and rural-urban flows in which women are represented in large numbers, is usually ascribed to marriage or 'association'. Only recently has such data been questioned since it appears to be a conclusion linked to sex based stereotypes regarding economically active women. Several research studies on the micro-level, as noted by Singh, show that women also tend to migrate for economic reasons and not merely because of marriage and association.

Census data provide unreliable data on women largely because women interviewers have not been used in the data collection process. The practice of obtaining information on the work done by women from a male member of the household leads to under-reporting of the activity of women particularly those who are engaged in part-time work. The use of female enumerators, as Stan D'Souza reports, contributes greatly to the improvement of the quality of data and, on the basis of his experience with the Afghan Demography Survey, he found 'the extra financial involvement—as women had to go in pairs or required a male guide—was more than compensated for by the type and quality of data obtained'. He further stresses the importance of a mix of male and female professionals among both 'users' and 'producers' of data so that a fruitful dialogue could be set up between these two separate groups. Shah and Shah provide a telling example of how the overall activity rates of women in Pakistan, when they were reported by women themselves, were twice as high as when a male respondent reported on female economic activity. Cultural norms and social practices which determine the expectations and behaviour of women require data collection methods and tabulation procedures to be sensitive to the changing roles of women in society. Thus, as Shah and Shah point out, 'there is a great need for specially designed methodological studies aimed at assessing the quantum of female participation in various activities in order to undertake effective human resource planning, development and utilisation'.

It is commonly recognised that there is need of using qualitative techniques in order to refine data particularly on women's work. Stan D'Souza has highlighted the importance of 'time use' surveys which, though they are costly and require experienced interviewers, are 'useful for obtaining a more realistic estimate of actual work schedule in societies where cultural norms inhibit married women from being recorded as being economically active'. A fine example of the richness of information that becomes available through 'time use' techniques can be seen from Chen and Ghuznavi's report on rural women in Bangladesh whose activities, according to conventional data collection methods might appear to be economically insignificant.

> The Bangladeshi village woman is busy from before sunrise until after dark. She rises early to wash the previous night's dinner dishes and to prepare and serve breakfast. After breakfast, she must care for the milch animals and poultry, fetch water, and clean the house and kitchen. There are spices to be ground, fruit trees and vegetables to be tended, clothes to be washed. Some part of each day is spent processing rice. Threshed paddy must be boiled and then spread on a bamboo mat in the open air to dry. The parboiled paddy must then be husked and winnowed before being cooked and eaten. At least one half day a week goes into husking the family's weekly paddy requirements. At harvest time, the village woman must also thresh, winnow, dry and store large quantities of rice. She prepares the rice storage bins, separates some paddy for seed. The village woman stores and sprouts the seed (not only for paddy but

also for wheat, pulse, and oil seed crops). She collects fuel and water, makes implements (including the mud stove on which she cooks), cleans and repairs the house and kitchen. In weaving and fishing communities, village women contribute substantially to the work load by making nets and spinning thread.

The critical evaluation of data on women from census operations, national surveys as well as conventional micro-level research is making scholars and social planners increasingly aware of the limitations of present data collection and tabulation procedures. At the same time, new research techniques sensitive to women's special requirements as well as more data are needed to broaden our understanding of various aspects such as the dynamics of occupational and social mobility of women, the relationship between changing family structures and the status of women particularly with respect to freedom of movement, choice of occupation and the role of kinship as a support structure for women migrants in the informal urban sector. This information is important because cultural and social stereotypes generate data which, when used in planning programmes and services specifically oriented to women, tend to reinforce rather than transform the subordinate and inferior status of women in the sex segregated societies in South Asia.

Employment and Income

The disadvantaged situation of women in the labour market is a consequence of their position in the social system, particularly their almost total exclusion from the structures of decision making and power. It is within this structural framework that the institutional and historical aspects of discrimination against women workers in society and in the labour market can be better understood. The sex typed labour market which has, until recently, been taken for granted, is opposed to equality of opportunity understood in a comprehensive sense to include equality of employment, training and promotional opportunities. In this sense it is not possible in the sex segregated labour market whose structures ensure that the career patterns of women will normally be marked by discontinuity, unlike the normal male career patterns which assume continuity.

Because of the constraints of the sex segregated labour market women tend to cluster in a limited range of occupations, which have low status and are poorly paid. As a consequence of the concentration of women in a limited range of occupations, women are forced to compete with women for limited job opportunities and this also has the effect of driving down the wage rate. In India as in other countries of South Asia, women are less likely than men to continue their education to higher levels and are more likely to be found concentrated in female occupations like teaching, nursing, social work, secretarial and clerical occupations—all of which have low status and low remuneration. Even those women who have surmounted the hurdles to professional education are disadvantaged as women because of the difficulty of reconciling the competing, and sometimes incompatible, demands of a professional career with culturally defined family responsibilities.

In Pakistan educated women are clustered in two or three professions, the most important being teaching and nursing. Among the reasons why educated women in India and South Asia tend to cluster in a limited range of occupations are preferences based on cultural definitions of employment considered appropriate for women. In addition, as Stan D'Souza points out, women are restricted to the arts stream of education whereas men are more evenly spread over arts and science. In countries such as Pakistan, as Shah and Shah suggest, the occupational concentration in two or three professions is 'largely because of sex segregated educational facilities and the strict preference for female doctors and nurses'.

Because of occupational segregation, education is more directly linked with occupation in the case of women than it is for men, though the level of education is not correlated in a linear fashion with propensity to enter the labour market. The relationship between employment, education and status of the family is a complex one and, as Victor D'Souza shows from a study of women in Chandigarh, there is a curvilinear relationship between female work participation and the education of women. The remarkable association between the occupational prestige of wives and husbands leads him to consider the asymmetry hypothesis or family status consistency, according to which a wife tends to enter an occupation which is almost equal in prestige to that of her husband's or slightly inferior to it. If the wife is not able to fulfil this condition her tendency is to withdraw from the work force. Thus, this study suggests that legislation on the right of women to work and to equal employment opportunities may not be effective if the social structural factors are not taken into account.

It is largely in the context of women in professional careers that the issue of the conflict between marriage and career has been considered. In the countries of South Asia marriage is universal and it is difficult for women to remain single or to combine marriage with career. Apart from the general expectation that all wives must be housewives, it has been noted that 'when occupational sacrifices have to be made, the wife is usually happy to be the one to make them, subordinating her own career to that of her husband's'.[2] It has been widely assumed that household chores are the responsibility of the wife, irrespective of whether she is employed outside the home for the benefit of the family. In effect, with the belief that child-rearing and housework are 'women's work', women are compelled to manage two full-time jobs with little or no support of the husband. In a study[3] of the role conflict experienced by nurses, social workers and researchers in Delhi with regard to their family responsibilities, it was found that all these women experienced the greatest difficulty in combining their professional work with their role as *mother*.

Two approaches have been suggested for the resolution of the conflict experienced by working wives. One is to reorganise the traditional division of work in the home so that husband and wife share in the rearing of children and the various household tasks which so far have been considered to be female

---

2. Jessie Bernard, *Social Problems at Midcentury* (New York: Holt, Rinehart and Winston, 1957), p. 350.

3. Rama Kapur, 'Role Conflict Among Employed Housewives', *Indian Journal of Industrial Relations*, 5 (July, 1969), pp. 39-67.

Introduction 9

work. A pioneering effort in this direction was made by Szalai[4] through 'time-budget' studies to document the prevailing sexual division of labour within the home in several developed countries. His general conclusion was that, when the wife is employed outside the home, there is a tendency for the husband to help her in the housework. As a result, there is a trend in urban-industrial societies towards a 'symmetrical family' in which a more equitable sexual division of labour prevails. He reports that a time-budget study of ten countries with regard to child care activities showed that fathers were only minimally involved in the basic child care services of feeding, washing, clothing and other tasks such as playing, talking or walking with the child or supervising schoolwork. 'Mothers, be they full-time employed women or housewives, have no choice except to do all the rest'. Szalai notes that working women adjust to this inequitable distribution of parental tasks by having recourse to 'preferences and prejudices about feminity'. In India traditional concepts about women's work persist and, according to Kapur,[5] the tendency of husbands to act on the belief that household jobs and child care are the wife's duty, is one of the 'most significant factors' in marital discord. Though the tasks associated with housework and child care are looked upon as women's work, it is likely that husbands in the countries of South Asia will be under increasing pressure to assist their employed wives. It seems doubtful, however, if the 'symmetrical family' will develop in the near future in cultural settings such as India because, apart from the cultural attitudes to the wife-mother role, women themselves in the prevailing system of arranged marriage tend to find their emotional fulfilment in the mother-son relationship.[6]

The second approach to the resolution of the conflict between

4. Alexander Szalai, 'The Situation of Women in the Light of Contemporary Time-budget Research' (United Nations: E/CONF./66/BP/6, 15 April, 1975).

5. Promilla Kapur, *The Changing Status of the Working Woman in India* (New Delhi: Vikas Publishing House, 1970), p. 27; *Draft Plan of Action*, n. 102.

6. Aileen D. Ross, *The Hindu Family in its Urban Setting* (Toronto: University of Toront) Press, 1967), p 177; See also M.S. Gore, *Indian Youth: Process of Socialisation* (New Delhi: Vishwa Yuvak Kendra, 1977).

family responsibilities and employment outside the home is to consider working wives as a 'special employment group' and to reorganise the conditions of work. Some suggest that employers should provide working wives with flexible working hours, housing facilities, transport and facilities for child care. These improvements in the conditions of work within the existing pattern of occupational segregation, it is believed, could ease the working wives' burden of two full-time jobs. Even if this were so, it is not often realised that career patterns of high status that are tailored to male life styles are a pervasive source of inequality because they discriminate against women who have family responsibilities and force them into female occupations.[7] In view of this institutionalised inequality in the structure of occupational opportunities, it seems unrealistic to expect relatively minor changes in working conditions to widen the scope of occupational choice and career mobility for working wives.

Largely because of the difficulty of reconciling the demands of employment outside the home with family responsibilities, large numbers of educated women tend to take up part-time employment which is seen by many, including women themselves, as a solution to this problem. However, as recent studies[8] show, part-time employment has severe consequences for career advancement and tends to perpetuate the image of women as lacking in commitment to career responsibility and employment in the way in which men are. Part-time employment also leads to the exploitation of women since their income appears to be merely supplementary and therefore employers tend to underpay such work. If women are part-time workers this also affects their participation in trade union activity and they do not enjoy the same protection, notwithstanding protective social legislation in industrial work. Thus, although the value of protective social legislation for women in industry is recognised, it is being increasingly recognised that protective

7. *Education and the Working Life in Modern Society* (Paris: Organisation for Economic Cooperation and Development, 1975), p. 16.
8. See *Women Workers and Society: International Perspectives* (Geneva: International Labour Office, 1976).

legislation tends to lead to the deterioration of wages of women workers and to lower paid work.

Largely because of cultural perceptions regarding the mobility of women in the public domain, women in the informal urban sector and in the rural areas have a decided preference for self-employment in the home. In Pakistan, as Shah and Shah point out, tailoring, spinning, carpet weaving tend to be popular occupations for both rural and urban women because they can be practised within the home. However, the preference to work at home tends to place these women outside the scope of protective social legislation and opens them to systematic exploitation. In a study of women in North India, Sharma found that the preference for tailoring in the home forced women to accept much lower remuneration than tailors who sat and stitched in the village shops. As Sharma points out, 'women literally pay for their public invisibility'; and, because they have to depend on a male intermediary, they become more vulnerable to exploitation.

The tendency of South Asian women to prefer self-employment within the home is also seen among Indian and Bangladeshi migrant women in Britain. These migrant women are exploited when they work at home because they are poorly paid and are unprotected by legal norms affecting wages or working conditions. Employment opportunities in the handicrafts industry have been vigorously promoted as a home industry for women in South Asia. However, there has been a failure to take into account the structural determinants of employment in handicrafts as a home industry. Thus, the handicrafts exported to the developed countries are the products of sweated labour and though women are given employment and earn an income that is useful for maintaining the family, it is the middlemen who benefit. The conventional notion that to support handicrafts as a cottage industry is to promote the employment of women and to eliminate poverty in South Asian countries is quite unrealistic since the handicrafts industry thrives on the exploitation of women workers.

Another way to solve the conflict between work outside the home and family responsibility is the provision of day care centres and creches. In a study of day care for the urban poor in Delhi[9] it was found that creches were indeed a social necessity even for women belonging to the lowest income groups. Even housewives used the creches because this enabled them to engage in a variety of unpaid work that had important economic implications for the well-being of the family. However, it is not yet clear from the little research that is available, if separation for long hours from the mother is detrimental to the development of the child. If creches are combined with structural changes in the labour market women will be in a better position to combine family and occupational responsibilities; yet it would seem that decisions related to day care facilities for working women look on the creche and other arrangements for child care more from the point of view of the convenience of the mother than the development needs of the child.

In the countries of South Asia between 70 and 80 per cent of the total female work force is employed in agricultural activities either as cultivators or farm labourers. Women usually perform unskilled or semi-skilled task that are poorly paid but they are also involved in different ways in dairying, poultry and gardening. Rural women have not only to do their share of subsistence farming for the survival of the family but they are also entirely responsible for the female tasks of child care and housework. Very little attention has been paid by social planners to improving the social situation of the rural woman. For example, it has been pointed out that agricultural extension services are directed to men though women are heavily involved in agricultural production and marketing. Instead of formal education that is largely irrelevant to their needs, the situation of rural women could be improved if they are given opportunities for informal education in production, marketing, nutrition, hygiene, cooking and basic child care skills.[10] In the sex typed division of labour in the village, women are primarily responsible for the supply of water for drinking and other needs of the

---

9. Alfred de Souza, *Children in Creches: Day Care for the Urban Poor* (New Delhi: Intellectual Publishing House, 1979).
10. See *Women in India: A Compendium of Programmes* (New Delhi: Women's Welfare Division, Department of Social Welfare, 1975).

family.[11]

Largely because of the methodological limitations of census and research data, women in the agricultural sector have been 'invisible' and their important social and economic contribution appears on the surface to be unproductive work. Unfortunately the definitional changes in the 1971 Census led to the underestimation of the involvement of women in the agricultural sector because of the exaggerated emphasis it gave to full-time workers. Several studies[12] have shown that in India and Bangladesh, for example, women in the agricultural sector may work 12 to 15 hours—much longer than men who are full-time agricultural labourers or cultivators. Chen and Ghuznavi report that 50 per cent of the women who participated in a food-for-work scheme in Bangladesh were the sole income earners for their families, each of them having an average of 3.7 dependants. These women were committed to work—'It is not work that I am afraid of, but the lack of it'. one woman said—nevertheless they tend to be less 'visible' than men because men are 'visible' as paddy growers whereas women tend to be 'invisible' as paddy processors in the *bari*.

In the rural sector there is also a sex typed division of work though this may undergo changes in response to new technology and occupational changes because of migration and urbanisation. Ullrich reports that in a village in Karnataka, South India, Divaru women were heavily involved in agricultural work which was specialised: men did the ploughing and women the sowing and transplantation of rice. Chen and Ghuznavi report that in food-for-work programmes in Bangladesh when women worked in mixed gangs men dug the earth and the women carried and dumped it; but in female gangs women dug, carried and dumped the earth. In a study of an urbanised village

---

11. George Macpherson and Dudley Jackson report that a village in northern Tanzania had been supplied with about 32,000 gallons of water annually by village women and children who carried it in four gallon containers from a pipe nearly a mile away from the village, 'Village Technology for Rural Development: Agricultural Innovation in Tanzania', *Internatianal Labour Review*, 111 (February 1975), p. 112.

12. See, Shanti Chakravorty, 'Farm Women Labour: Waste and Exploitation', *Social Change* (March-June, 1975).

on the outskirts of Delhi, Vatuk found that the care of milch animals was relegated to women though in the village it was the task of men. Apart from sex typed occupational activities among rural women in South Asia, there is also, Palmer points out, 'a clear class stratification among rural women with some leaving the fields and confining themselves to the home, others working on family homesteads, others landless labourers'.[13]

Education

According to Standing[14] 'empirical research has so far not adequately demonstrated any consistent association between education and female labour force participation'. Studies by Nath[15] on the 1961 Census data and by Singh on the 1971 Census data suggest that women's participation in the labour force tends to decline with increase in literacy. In fact Singh states that 'those women with the least amount of education, whether gained in the formal system or not, were the ones most likely to work'.[16]

The relationship between education and propensity to participate in the labour force tends to be non-linear for women with high educational attainments. Several reasons for this have been suggested such as the operation of the asymmetry hypothesis or that relatively few job opportunities are available to higher educated women or else that, while jobs may be available and women may have even the skills for them, these employment opportunities are not used because of cultural preferences.

13. Ingrid Palmer, 'Rural Women and the Basic Needs Approach to Development', *International Labour Review*, 115 (January-February, 1977), p. 99.
14. Guy Standing, 'Education and Female Participation in the Labour Force', *International Labour Review*, 114 (November-December, 1976), p. 295.
15. Kamla Nath, 'Female Work Participation and Economic Development: A Regional Analysis', *Economic and Political Weekly*, (May 23, 1970).
16. Andrea Menefee Singh, 'Rural-Urban Migration of Women Among the Urban Poor in India: Causes and Consequences', *Social Action*, 28 (October-December 1978), p. 332.

Standing[17] suggests the alternate hypothesis of 'sexual dualism' which he explains as follows:

> To the extent that there is a dualistic development of human potential based on sex, women are likely to be increasingly channelled into secondary jobs (when they are not discouraged from participation in the labour force altogether), largely because of their limited access to education and training. Because lack of training and on-the-job experience keeps their productivity low, moreover, the initial discrimination against them is reinforced by 'statistical' discrimination. In this way employers come to regard women workers in general as having low productivity and a lower degree of labour force commitment than men, so that they discriminate against women in general and screen workers on the basis of sex, preferring to hire men even when an individual woman seeking employment may have a high level of education, training and labour force commitment. A cumulative pattern of discrimination is thereby gradually built up which forces large numbers of women into low-status, secondary jobs and induces a status frustration effect among the educated.

Even in the informal urban sector where educational opportunities may be available to girls and women the perception of female education as unrelated to improvement either in wages or in conditions of work or occupational mobility leads to parental unconcern for the education of girls. Since in the case of girls primary education is not significantly related to occupational improvement and may even create problems with regard to marriage, the urban poor readily limit education for girls even when opportunities are available. In families belonging to the middle and upper classes of the society, there is greater use of access to education but even here there is a tendency because of cultural reasons to opt for the kinds of education related to female types of employment. Thus cultural and religious influences may determine not only access to educational oppor-

---

17. Standing, op. cit., p. 294.

tunities but indirectly employment opportunities and the very propensity to participate in the labour force.

The interest in women's education increased as a result of studies on the relationship between education and fertility. In sex segregated societies in South Asia, Papanek[18] notes, there is a preoccupation with the sexual and reproductive behaviour of females. Allowing for variations of behaviour across regions and between higher and lower castes, it is generally true that in India and South Asian societies a woman's sense of personal worth is related to her fertility performance and the social standing she achieves as a mother of sons. The typical Indian woman, Mandelbaum[19] points out, 'knows of no acceptable alternative role for herself than that of wife-mother' and the 'mark of her success as a person is in her living, thriving children'. By the time she has completed her reproductive span an Indian woman has an average of five to six live births. Chen and Ghuznavi report that the average Bangladeshi woman has eight pregnancies and six live-born children. In the rural areas where the economic advantages, of having many children, particularly sons, is widely recognised, high fertility becomes less a personal choice of the woman than an outcome of a combination of socio-economic factors such as poverty, high infant mortality, the requirements of the family work force and old age security. In a study of aging women in an urbanised village near Delhi, Vatuk reports that great effort goes into the preparation for old age, and the first step is to have a son to care for one's needs in old age; various alternative arrangements are made if there are only female children such as remarriage, adoption or the taking of a *ghar jamāī*.

High fertility in a sex segregated society affects the status of women in several ways. First, the birth of the first child at a very early age and repeated pregnancies combined with malnutrition lead to high maternal mortality and fetal wastage. The maternal mortality rate (1971) was estimated at 376 for 100,000

18. Hanna Papanek, 'Men, Women, and Work: Reflections on the Two-Person Career', in Joan Huber (ed.), *Changing Women in a Changing Society* (Chicago: University of Chicago Press, 1973), pp. 90-110.
19. David G. Mandelbaum, *Human Fertility in India* (Berkeley and Los Angeles: University of California Press, 1974), p. 16.

live births; in Bangladesh one-third of all adult female deaths were maternally related. Second, women are so completely tied down by child care, housework and agricultural labour that few options are open to them for their personal growth apart from their main role of wife-mother. Third, since such a high value is attached to the reproductive function, formal education tends to be seen as irrelevant for girls who are destined for marriage and motherhood at an early age. Though the mean age at marriage for females in India is reported to have increased from 16 years in 1951-61 to 18.3 in 1961-71, girls continue to be married before puberty and, especially in the rural areas, the age at effective marriage is at least two or three years lower than the mean.[20] This pattern of early marriage and the attitude to female education is largely responsible for the high female illiteracy rate. According to the 1971 Census, the literacy rate for females was only 18.7 per cent in contrast to 39.5 per cent for males.

In Indian cities, excluding the urban slums, it has been found that high school education for girls is significantly associated with smaller family size.[21] Though education of women has tended to raise the age at marriage and lower the birth rate, it has not brought about any radical change in the traditional pattern of arranged marriage with dowry. In a study of three villages in the Punjab that was made to assess the impact of education on marriage, caste and occupation, Bhatnagar[22] found that most of the educated villagers were in favour of intercaste marriage and marriage without dowry, but in actual practice there was not a single intercaste marriage in these villages and in all cases dowry was accepted. In a study of Indian students, Cormach found that girls were ready to go to college and mix with boys but they wanted their parents to arrange their

---

20. *Country Statement: India* (Bucharest: World Population Conference, 1974); A.P. Barnabas, 'Population Growth and Social Change', in Anthony A. D'Souza and Alfred de Souza (eds), *Population Growth and Human Development* (New Delhi: Indian Social Institute, 1974), pp. 57-66.

21. Mandelbaum, op. cit.

22. G.S. Bhatnagar, *Education and Social Change* (Calcutta: The Minerva Associates, 1972).

marriage. 'Many want new opportunities, old securities; new freedom, old protection'.[23]

Apart from the fact that viable alternatives to arranged marriage are not easily found in a sex segregated society, it would appear that arranged marriage is an important mechanism for ensuring compatibility of life styles of husband and wife within the framework of caste and religious norms regarding the traditional roles of men and women within the family.[24] Though educational and occupational opportunities are providing women with new roles outside the home, their social position in the family remains largely unchanged because the system of arranged marriage reasserts the authority of caste norms and the obligation of conformity to the traditional image of woman as wife-mother with low ritual status. It seems most unlikely that the requirement of dowry will be discontinued with the education and employment of women. The problem of dowry is rooted in the system of arranged marriage and, while it may provide the bride with security and facilitate upward social mobility, it also encourages a view of woman as a commodity with a market price that varies according to her education and complexion and the boy's occupation.

Marriage and the Family

In South Asian countries marriage is universal and there has been a tradition of early marriages particularly for females.[25] The mean age of marriage in India, 1891-1971, shows a steady increase in the age at marriage from 19 to 22 years of age for males and 12 to 17 years of age for females. This has also been the case in Pakistan where the mean age at marriage for both males and females has increased from 21.5 to 23.1 years for males

---

23. Margaret Cormach, *She Who Rides a Peacock* (Bombay: Asia Publishing House, 1961), p. 109.

24. See Papanek, op. cit.; Cormach, op. cit., p. 128.

25. For a fine analysis of South Asian data on this theme, see Stan D'Souza, 'Fertility Implications of Nuptiality Patterns in South Asia', *Social Action*, 29 (October-December, 1979), pp. 341-76.

and 13 to 15.5 years for females over the period 1921-61. In Bangladesh the mean age for males was 24 years in 1974 compared to 15.9 for females. In all these countries the age at marriage tends to be higher in the urban than in the rural areas.

The recent (1978) amendment to the Child Marriage Restraint Act has increased the legal age of marriage for males to 21 and females to 18. However, legal deterrents notwithstanding, the percentage of child marriages continues to be high and Vatuk reports that the majority of old women she studied in an urbanised village near Delhi were married before the age of 12 or 13 and consummated their marriage within two or three years. Several of the women who participated in the food-for-work programme in Bangladesh contracted child marriages. One women was barely six years old when she was married while her husband was nine years of age. Another woman in this group was married when she was ten years old. However, the age of marriage tends to rise not only with residence in urban areas but also according to position in the system of social stratification. A study[26] of a group of divorced women reported that the average age at marriage of 25 women belonging to the upper middle class was 21.9 years whereas for 25 women belonging to the lower middle class the average age at marriage was 19.

Since society in South Asia is sex segregated, most marriages are arranged and this preference is carried over by Indian and Pakistani migrants when they migrate to other countries. Khan notes that the preference of Asian migrants in Britain for the 'sons to have an arranged marriage with a girl from home', is a 'preference for a less independently-minded, domestically orientated and submissive girl'. In the system of arranged marriages many of the traditional social and cultural factors which affect the status of women come into play and reinforce the patterns of behaviour that tend to restrict their freedom of movement and social mobility and life styles. As Singh notes, 'The system of arranged marriages appears to be at the core of the society's ability to sustain traditional images and roles for women,

26. Rama Mehta, *Divorced Hindu Woman* (New Delhi: Vikas Publishing Huose, 1975).

despite revolutionary changes in the economic and political spheres of the wider society'.

A distinctive feature of arranged marriages is dowry, or 'mehr' among Muslims, and in recent years there have been several case of women who have committed suicide or been harrassed for reasons related to dowry. Minattur observes that 'a large number of young men and their parents consider dowry a legitimate stepping stone to higher rungs in the social ladder and possibly a passport to domestic comfort, if not happiness'. One of the women in the food-for-work programme in Bangladesh stated that her daughters had been divorced and deserted because 'I have no money to buy the radios and watches demanded by my sons-in-law. They expect dowry and have no sense of social obligations. The sons-in-law if they cannot get anything material out of you do not stay with your daughters. Marriages have become very unstable'.

Because arranged marriage is an alliance between families rather than between individuals, divorce and remarriage lack social acceptance. Though there is provision for divorce in Indian legislation it is relatively more difficult for the wife to divorce her husband. As Minattur points out, a single isolated act of adultery by the wife is a valid ground for granting a divorce to her husband. But if the wife is to be granted her petition for divorce she has to prove not merely adultery but also an additional ground such as desertion or cruelty. Among the upper class Muslims divorce carries a social stigma but this is less so for women belonging to the lower social strata. In a study of Muslim women in Uttar Pradesh Bhatty found that divorce and remarriage after divorce were more frequent among non-Ashrafs than among the Ashrafs.

While the ideal pattern of the family in the sex segregated societies of South Asia continues to be the joint family, in actual fact a high proportion of families, both in the rural and the urban areas tend to be nuclear in composition. The structure of the family has important implications for the status of women particularly with respect to education, life styles and entry into the labour market. In the informal urban sector a majority of the women live in nuclear families, yet, a recent study of migrant women in the *bastis* of Delhi reported that 'more than half of the women interviewed said that they considered the joint family the ideal, viewing it as a source of togetherness, protection, help in time of crisis and economic and social security.'[27]

Since relations within the family have great significance for the status of women rather than their participation in the formal social, economic and political institutions of society, it is important to examine the distribution of power within the domestic domain. Particularly in the joint family there is a feminine division of labour and, according to Vatuk, the daughter-in-law works *inside* the home concerned with a variety of tasks oriented to the welfare of the family and personal service of her mother-in-law. Usually, when the daughter-in-law enters the family, she takes over most of the domestic tasks formerly done by her mother-in-law. On the other hand, the mother-in-law takes up family tasks outside the home such as shopping. In a study of Muslim women in Uttar Pradesh there was also a division of household responsibilities among non-Ashraf families that had improved their economic situation. Among such families the daughter-in-law who was formerly working the oil press or self-employed as a vendor in the village streets withdrew into *purdah* to become a prestige symbol while the mother-in-law continued to work outside the home.

Just as among the women in the household there is an unequal distribution of work and power between daughter-in-law and mother-in-law, so too is there an imbalance of work and power in the household between husband and wife. Even when women are employed outside the home they have to combine the double work-load of occupation, housework and child rearing without, however, enjoying a corresponding increase of power in decision making within the family. It has been pointed out that the perception of disparities in labour productivity—the wife in housework and child-rearing and the husband in agri-

---

27. See Andrea Menefee Singh, 'Women and the Family: Coping with Poverty in the *Bastis* of Delhi', in Alfred de Souza (ed.), *The Indian City: Poverty, Ecology and Urban Development* (New Delhi: Manohar, 1978), p. 71.

culture or industrial occupation—fosters the operation of the principle of unequal exchange in the productive relations within the household.[28] Within the household unit the relationship between the husband and wife is characterised by dominance and dependency and this is particularly seen in decisions regarding the disposition of family income. Because child care and housework are attributed low productivity and are consequently devalued, the wife appears to be totally dependent on the productive activity of the husband.[29] On the other hand, even when the wife is working outside the home, her income is perceived as being supplementary and uncertain and therefore not related to the basic needs of the family. Because of this perception of the income of the working wife, it is understood within the family that should she withdraw from the labour force, the family would depend on the primary income derived from the occupation of the husband. Because of this the wife's employment outside the home seems 'voluntary', unlike her husband's, which appears to be essential and this reinforces the ideology of the woman as a homemaker.

In the rural areas where women are also engaged in productive work outside the home, their work also is associated with low productivity largely because they have to spend several hours in child care services. In the food-for-work programme in Bangladesh women were unable to meet the performance norms set for men not merely because of biological differences but because women had other demands on their time. Thus while men were able to average 70 cft of earth moving daily women averaged only 44.5 cft. As Chen and Ghuznavi observe, 'part of the difference reflects the fact that women cannot work as many hours a day as men because they have household responsibilities, which include the care of men and children'. It must also be noted that even when women are fully occupied in agricultural tasks with men, the allocation of power in the

---

28. Palmer, op. cit.
29. See Pauline Hunt, 'Cash-Transactions and Household Tasks: Domestic Behaviour in Relation to Industrial Employment', *Sociological Review*, 26 (n. 3, August 1978).

rural household continues to be unequally distributed between husband and wife. The reason for this, as Palmer[30] notes, is that tasks outside the home such as marketing and negotiations with financial institutions for credit are monopolised by men so that, even though they may work less hours than women in agriculture, their contribution seems much more valuable. In this situation where women tend to be excluded from the benefits of marketing, technology and training, it is important, Palmer[31] suggests, to create 'institutions specifically directed at women as producers and not merely as procreators or dieticians or child care practitioners'.

Cultural context

The family is the social context in which girls are socialised in their roles of dependency which they will later carry out after they are married and have a family. Since the transmission of culture is the prerogative of women they tend to be instruments for the maintenance rather than the transformation of values, norms and patterns of behaviour. Within the family it is the women who perpetuate the preference for a male child though there may also be valid economic reasons for this. In the countries of South Asia the status of a woman is enhanced when she becomes the mother of a son and this cultural and economic preference is seen to have serious implications not only for the status but even the survival of females. A study of infant mortality in North India, found that post-neonatal mortality seems to be strongly sex specific and is much higher for females than for males. It suggested that 'this pattern may reflect cultural practices and patterns of nutrition which place lower priority on female than male children'.[32] Census data also showed a declining sex ratio in India (females per 1000

---

30. Palmer, op. cit.
31. Ibid., p. 105.
32. George Simmons et al., 'Some Aspects of Infant and Child Mortality in Rural North India', in Alfred de Souza (ed.), *Children in India: Critical Issues in Human Development* (New Delhi: Manohar, 1979), p. 104.

males) but this did not evoke much comment until recently.[33] As Stan D'Souza points out, the declining sex ratio revealed in successive censuses in India cannot be explained merely by under-enumeration but should be interpreted in the light of the social and cultural devaluation of women in society.

The socialisation of women in the family and in the school reinforce 'gender roles', that is, cultural definitions of the traits and behaviour that are considered appropriate for men and women. As a subordinate group in society women, it has been suggested, have internalised 'self-sacrificing' and 'expressive' values and developed a 'false consciousness' which includes 'beliefs in the appropriateness of lower pay and of eschewing leadership positions and politics'.[34] Thus women are expected to seek occupational roles which stress the aspect of service and cooperation with men, not competition. It is interesting to note that Gandhi whose salt campaign, he believed, had brought thousands of women 'from their seclusion and showed that they could serve the country on equal terms with men', expressed a strong belief in woman as the 'embodiment of sacrifice', and that 'equality of the sexes does not mean equality of occupation'.

The socialisation of women is influenced by the diversity of caste, region and religion. Ullrich's analysis of the forms of address used by women in a village in Karnataka show how three basic forms of address used by women express dimensions of ritual and economic power and reinforce the basic social divisions in the village as well as their hierarchical character. Within the family the relative position of the women is discussed with reference to the ways Havik Brahmin and Divaru wives address their husbands. In the Havik family the husband has complete authority in the running of the household in decisions regarding marriage and even food. The wife regards her

---

33. See Vina Mazumdar and Kumud Sharma, 'Women's Studies: New Perceptions and the Challenges', *Economic and Political Weekly*, 14 (January 20, 1979).

34. Wilma R. Krauss, "Political Implications of Gender Roles: A Review of the Literature', *The American Political Science Review*, LXVIII (December, 1974). pp. 1706-1923.

husband as a personal god and is completely submissive to him. Though Havik women tend to view their identity in terms of their husbands, there is tendency among educated younger Havik women to be more independent. Divaru women, on the other hand, are in charge of their household, work with their husbands in the fields and have no inhibitions about criticising their husbands in public. The more egalitarian relationship between Divaru husband and wife is reflected in the use of a common term for both boys and girls whereas among Brahmins the terms for male and female children are distinct. Ullrich's analysis suggests that the changes taking place in the forms of address are reflected in the changing relationships between the various caste groups that are moving from the more strictly hierarchical to what is more egalitarian.

The process of socialisation which encourages women to have a poor self-image of themselves and to relate to the men-folk in the family in terms of dependency is seen in the cultural modes of expression which identify women in terms of their husbands, rather than by their own name. In Bangladesh, the social and economic dependency of rural women is expressed through kinship terms such as *bou* (wife), *maa* (mother), *bhabi* (brother's wife). Thus one of the women engaged in a food-for-work programme in Bangladesh was called Samed Khaner *Bou* (Samed Khaner's wife) although her husband had died 15 years ago. As a result of their experience in the food-for-work programme many of these women who had been socialised to economic and social dependency were able to manage efficiently the role of sole supporter of the family, much to their surprise. As Chen and Ghuznavi explain it, 'these women have fallen out of the traditional social web into a state of enforced independence. . . . Nothing in their upbringing or the rural economy prepares them for this independence or to be sole supporters'.

Another important factor which affects women's self-perception and maintains traditional images in spite of social and economic change, is religion. All religions, King suggests, are facing a new challenge. Women who have attained sexual equality with men in the secular sphere are questioning the secondary status accorded to them in the major religious traditions of the world. Women have not always and everywhere been excluded from active participation in religious life as can be seen from the presence of women magicians, healers, seers and priestesses in both primitive and ancient religion. With the institutionalisation of religious roles in the higher religions, sacred authority, like secular authority, was invested in man and the exercise of religious functions became a male prerogative. This regressive trend can be found in all the major religious traditions—Hinduism, Jainism, Buddhism, Islam and Christianity. King's examination of the image of women leads to a threefold conclusion: whenever the ascetical ideal gained ascendancy in a religion, the position of women deteriorated; no religion appears to have a model that corresponds to contemporary women's self-understanding; and an adequate theology or religious interpretation is only possible if both men and women participate in its elaboration.

The participation of women in the religious sphere is complex since a popular religious tradition may provide women with greater scope for self-expression in rituals and other religious practices than the 'great tradition' which tends to restrict the participation of women in the religious sphere to rituals in the private or domestic domain. Thus religion acts as an important cultural factor which reinforces the ideological perception of women as subordinated and under male control.[35] In a variety of ways religion also tends to provide support for the system of *purdah* (seclusion of women), elements of which are to be found in all the countries of South Asia. In sex segregated societies where interactions between men and women are influenced by considerations related to the society norms of the *purdah* women, as Sharma notes, 'experience social space as divided into zones of differential danger or risk'. In this system of evaluation of private and public space, domestic space is considered to be a woman's place and within it the kitchen is 'the moral centre of the household . . . even if

---

35. For an interesting discussion of the Hindu perception of woman in the roles of wife and mother, see 'Women and the Hindu Tradition', by Susan S. Wadley in Doranne Jacobson and Susan S. Wadley, *Women in India: Two Perspectives* (New Delhi: Manohar, 1977).

(the woman) spends much of the day at work outside the home'. Because the kitchen is the 'epitome' of domestic space women have the fundamental duty of supervising the cooking and serving of food. Thus it would seem that because of cultural perspectives influenced by the values of the *purdah* society, strategies to bring about greater balance in the distribution of housework between men and women in the domestic domain may not be the most effective way to enable working women to reconcile occupational and family responsibilities.

Apart from religion, the pattern of socialisation within the family and the range of occupations available to women are limited by factors such as caste and region. As we have seen above, various studies have shown how the range of occupations available to migrant women in the informal urban sector are determined not so much by their availability as by cultural considerations related to religion, caste and region.[36] The requirements of *purdah* place great barriers to social mobility and freedom of movement of women in the countries of South Asia. Saleha who was involved in the food-for-work programme in Bangladesh said she was embarrassed at first to work in the open. She said, 'I worked in the fields at night, by moon light, or at times when there is the least likelihood of being seen'.

This cultural requirement that women should not of seen by unrelated men influences the occupational behaviour of women even when they migrate to Western countries such as Britain. Both at home and abroad the tendency is to prefer occupations, as Bhatty and Khan point out, in which they will be able to work with other women and, if possible, of the same ethnic group. It is this notion that encourages women to prefer cottage industries, even though they are exploited, to work outside the home. While some form of segregation prevails in the Western industrialised and Asian countries, religion, caste and regional influences tend to act in a cumulative

36. T. K. Majumdar, 'The Urban Poor and Social Change: A Study of Squatter Settlements in Delhi', in Alfred de Souza, *The Indian City*. op. cit.

fashion to exclude women from the public domain which is monopolised by men who dominate its economic, social and political institutions.

Conclusion

The persistence of traditional images of women in India and other countries of South Asia tends to mask the significant changes that are taking place in the self-understanding, values and roles of women whatever their position in the social structure. A female landless labourer in Bangladesh is reported by Chen and Ghuznavi to have recalled that her mother had no need 'to step out of her secure home for anything'; yet these women had broken with traditional roles and expectations by participating in the rural wage economy. As one of them said: 'People with empty stomachs do not have to worry about social norms. If begging does not hamper my self-respect, why should hard work erode my dignity'? In her study of women in rural Karnataka, Ullrich reports that 'While the old model where the woman is helpless and incapable of managing on her own is true for many older women, younger women have become much more independent'. Even in the tradition-bound sphere of religion, King asserts that 'at present no religion can offer an adequate model for contemporary women's self-understanding'.

Nevertheless, the significant social and economic contribution women, particularly those in the rural and informal urban sector, make to society tends to be as 'invisible' as the women themselves and it is hardly taken into account in social, economic and educational planning and policies at the national level. Particularly in the countries of South Asia, the problems women experience in employment cannot be considered in isolation from the social and cultural context, nor must their solutions be considered the sole responsibility of women. The new trend for both urban and rural women to unite in interest groups for organisational strength is important not only because it may make the implementation of social legislation more effective, but also because it could initiate a process of re-education of the women themselves who are pressured by early socialisation and social institutions to accept their own exploitation. Yet, for women's movements to be successful, the family, educational, economic and political institutions and society must collaborate in creating a social environment in which women will be able to enjoy genuine freedom and equality of opportunity.

1 The Data Base for Studies on Women: Sex Biases in National Data Systems*

Stan D'Souza

In connection with the Mexico Conference held from 19th June-2nd July 1975, a World Plan of Action was drawn up in order to realise the objectives of the International Women's Year. Paragraphs 161-169 of this plan—later endorsed by the General Assembly Resolution (XXX)—stress the importance of research, collection and analysis of data on women and the role the UN could play in this task.[1]

An interim report (dated July 30, 1976) on the 1980 World Population and Housing Census prepared for the 19th Session of the Statistical Commission held in New Delhi from 8-19 November 1976, took note of the problem of sex based stereotypes, particularly in connection with the concepts of 'heads of households' and the 'economic activity of women'.[2]

---

*The author wishes to thank Mr. W. Seltzer and Ms. B. Diamond of the UN Statistical Office, New York for their assistance in the preparation of this paper. He also wishes to thank the editor, Dr. Alfred de Souza, for his helpful comments and valuable suggestions. The secretarial services of Ms. Loretta Saldanha are gratefully recognised. The views expressed in this paper are those of the author and do not represent necessarily those of the United Nations Statistical Office or of any agency.

1. UN Declaration of Mexico, Plan of Action (New York: United Nations World Conference of the International Women's Year, June 19-July 2, 1975).

2. UN Social and Demographic Statistics, 1980 World Population and

At its 19th Session the Statistical Commission, 'agreed that all possible precautions should be taken so that the use of concepts or methods involving sex based stereotypes would not prejudice census results. In that connection, the problem posed by the term 'Head of Household,' in a number of countries was noted. The concept was largely out-of-date in the context of modern social and labour force conditions in many countries. The Commission agreed that whatever solutions were developed for that or other problems the census instructions for enumerators should be clear and should not leave any room for variations in interpretation by individual enumerators.'[3] Incorporating suggestions made at the 19th Session an 'Interim Report of the United Nations Recommendations for the 1980 Population and Housing Census' was prepared by the UN Statistical Office which was circulated to member States in 1977. Paragraphs 26-29 of the Report deal with the question of sex-based stereotypes.[4]

Meanwhile the Economic and Social Council resolution 2061 (xii) of 12th May 1977 called on the United Nations Statistical Commission to continue action aimed at the improvement of the data base for measuring implementation of the objectives of the International Women's Year. It requested 'The Statistical Commission at its twentieth session, as a contribution to the success of the United Nations Decade for Women: Equality, Development and Peace, 1976-1985, to continue its action in co-operation with national statistical offices, regional commissions, and inter-governmental organisations, organs of the United Nations and the specialised agencies, especially the International Labour Organisation, the United Nations Educational, Scientific and Cultural Organisation, the World Health Organisation and the Food and Agriculture Organisation of the United Nations. . . .'

Housing Census Programme, Report of the Secretary General (New York: United Nations. E/CN. 3/480, July 30, 1976).

3. UN Statistical Commission. Report on the 19th Session, Supplement No. 2/E/CN. 3/500 (New York: United Nations, November 8-9 1976).

4. Interim Report of the United Nations: Recommendations for the 1980 Population and Housing Censuses (New York: United Nations, ST/ESA/STAT 71, 1977).

The effect of the Mexico Conference document was felt in other UN agencies too. The UNFPA, which is responsible for funding a variety of projects in the population area found it necessary to provide 'guidelines' that would be utilised for its programme. The guidelines stress that a major area of the UNFPA activities is data collection and analysis; it is very important to collect full and accurate statistics on women—particularly on their occupation, levels of education, economic conditions and their effectiveness in social, economic and political decision-making. The revision of discriminatory legislation and the distribution of social welfare benefits are two examples where accurate and complete data have a considerable impact on improving the status and conditions of women.[5]

This paper presents material from a consultancy report[6] with a focus on developing countries in general and S. Asian countries in particular. The examples presented in this paper are not intended to reflect adversely the situation in any particular country. They are given as illustrations which statisticians in other countries would find useful for tabulation purposes or to unearth similar problems in their own country. On the whole, while statistical centres were ready to assist in the development of better techniques for the collection of data on women's characteristics, the general impression given was that this did not constitute one of their central priorities. In fact, one encountered concern about the quality of data on women only when one visited specialised research institutes within the country.

5. UNFPA, Women, Population and Development, Guidelines for Programme Development Project Formulation, Implementation and Evaluation (New York: UNFPA N/76/119/Rev. I, January 1977).

6 'Sex Biases in National Data Systems' December 1978 by Dr. Stan D'Souza. This consultancy report based on visits to 17 countries from Asia, Africa, Europe, North and South America has been prepared on the question of sex biases for the UN Statistical Office. The purpose of the visits was not intended to make an evaluation of the statistical activities of particular countries but rather to obtain information regarding relevant practices which will be useful to other counties tackling the same problem of sex-based stereotypes and its effect in national data systems. The report has been recommended for distribution to the member countries by the 20th session of the UN Statistical Commission, held in New York from 20th February to 2nd March 1979, and may be published as a technical report.

This could be due to the fact that 'users' of data and 'producers' constitute two separate groups and a dialogue between them does not always exist. While statistical organisations were awaiting concrete and practical requests for data on women, women's organisations were often unable to specify their needs.

Producers tend to insist on continuity of time series whereas users, facing rapid changes in society, require complex tabulations of data at levels that are usually not available through census producers. Some of the elements required to monitor progress of women are of a qualitative nature and as such do not fall within the framework of national statistical data collection systems. While most of the statistical centres in the developed countries have the resources and technical capacity to initiate studies on better collection of data on women, the same cannot be said of some of the developing countries visited. Outside assistance may in fact be necessary for such countries. Such assistance has been forthcoming for fertility surveys. The measurements of woman's status in society, her economic activity etc., form a range of problems wider than a mere study of her fertility-capacity. The assumption that data collection methods applicable for men will automatically suit women is open to serious doubt. This does not imply that such methods have been designed for men only but cultural and social stereotypes exist distorting both data collection methods and tabulation procedures. A basic understanding of women's status and role in a country as well as the particular stage of her family-life cycle are important prerequisites for the collection of quality data on women, that can be utilised for planning purposes.

The Report of the Committee on the 'Status of Women in India' has pointed out problems that exist in national data sets on such questions as employment.[7] In Pakistan hard data in the women sphere are also not available.[8] The situation in

---

7. *Towards Equality:* Report of the Committee on the Status of Women in India (New Delhi: Department of Social Welfare, Government of India, December 1974).

8. Miriam Habib, 'Pakistan Women in Transition,' paper presented at

Bangladesh and Afghanistan is not much brighter. The problems facing statistical centres in developing countries are diverse. These centres often lack technical and administrative staff. Due to financial constraints, transport and other logistic support are far from adequate. At the technical level, maps and cartographic inputs are of poor quality. It is against such a background that these countries will have to determine their priorities in terms of collection of better data on women. Census and national surveys are the main sources of data. The registration of vital events is often lacking or at best fractional in its coverage. Some topics are now considered that are mainly relevant to data collection on women in developing countries.

The topics to be discussed will be presented under three broad headings. In the first section, the measurement of some demographic characteristics are dealt with. These characteristics are—sex ratio and age, head of household, household and family, marital status, education and migration. Some of the problems associated with indirect estimation—methods, relevant to data on women, are also mentioned. In the second section problems related to the measurement of economic activity of women are cited. Under methodological problems, four areas of underenumeration are indicated—agricultural farm workers, unpaid family workers, female workers in the informal urban sector and the non-farm rural sector. Time use surveys are discussed as a possible method to reduce some of the biases in the data. In the third section the question of staffing patterns of national statistical offices is raised. It is proposed that the use of women at all professional levels would go a long way to ensuring better data collection on women. Finally some conclusions are drawn, which while requiring scrutiny at the operational level of each country, do indeed surface as appropriate at a general level for the countries considered. A note on the terminology used is appropriate: *Sex based stereotypes:* A preconception, often cultural, regarding the role, status etc., of a person based on sex; *Sex biases:* Biases which are sex based, occurring in measurements.

the Pakistan Administrative Staff College Seminar, Lahore, October 1975.

1. Measurement of Demographic Characteristics

Sex ratio and age

Demographic data in developing countries are defective for both men and women. However, sex biases do exist in such data and some of the problems are discussed here. The sex ratio (number of males per 100 females) is high in several countries belonging to the Indian sub-continent. The Bangladesh census of 1974 shows a sex ratio of 108. The Afghan Demographic Survey (1971-73) estimated the sex ratio at 116. Reasons for these high values remain obscure in many countries and could be due to under-enumeration of females or higher female mortality. In fact, the 1974 Bangladesh data show age-specific under-enumeration of females e.g., those in the marriageable age group.[9] Higher female than male mortality has been noticed in connection with Afghan data. In India, the sex ratio has been increasing steadily. Studies would indicate that under-enumeration alone is not sufficient to explain this phenomenon. In fact, some authors believe that the improvement of health standards of females in India is not advancing at the same pace as that of males.[10] These countries could be exceptions. In several ESCAP countries there has been a post-war rapid decline in mortality especially of females. Changing sex-ratios with implications for future social, political, and economic status of women could result. Studies in Africa show that reported sex ratios do not necessarily represent the actual balance of the sexes.[11]

The Whipple's Index is a test used to examine age preferences for '0' and '5' as compared to other digits. For Bangladesh this index shows that the data are worse for females than for males. This, of course, could be due to lower educational levels

---

9. S. D'Souza and S. Rahman, 'Estimates of Fertility in Bangladesh,' *Social Action*, 28 (n. 4, 1978), pp. 336-390.

10. M.K. Jain, 'Growing Imbalance in the Sex Composition of India,' *Demography India*, 4 (n. 2, December 1975), pp. 305-315.

11. W. Brass *et al.*, *The Demography of Tropical Africa* (Princeton: Princeton University Press, 1968).

attained by women there. The ages of women are often estimated by the interviewer on physical characteristics, as well as marital and child-bearing status.

The UN Manual[12] has noted the following typical errors in age data of females in Africa, Indonesia and the Indian subcontinent:

'1. A tendency to over-estimate the age of young children, contributing to the typical excess proportion at ages 5-9, and the relative deficit at 0-4.

2. A tendency to over-estimate the age of girls 10-14 who have passed puberty, especially if they are married, combined sometimes, but not universally, with a tendency to under-estimate the ages of girls 10-14 who have not reached puberty, causing a net transfer downwards across age 10, and contributing to the peak at ages 5-9.

3. A tendency towards over-estimation like that affecting some of the 10-14 year old, for females 15-19, 20-24 and 25-29, causing deficits at 10-14 and 15-19, and excessive proportions at 25-29 and 30-34. This over-estimation of the age of young women may be caused by an unconscious upward bias associated with marriage and child-bearing, or from a mechanical assumption that women were married at some alleged conventional age at marriage and have then experienced an allegedly typical passage of time between marriage and first birth, and in each subsequent interbirth interval.'

Head of Household

The question of sex-based stereotypes has been raised in a serious way in some ECE (Economic Commission for Europe) countries like the United States, Canada, and the Scandinavian areas with regard to the question of 'head of household'. Census questionnaires usually start with the selection of 'head

---

12. UN Manual IV, Methods of Estimating Basic Demographic Measures from Incomplete Data (New York: United Nations, ST/SOA/Series A/42, 1967), p. 21.

of household' and the relationships of the other members of the household to this person are then noted. This has been opposed in these countries by activist groups that consider the designation of 'head' a repugnant procedure smacking of authoritarianism. Against a background of protest the various statistical offices have been under pressure to experiment with a new questionnaire design that would be acceptable to the general public. In several of these countries self-enumeration is the usual practice. Census slips are mailed to various addresses and it has been a prime necessity that the questionnaire should not raise negative reactions as the whole purpose of the Census could be frustrated through increasing non-response.

In countries outside the ECE region the problem of 'head of household' has been raised in a different way. In a study of 74 developing countries it has been shown that the percentage of potential household heads who are women among the total potential household heads varies from a low ranking of 10 to 48 per cent. In these countries it is important to know whether women are heads of households, because such households have serious problems of poverty. Women heads are often widows or persons who are separated from their husbands or partners such as divorced women and single mothers.[13] Thus while the discussion in ECE countries has revolved around selection of new terminology to replace the 'head of household' concept, in some developing countries it has become an important aspect of government social welfare planning to identify the households with women heads.

The cultural setting is of great importance in many developing countries determining whether the use of the 'head of household' question can have meaningful results. In countries like Afghanistan the dominant religious factors could inhibit women being nominated as heads of households. On the other hand, in the West African countries, like Ghana, where matrilineal traditions do exist, statistical offices would find their task of recording women heads facilitated. Women in such countries have assumed important roles traditionally. In the latest

13. M. Buvinic, N. Youssef and B. von Elm, *Women-Headed Households: The Ignored Factor in Development Planning* (Washington DC, International Centre for Research on Women, 1978).

Ghana census 31.9 per cent of heads of households having children, without spouses present, are females. Due to the rapid changes in economic structures occurring in the Middle East area, and the consequent movement of males to work-sites in such countries as Saudi Arabia, *de facto* women 'heads of households' are increasing in rural areas. A similar situation is developing in Kerala where there is a large exodus of males to the Gulf area for employment.

Among the various types of women heads of households in developing countries, widowhood remains the structural position to which the greatest institutional support is accorded. A distinction, however, has to be made between the ideal system and actual behaviour. Widows often find themselves in tragic circumstances even if theoretically they should be held in high respect.

Divorced and separated women do not have well defined structural status. Institutional support or social acceptance may often be lacking. This group of women often has a heavy involvement in work for sheer necessity. In several parts of Central and South America, 'consensual' unions are common. Due to the lack of legal protection this group is often forced to assume family hardship under difficult circumstances as men can break such relationships without assuming much responsibility. The study shows that 'single mothers' form a large group in this area.[14]

Household and family

An understanding of the cultural settings in a country is important before one decides to make studies on the evolution of women's status. As a result of the cultural patterns existing in countries women may or may not undertake particular types of income generating activities. A woman's decision to work, for instance, has to be made within the context of the 'life stage' of her family whereas a man's decision under similar circumstances would be very much less restricted. The ability to measure

14. Ibid.

some of her roles, for instance her 'home role', will provide great insight into other consequences such as why women tend to have lower average income than men. The census tabulations required for the understanding of women's status are not only as 'characteristics' presented in national and international tables with breakdown by sex, but must also include tables by 'family stage' background. This would help explain, for example, why an educated woman with a degree similar to that of her husband, may in fact, opt not to work because of her preoccupation with child rearing at a particular stage of her family.

Interest in the family data is beginning to manifest itself in both affluent and less developed countries. Changes in family structures from the extended family to the nuclear family during the processes of industrialisation and urbanisation are the focus of sociological studies.[15] In many developing countries, whether in Africa or Asia, family structures are quite complex. Appropriate research indicating how census data on the household can be utilised to understand actual social realities are rarely available. In fact, some sociologists tend to bypass the whole set of data collected by the census organisation and base their inferences on micro-studies. The need for a conceptual framework that would link micro-studies with data from available censuses and national surveys has been pointed out by some authors.[16]

The Indian concept of 'joint family' is complex and many studies have been devoted to the subject. The definition of the household used for the 1971 census was 'a group of persons who commonly live together and would take their meals from a common kitchen unless the exigencies of work prevented any of them from doing so'. There may be one-member households,

---

15. The Family as a Unit of Welfare in National Planning was the theme of a recent Asian Regional Conference in New Delhi, October 17-21, 1977. See *Family As a Unit of Welfare in National Planning* (New Delhi: Indian Council of Social Science Research, 1977). In Latin America requests for 'family data' are now being expressed by research groups. See, for example, S. Torrado, *Algunas Reflexiones sobre los Censos de 1980 en la Perspective de la Investigacion Sociodemografica y las Politicas de Poblacion en America Latina* (CELADE: Santiago de Chile, April 1977).

16. A.M. Shah, *The Household Dimension of the Family in India* (New Delhi: Orient Longmans, 1973).

two-member households, or multi-member households. For census purposes each one of these types is regarded as a 'household'. Again, there may be a household of persons related by blood or a household of unrelated persons, the latter are boarding houses, hostels, residential hotels, orphanages, rescue homes, ashrams, etc. These are called 'Institutional Households'.

The definition presented above considers the concept of a household as a 'house-keeping unit'. The identification of families within households is not always simple. The latest UN recommendations distinguish between 'family' and 'census family' within a household. According to the document the 'family' is defined as 'related persons having a common budget although not necessarily living together'. On the other hand, the 'census family' is defined as 'those members of the household who are related, to a specific degree, through blood, adoption or marriage. The degree of relationship used in determining the limits of the census family is dependent upon the uses to which data are to be put and so cannot be set for world-wide use'.

The diversity of cultural conditions is thus recognised in the recommendations. In view of the changing roles of women and the family some countries have initiated studies and the development of data sets implying new conceptual frameworks.

Marital Status

A consistent feature of the censuses of the Indian sub-continent has been that the number of married women has exceeded the number of married men, usually 1005 to 1011 females per 1000 males. It would be interesting to know whether the excess is due to polygamy and/or absence of husbands at the time of census, or merely erroneous information due to cultural reasons. Perhaps women in consensual unions refer to themselves as 'married' whereas men in such unions call themselves 'single'.

The categories divorced/separated/widowed are often combined under one heading for statistical convenience. While there may be reasons for this from a tabulation point of view—the social circumstances of the women in these categories can be quite different.

Questions regarding the rising 'age at marriage' for women noticed in Sri Lanka—possibly as a result of imbalances in the number of males and females in the marriageable age groups—should be carefully studied as they can have important repercussions on fertility and population control.

Education

The level of education of women is an important indicator for the understanding of the present and future status of women in a country. Literacy rates are usually available for most countries of the world. Differences in literacy rates are quite large in the developing countries—women's rates being much lower than those of men. Conceptual differences in definitions from census to census often make comparisons difficult. School enrolment, the number of years of schooling and the highest level of education attained, are usually other educational characteristics that appear on census questionnaires.

With the impetus towards universal education successive censuses tend to show gains by women in literacy over the last decades. However, the fact that women are restricted either by choice or social customs to particular streams of education is not clearly brought out by census data.

TABLE 1
Percentage of Total Enrolment of Each Sex in Type of Secondary School Stream Forms 4-Upper 6, 1973-74 Stream

Sex	Type of Stream		
	Science	Arts	Commerce
Female	19	69	12
Male	43	48	9

Source: A. Smock, op. cit.

Table 1 taken from the Ghana Teaching Surveys, 1975 ind-i

cates that women tend to concentrate in the arts stream whereas men tend to spread more evenly over arts and science.[17]

Tabulations of this type show that even though the levels of education of women might increase in a country, their role in decision making does not really increase. The job market is open to them in very restricted areas. In some developing countries the educational system—built on Western models—tends to inhibit some of the traditional equality that may have existed in those societies.

The importance of educational standards has repercussions in various spheres of activity including the choice of enumerators for census data collection. In some countries, where teachers are selected to collect census data, the fact that the proportion of women teachers in the rural areas is low implies that mostly male enumerators are employed. This results in distortion of data in societies where women are not ready or are not allowed to meet with male enumerators, and census counts are done by the heads of households without reference to the women.

Migration

Migration studies assume great importance in developing countries where rapid and unplanned urbanisation has been generally present. The selectivity of migrants is as important as the volume. The sex ratio of migrants is rarely the same as that of the residents of the urban areas into which they migrate. In countries of South Asia rural-urban migrants are predominantly males whereas in Latin America the proportion of women in the migration stream to cities is greater than that of men. Given the unstable character of the occupations, housing etc., available to migrants, especially women, it is important that development planners have at their disposal reliable data regarding migration. In South Asia rural migration is important for women but such migration is usually

---

17. A Smock, *Women's Education in Ghana and Its Impact on their Roles: A Consultancy Report* (New York: Ford Foundation, 1978).

due to 'marriage' or by 'association'—accompanying migrant husbands. At the international level, studies on migrant women are also important. Women migrants from developing countries tend to adapt more slowly to the new cultural settings, than men, into which they have been immersed. For Asian immigrants to the UK, for instance, languages are learnt more rapidly by men due to their greater contact with the resident population, whereas women tend to be more restricted to a domestic setting.[18]

A study of migrant women in the slums of Delhi shows the limited nature of employment opportunities offered to women as compared to men. In the table below women form 87 per

TABLE 2
Occupation According to Sex of Migrants to Delhi

Occupational Category	Male Number	Male Per cent	Female Number	Female Per cent	Per cent female out of total workers
Domestic	57	9.33	372	84.35	86.7
Unskilled Labour	211	34.53	32	7.26	13.2
Semi-skilled	160	26.19	10	2.27	5.9
Skilled	80	13.09	2	0.45	2.4
Household Industry	13	2.13	6	1.36	31.6
Business	62	10.15	11	2.49	15.1
Technical Manager	16	2.62	2	0.45	11.1
Agricultural	6	0.98	4	0.91	40.0
Others	6	0.98	2	0.45	25.0
Total	611	100.00	441	100.00	41.9

Source: A.M. Singh, op. cit.

18. See V.S. Khan, 'Asian Women in Britain: Strategies of Adjustment of Indian and Pakistan Migrants' in this volume.

cent of all domestic workers. Among occupational categories, women in domestic services form 84 per cent of the total female labour force. In occupations of high prestige and income, migrant women are hardly represented. With regard to income, women worked on an average 40 hours per week as compared to 48 hours per week as men worked but their monthly income was only Rs. 75 as compared to Rs. 192 for men. Participation of migrant women in the labour force is much higher (40 per cent) as compared to resident women (5 per cent). The type of jobs available to them, however, are of the lowest status and pay.[19]

A study made in Ethiopia examined female migration into Addis Ababa along with the structure of female employment. It showed that formal labour market employment opportunities are inaccessible to the majority of Ethiopian women. The incidence of prostitution and the rate of absorption into the formal labour market are inversely related.[20]

Indirect methods

In developing countries even when serious efforts are made to collect accurate data, several problems inherent to the level of development exist, which vitiate the quality of the data. Vital registration systems hardly exist, and when they do, under-enumeration of births and deaths is quite prevalent. The heaping of average data at ages 0 and 5 as well as the omission of individuals at certain age groups have been mentioned. It is against the background of such incomplete data that indirect estimation techniques have been developed.[21] The development

---

19. A.M. Singh, 'Women and the Family: Coping with Poverty in the Bastis of Delhi', *Social Action*, 27 (n.3, July-September, 1977), pp. 241-265.

20. L. Dirasse, 'The Socio-Economic Position of Women in Addis-Ababa: The Case of Prostitution', unpublished Ph. D Thesis, Boston University, 1978.

21. The UN Manual IV shows how census data can be utilised for the estimation of birth and death rates. The use of stable and quasi-stable population methods has increased the value of inadequate census data. Further, when information on 'children ever born and children

of indirect methods does not eliminate the need for careful data collection and often conceals underlying problems due to the availability of model tables etc. A case in point is the Bangladesh Retrospective Survey on Fertility and Mortality (BRSFM) held in 1974 immediately after the 1974 Census.[22]

An important feature of the results shown in the report is that the expectation of life at birth for women is slightly higher than for men. The evidence of previous surveys and the data from the subcontinent indicate the contrary. Crucial to the results is the estimation of $2q_0$—the proportion of children dying by age 2. For the BRSFM the value of $2q_0$ is higher for males than for females. This result is open to criticism since the report itself indicates that under-reporting for female deaths is higher than for male deaths. This difference in under-reporting has not been taken into account in the estimation of $2q_0$. Since several demographic parameters depend on the choice of the stable population model, and consequently on $2q_0$, the results presented in the report must be treated with some caution.

Information on 'children ever born and children dead' is obtained by retrospective methods. Omission of female children deaths may be more frequent in countries where a higher value is placed on male children than on female children, resulting in more accurate reporting of the deaths of male children. Female deaths are often more easily forgotten. At a recent meeting on census techniques held in Beirut, Lebanon (December, 12-16, 1977) a paper dealing with the 'Census data required for indirect methods' recommends as 'second priority' breakdowns by sex of child when Brass questions are proposed.[23] In view of the fact that most of the countries in the ECWA (Economic Commission for West Asia) region have

dead'—the so called Brass questions—are available, a wide range of analytical methods can be applied.

22. Report on the 1974 Bangladesh Retrospective Survey on Fertility and Mortality (Dacca: Census Commission, Ministry of Planning, 1979).

23. K. Hill, 'Census Data Required for Indirect Methods of Estimating Demographic Parameters, 1980 Round of Censuses' (Beirut, Lebanon: ECWA, Expert Group Meeting on Census Techniques, December 12-16, 1977).

poor data on women, it would be extremely important to obtain separate mortality estimates for males and females, as first priority.

In his paper on 'Characteristics of African Demographic Data' van de Walle presents a table showing that sex ratios recorded by retrospective methods increase with the age of the mother, implying greater omission of female children by older women.[24]

TABLE 3

Observed Sex Ratios for Children Ever Born, by Age of Mother, in four African Censuses and Surveys—1940-1960

(Males per 100 Females calculated from a question on Children Ever Born asked separately for each sex)

Age of Mother	Mozambique 1940 Census*	Mozambique 1950 Census	Niger Survey, 1960	Guinea Survey, 1954-1955
14-19 yrs	103	99	101	103
20-24	101	102	104	102
25-29	104	103	105	104
30-34	106	105	108	106
35-39	108	104	103	104
40-44	109	106	108	102
45-49	112	106	112	102
50-54	111	107	118	101
55-59	118	108	119	103
60-64	118	109	110	100
65 and over	119	109	122	103

*Based on age groups 16-20, 21-25, 26-30...66 and over
Source: van de Walle, n. 11 on page 36.

Retrospective questions were used in the National Demographic Survey of Honduras.[25] Analysis of results shows that

---

24. See footnote 11 on page 36.
25. K. Hill, G. Maccio, A. Packer and J. Somoza, *National Demographic Survey of Honduras: Methodology, Results, Indirect Estimates* (CELADE: Santiago de Chile, 1977).

female infants were systematically omitted and deaths of female infants were even more seriously under-reported. The result of these omissions was that very low infant mortality rates for females were obtained. The sex differential infant mortality for this survey was 139 per thousand for males and 92 per thousand for females. Results such as these indicate the necessity for careful data collection methods as indirect estimate procedures would tend to mask underlying problems and could show apparently higher values for the expectation of life of females than males, when the reverse is in fact the case.

II. Economic Activity

Since the development of a data base to measure women's economic activity also suffers from various defects, this section will restrict itself to problems affecting data of particular concern to women. In many developing countries women's work is difficult to measure since it takes place mainly in the informal sector so that the usual methods of estimating labour force participation are not effective. In developed countries, too, the problem of measurement exists since the acceptability of such roles as 'housewives' makes it difficult to ascertain real employment. Women, who otherwise may have declared themselves as 'looking for work' find it socially convenient to declare themselves as 'housewives'. Further, given the intrinsic differences in responsibilities at different life stages between men and women—the burden of child rearing falling largely on women—and the lack of adaptation of the industrial sector to such realities as the need of child care centres etc., it is not surprising that many women may not be interested in working full-time. Measures for part-time work are not always adequate.

Reliable statistics of economic activity are a prerequisite to development planning. In developing countries the lack of an adequate data base may result in planning that fails to take into account the economic activities of substantial numbers of women. This can lead to the displacement of women workers from traditional work patterns by modernisation and large scale industrialisation. This displacement goes largely unnoticed in national statistical systems resulting in great hardship and suffering to the women concerned and consequently to their families. A recent example in South India is the setting-up of a factory for the preparation of nylon nets which threatens to displace 10,000 women workers who prepare fishing nets at home. Such displacement of women workers has also occurred in Latin America in the agricultural sector, due to the introduction of a dairy farm by a multinational corporation.[26] These modernisation programmes often have strong governmental support. Due to an inadequate data base, planners fail to realise that such 'improvement' which theoretically is intended to create employment opportunities does in fact increase the difficulties of marginal families where the income derived by the women often maintains the family above the poverty line. Against this background of social realities and the need to assess not only the benefits but also the negative or unintended aspects of industrialisation, the participation of women in the labour force has to be more effectively measured.

While international recommendations have generally been free from the effect of sex-based stereotypes,[27] at the *operational level* in various countries sex-biases have been introduced into economic activity rates of women. Special difficulties in the measurement of these rates stem from the fact that women frequently have dual activity statuses—one of 'home-maker' and another covering activities of a productive nature. In several countries these latter activities are usually 'unpaid'. The UN recommendations for this problem are clear enough—'In classifying the population by activity status, participation in economic activity should always take precedence over participation in a non-economic activity'.[28] However, sex-based stereotypes operative in countries would result in classification of

26. C.D. Deere, *The Agricultural Division of Labour by Sex: Myths, Facts and Contradictions in the Northern Peruvian Sierra* (Amherst: University of Massachusetts, Economics Department, 1977).
27. *International Recommendations on Labour Statistics* (Geneva: International Labour Office, 1976).
28. Draft Principles and Recommendations for Population and Housing Censuses (New York: UN Statistical Commission, E/CN.3/515, 20th Session, Feb 20-March 2, 1979).

women engaged in dual activities, as 'home-makers', especially if women perceived 'home work' as their main activity. A further difficulty stems from the fact that the concept of 'homemaker' as a non-economic activity has been questioned. Current research is being undertaken on the subject, the scope of which is beyond the framework of this paper.[29]

Methodological problems

The levels of female economic activity are not as low as the censuses indicate. Some of the problems inherent in census data regarding the female labour force have been treated by Durand. He focuses on two areas of under-enumeration—*agricultural labour force workers* and *unpaid family workers*.[30]

Problems in the implementation of standardised concepts as well as changing definitions make international comparisons difficult and sometimes meaningless. Boserup indicates that two statistical procedures are used in developing countries regarding women. In one procedure nearly all farmers' wives are counted in the agricultural labour force resulting in the fact that about half this group is female. The other counts all farmers' wives as 'housewives'. Thus the recorded share of women in the agricultural labour force is very small. 'The use of the first system would mean that female activity rates decline in the process of urbanisation, whereas an increase would be registered if the second system were used'.[31]

With regard to unpaid family workers Durand states that 'it is especially the females who assist without pay in the work of the family farms and other family-operated enterprises, whose participation in the labour force goes to a large extent un-

29. The Feasibility of Welfare Oriented Measures to Supplement the National Accounts and Balances: A Technical Report (New York: United Nations ST/ESA/STAT/Ser. F/22, 1977).

30. John D. Durand, *The Labour Force in Economic Development: A Comparison of International Census Data (1946-1966)* (Princeton: Princeton University Press, 1975).

31. E. Boserup, *Women's Role in Economic Development* (London: George Allen and Unwin, 1970).

reported in the censuses of many countries, while it is more fully reported in others'. Differences in levels of female economic activity may be due to a 'large extent unreal-artifacts of the definitions and enumeration procedures and of reporting biases rooted in the institutions and values of different cultures':[32] Male subsistence workers are usually classified in the national labour force in developing countries. Females, however, tend to be classified differently according to particular countries.

Important areas of under-enumeration where little data exist are in the *informal urban sector* and the *non-farm rural sector*. Problems arise in the informal urban sector due to the fact that workers lack stable residence or employment. There is a great need to obtain measures of economic activity, especially in developing countries with rapid urban expansion. Special social welfare problems are common among women in this sector including the neglect of small children where child-care facilities are not available. In Delhi, female construction workers face such problems. Non-farm activity of women in rural areas is of great importance though due to cultural reasons this may be perceived as 'home work'. Handicrafts have proved to be an important source of income generated by women, though this activity has often not been recorded in the national data sets.

The census definition with the *reference period* of a week, is unsuitable for agricultural workers given the seasonality of agricultural work. It is suggested that studies be made with regard to longer reference intervals. This would also be desirable for urban areas where a high percentage of economically active women exist in unstable occupations and in family enterprises. The UN recommendations discuss the need for an additional reference period besides the one-week criterion and suggest that countries should take into account relevant regional recommendations.[33]

Serious errors arise also from *women's own perception* of their work. They identify themselves as mothers and wives. Results from a Post Enumeration Survey in Ghana after the 1960

---

32. John D. Durand, op. cit.
33. See footnote no. 4 on page 32.

Census showed 45 per cent of the women in a matched subsample as 'employed' in the PES whereas they were enumerated as 'home-makers' in the Census.[34] While these differences could be due to the fact that the PES was conducted during the 'on-season' and the census during the 'off-farming season', the instability of estimates of women's economic activity is patent.

Unemployment rates for women do not reflect accurately the pool of women who desire employment. Much of women's employment is concealed due to inadequate measurement techniques. 'To what extent it is under-recorded by the official statistics depends of course on the definition of unemployment, but it may take the form of young women dropping out of the labour force at a time when their skills would have developed. One implication is that the threat and reality of unemployment frequently encourages women to orient their lives to domesticity and what is described as economic inactivity'.[35] As some women are interested in obtaining part-time work, the development of measures of unemployment relating to 'part-time' work should receive consideration.

Census interviewers in several countries do not approach the women themselves, but only a male relative, causing distortions regarding the work done by women. The importance of using *women interviewers* for the collection of data on women should be stressed.

Female economic activity rates are usually presented at the national level. Serious efforts should be made to study labour force problems at the *regional* level, since whole countries are too heterogeneous with regard to cultural and social institutions. In Yugoslavia, for instance, in 1971 female activity rates were 40.8 in the Republic of Slovenia and 8.4 in the Republic of Kosovo. The national female activity rate of 30.7 masks the wide differences existing in the country with regard to women's participation rates. Male activity rates do not exhibit such a

34. J.G.C. Blacker, *A Critique of International Definitions of Economic Activity and Employment Status and Their Applicability in Population Censuses in Africa and the Middle East* (London: London School of Hygiene and Tropical Medicine, Centre for Population Studies, December 1977).

35. M. Darling, *The Role of Women in the Economy* (Paris: OECD, 1975).

wide difference—63.2 and 42.7 being the highest and the lowest rates.[36] Regional statistical tabulations should be available to policy makers engaged in the alleviation of some of the underlying problems facing women in backward areas of a particular country.

Time use surveys

Some of the problems mentioned show that the conceptual framework required to measure the number of women in the labour force is not identical with that of men. The ability to measure time spent on activities which may not have an overtly economic value is quite important. In developing countries researchers are becoming increasingly aware of the necessity to collect information on the allocation of time for all types of activities. Detailed time use surveys have been set up without previous judgement of what is and what is not economic activity. Such an approach is useful for obtaining a more realistic estimate of actual work schedule in societies where cultural norms inhibit married women from being recorded as 'economically active'. Thus, for instance, in some countries with Islamic culture, a male respondent might claim his wife was doing 'housework' whereas more detailed probing would show that the woman was really doing work which could be considered economic activity. Time use surveys can also produce lower estimates where erroneous classification of domestic activities as agricultural work has been made. Since women's work is often on a part-time basis such an approach often does give better results.[37]

The drawbacks of time use surveys are that they are very expensive and require highly trained interviewers. They require a lot of time to execute and can only be done on a small sampling basis. The insights, however, provided by such use could

36. Demographic Research Center, *The Population of Yugoslavia*, CICRED Series (Belgrade: Institute of Social Sciences, 1974).

37. G.M. Standing, Concepts of Labour Force Participation and Under-Utilisation, Working Paper No. 40, World Employment Research Working Papers (Geneva: International Labour Office, July, 1976).

supplement the macro-level information provided by censuses and questionnaire-type surveys.[38]

An expert group meeting (4-10 December 1977 at Tehran) on the identification of the basic needs of women of the Asian and Pacific area has taken a negative view of time allocation in their draft report entitled 'Identification of Critical Needs of Women'.[39] It thus seems appropriate to utilise time use studies to investigate work of women in countries like Ethiopia with regard to 'fetching water' etc., and rural development activities in some countries that have not taken into account that some of the 'improvements' have displaced women from traditional work or chores. National planners with adequate time-use data at their disposal would have been in a better position to arrange alternatives and more productive utilisation of women's time.

III. Staffing Patterns

In previous sections some of the biases resulting from the collection of data on women without serious reflection on the underlying difficulties in the collection of such data, have been mentioned. The cultural setting of countries and the status of women there must be understood before an efficient data collection system can be designed relating to the real requirements and needs of women. Women should be adequately represented in the long chain of professionals required in a data collection organisation—at the questionnaire-design stage, interviewers, supervisors and data processors, and finally at the analysis stage. The careful selection of such staff, sensitive to women's data requirements is an important requisite of statistical offices.

38. At the request of the Statistical Commission, the UN Statistical Office has recently prepared a report on the development on statistics of time use. See United Nations, Progress Report on the Development of Statistics of Time Use (New York: United Nations, E/CN.3/519, 18th April, 1978).

39. UN Asian and Pacific Centre for Women and Development, 'Report: Identification of Critical Needs' (Tehran: APCWD Expert Group Meeting, 9/Draft Report, December 4-10, 1977).

Women interviewers are commonly used in most of the affluent countries visited, partly because a pool of educated housewives exists, which is available for part-time work. In developing countries the use of women as interviewers is much less frequent. In the countries visited, with Islamic cultural traditions, women interviewers were employed mainly in urban areas. Since much of the population in these countries live in the rural areas, it is clear that the data collection machinery could be improved.

Afghanistan is an example of a country, where the use of women interviewers was essential to the conduct of a national demographic survey. As a census had never been taken in the country the Afghan Demographic Survey (ADS) conducted a national sample survey during the period 1971-73, to obtain estimates of population size as well as KAP type of data.[40]

When this survey was being prepared it was realised that many of the questions could not be asked by male interviewers and the use of women interviewers was considered. Several objections were raised: (1) The cultural context—a male dominated society with strong Islamic traditions—was not conducive to the use of women interviewers; (2) Afghan women had rarely worked outside their homes. Logistics were difficult as many of the interview sites were villages in the mountains; (3) Travel with male co-workers had not been done previously on a nation-wide level in Afghanistan. Further, as overnight stops would be required special provisions would be needed for lodging women interviewers.

Against this background the appropriate selection of women interviewers and supervisors did, in fact, succeed in obtaining quality data on various aspects of fertility of women in Afghanistan that hitherto were not available. Women interviewers were able to enter homes and were generally well received. The extra financial involvement—as women had to go in pairs or required a male guide—was more than compensated for by the type and quality of data obtained.

The Bangladesh Fertility Survey organised under the auspices

---

40. *National Demographic and Family Guidance Survey of the Settled Population of Afghanistan* (Kabul: Government of Afghanistan, 1975).

of the World Fertility Survey also employed women interviewers and supervisors. Preliminary results from the survey indicate that the fertility data are of better quality than has been collected previously. Similar results have been found in Pakistan where overall activity rates for women in the Pakistan Fertility Survey are much higher than those obtained from census data.[41]

In Ghana, women are being used in the Ghana Fertility Survey. My enquiry regarding the differential quality of data collected by men and women in Ghana received as response that basically there was no great difference since social mores allowed men and women to move freely in the country. The absorption of women staff employed in fertility surveys into the ordinary statistical cadre should be seriously considered.

The problems of high sex ratio in several countries including those belonging to the Indian sub-continent have been mentioned. Quality control and post-enumeration check teams which, in theory, are expected to obtain better data than census enumerators, are often similarly constituted in terms of sex composition. As a result the post enumeration check is unable to correct for sex selective under-enumeration in the areas where women tend to remain within the household when male interviewers are utilised. Female enumerators employed on a sampling basis could be of great value. Correction factors could be developed by comparing data obtained by women having entry into households with data obtained by 'proxy' methods—male interviewers who have to collect their data outside the homestead. Tabulations of post-enumeration survey data should provide breakdowns of under-enumeration by sex. Failure to do this has often meant that population totals are adjusted after a post-enumeration check but sex ratios remain distorted. Data on age of women and infant mortality can be substantially improved if some probing is done with regard to pregnancy histories. It is obvious that women interviewers would be more appropriate for such a task.

41. See Nasra Shah and Makhdoom Shah, 'Trends and Structure of Female Labour Force Participation in Rural and Urban Pakistan' in this volume.

Data on women regarding migration and economic activity are also better done by women interviewers. It is often difficult for male interviewers to have direct access to the living quarters of single migrant women into urban areas. Such women, especially in the informal urban sector, will often be missed from enumeration. With regard to economic activity, apart from stereotypes that might exist in the minds of male interviewers with regard to women's work, the ability to distinguish between housework and secondary occupations of economic significance requires types of questions or lengths of interviews that may be difficult for men to obtain from female respondents.

At the data processing and tabulation stage the use of women can ensure the problems of women are suitably highlighted. The coding of economic data, for instance, whether by occupation or industry is time consuming and coders must be convinced of the need for accurate classification of women before they would be ready to avoid the convenient stereotype of classifying women as housewives. Professional staff responsible for tabulation and for processing data are often in contact with users of data. Such staff must possess appropriate levels of sensitivity to women's problems if a dialogue with 'users' is to be undertaken since normal census tabulations are not immediately adapted to the requirement of research workers studying the status of women. The absence of women at this level can be a serious hindrance.

My visit to research centres regarding women's problems indicated that these areas are predominantly staffed by women professionals. While it is understandable that professionally trained women would be spontaneously interested in women's problems, the fact that few men are engaged in the study of such problems, means that the dialogue between 'users' (mainly women) and 'producers' (mainly men) of data is not very easy. In more than one statistical office visited, even where genuine openness existed with regard to the question of obtaining reliable data on women, it was felt that women's organisations have to specify their need for data more precisely before these organisations could focus more directly on women's questions. A 'mix' of male and female professionals in both 'user' and 'producer' institutions seems desirable.

In some statistical centres visited high-level women professionals form part of the statistical organisation. In these cases, the data collection machinery was directly open to research and experimentation on questionnaire design more in keeping with changing roles of women in society. Women, in technical positions, in statistical organisations are important for the improvements of concepts and classifications. However, in statistical offices in developing countries women professionals rarely existed except in a few countries like Brazil. This could be due to the educational biases of women in such countries, as indicated in the previous section, inhibiting women from entering statistical careers. In Brazil, as both research and data collection activities are undertaken under the overall auspices of the national statistics office, indications are that interaction between the two sets of activity was facilitated. In most countries workers tended to be independent institutions from national data collection offices. The advantage of this set-up was that they could focus on subjects of vital interests to women which had not yet necessarily become part of wider government programmes. The disadvantage of such a situation was that the research activity was often done in isolation from the national programmes and government approved plans of data collection.

IV. Conclusion

This paper has attempted to consider some of the problem areas with regard to the collection of data on women. Against the background of differing cultural, linguistic and census traditions, it would be presumptuous to present generalised solutions for the developing countries' problems. Even for the S. Asian area cultural and technical-level differences exist. However, the following points provide some conclusions that surface from the earlier presentation.

1. Data collection methods that have provided reliable data for men are not automatically capable of doing so for women. This does not imply that such methods

have been designed for men only but cultural settings and *sex-based stereotypes can inhibit the collection of accurate data.*

2. The objectives of the collection of data on men and women can also be widely different. In the case of special data on women, previously, population censuses and surveys have focused on fertility and mortality. In the context of the World Plan of Action formulated at Mexico, these objectives should be broadened to *include methods of estimating women's roles in the development process.*

3. In every country a *dialogue between 'users' and 'producers' of such data is absolutely necessary* to uncover the cultural and other problems that may prevent collection of quality data on women. While national statistical offices will remain preoccupied with large scale data collection methods like censuses and surveys, research units through micro efforts, which would include 'time use studies,' 'case studies,' and 'participation observation' methods, would be in a position to provide valuable information regarding the type of data required. New techniques would presumably evolve from such a dialogue that could link the 'representativity' that large scale methods provide with the 'depth' of micro studies.

4. The *use of women as interviewers*, especially in countries where the use of men would imply obtaining information by 'proxy,' should be encouraged. If logistic or cultural problems inhibit the use of women interviewers, at least at the Post Enumeration Survey (PES) level, women should be employed. The World Fertility Survey has shown that it is quite possible to use women interviewers even under difficult logistic conditions.

5. Tabulations of the PES should be made so that *underenumeration estimated separately by sex*—for most of the important characteristics of population and housing censuses—should be of 'first priority' in international recommendations.

6. When computer storage facilities are available, more

complex cross-tabulations should be made available when needed by research workers. In particular, *tabulations of the 'life stage' of families would provide important information for social welfare planning.* Linkages with other surveys should also be aimed at.

7. While *continuity of series* is important, rapid changes in the status of women require new data collection methods and tabulations even in countries with long census traditions.

8. *Internationally comparable concepts at the operational level should be arrived at in census data on women,* yet care has to be exercised that the cultural backgrounds of countries are taken into account both at the questionnaire and tabulation stages. The UN Statistical Office through its proposed meeting on the consultancy report could develop recommendations towards the standardisation of concepts.

A fertile ground for the application of some of these conclusions would be the 1980 round of censuses. While census pretests are already underway in several of the S. Asian countries, some modifications and possibly post-census surveys could be undertaken to eliminate sex-biases in the data. This paper has attempted to focus on specific problems of data collection on women, from a social and development-planning standpoint. The need to obtain better data on women arises both from a strictly neutral statistical point of view, and from an attempt to understand the vulnerable groups of society. The particular claims of activist groups have not been endorsed, but I have stressed the prerequisite of a good data base on which to build studies on women.

2 The Study of Women in South Asia: Some Current Methodological and Research Issues

Andrea Menefee Singh

The International Women's Year in 1975 in many ways marked an important turning point in the study of women in India and other Asian countries. Exercises, such as those carried out by the Committee on the Status of Women in India, which were aimed at putting together a basic statistical and social profile of women on a national level brought to light a myriad of problems and disturbing trends which had previously been obscured. For the first time scholars and policy-makers found their attention focused on the great majority, the women at the bottom of the status hierarchy, and the findings began to confront deeply ingrained myths and assumptions about the status and needs of women which were based largely on middle class and upper caste ideal role models. Sociological research on women, which had produced a fairly voluminous literature, had previously focused almost exclusively on role conflicts of middle class working women.

After 1975 there was a push by the Indian Council of Social Science Research (ICSSR), the research wings of social service agencies and university departments to broaden the base of knowledge of low-income rural and urban women. Now, as we approach the middle of the U.N. Decade of Women and Development, the results of some of these studies are beginning to appear, and the issues surrounding the status of women are no longer linked up to petty fears that the Western-inspired women's movement is in conflict with South Asian social and cultural norms and traditions. There is a growing data base which speaks for itself, and has begun to identify critical research and policy issues that are most relevant within the context of a developing country. Men as well as women are now making important contributions to the field of women's studies, and the study of women is no longer considered the exclusive domain of women. Economists, historians, demographers, lawyers and political scientists have joined the sociologists to contribute a broad base of expertise and knowledge about the status and needs of women. Research on women is no longer seen as simply a theoretical exercise, but is becoming increasingly policy oriented as the need is recognised for public action to reverse the trends observed over the last century towards the declining status and increasing exploitation of women.

In the following pages I would like to summarise what I consider to be some of the lingering methodological problems in the study of women in South Asia, the major social and cultural factors specific to this geographical region which need to be taken into consideration in the study of women, and the major research issues that remain to be addressed in the coming years.

Methodological issues

I think it is fair to say that most of the major methodological problems with research on women in this region are linked to deeply ingrained assumptions about their role and status. One such assumption that permeates the literature is that women are supplementary or secondary earners, and therefore their contribution to the household economy is minimal and insignificant. Because of the *dependency assumption*, i.e., that a woman is dependent on a man throughout her life (father, husband, son), data derived from household surveys frequently assume that a woman is only household head or primary earner if there is no adult male in the household.

This problem finds expression in a number of different types of studies. A recent study of self-employed women in two resettlement colonies of Delhi, for example, assumed that only 7.5 per cent of the women were primary earners because they had no adult male in the household, ignoring its own data that about 6 per cent of the husbands of married women (who comprised 86 per cent of the sample) were unemployed and 14 per cent had no husband to depend on.[1] In an otherwise fascinating study of women's migration in India based on the 1971 Census data, Premi[2] concludes that only about 3 per cent of the women who migrate do so for economic reasons. He assumes that all unmarried girls below the age of 20 have migrated with their parents for associational reasons, that widowed or divorced women below the age of 25 have returned to their parents and those above the age of 50 have moved with their sons or daughters, that married women below the age of 25 have migrated due to marriage, and married women above the age of 25 have accompanied their husbands to their place of work. Only widowed and divorced women between the age of 25 and 49, unmarried women aged 25 and above, and half of the unmarried women in the 20-24 age group are credited with economic motives for migration. Such assumptions about motives for male migration would certainly seem absurd.

Both types of studies ignore the fact that the mere presence of an adult male in the household is no proof that he provides the primary support. Ela Bhatt[3] believes that between 18 and 23 per cent of the self-employed women in Ahmedabad are sole supporters of their families, an estimate that not only includes widows, but also women with unemployed, chronically ill, handicapped, or irresponsible husbands. Her profiles of self-employed women[4] clearly show that a large proportion of them make a much larger contribution to household income than other earning members; women vegetable vendors are respon-

1. 'Report on Survey to Find Out the Occupational Structure of Self-employed Women in Resettlement Colonies of Delhi' (New Delhi: DGET, Ministry of Labour, August 1978), mimeo.

2. Mahendra K. Premi, 'Pattern of Internal Migration of Females in India' (New Delhi: Jawaharlal Nehru University, Centre for the Study of Regional Development, Occasional Papers No. 15, 1979), mimeo.

3. Ela Bhatt, personal communication, May 1979.

4. Ela Bhatt, *Profiles of Self-Employed Women* (Ahmedabad: SEWA, 1975).

sible on the *average* for 74 per cent of total household income. As for migration, a number of recent studies[5] indicate that a large proportion of women who migrate with their husbands do so because of some assurance that the wife will be able to find employment (however low the remuneration), or because of other personal resources such as the wife having kin in the place of destination who will help the family in the process of adaptation and adjustment. Single factor analysis obscures the often complex and interrelated factors involved in migration decisions for both men and women.

Another problem which continues to plague sociological and other kinds of development research is the *invisibility factor*. Urban planning agencies, for example, base their development strategies almost wholly on head counts and aggregate data which do not provide sex breakdowns even where this would have been possible, e.g., where the census provides the data base.[6] International agencies such as the World Bank and ILO which compile exhaustive statistics on income and employment around the world do not provide sex breakdowns in important areas such as employment and income in different industrial sectors.[7] Household surveys addressed to the household head (who nearly always is male due to the *dependency assumption*) end up reflecting the expressed needs and priorities of men with no thought being given to the fact that these might be very different from those of women.[8] As a result, relocation pro-

5. See, for example, Malavika Karlekar, 'Balmiki Women in the Development Process', Paper presented at the Xth International Congress on Anthropological and Ethnological Sciences, New Delhi, December 1978; Leela Kasturi, 'South Indian Domestic Workers in Karol Bagh', Paper in process of preparation for the Indian Council of Social Science Research; Ardrea Menefee Singh, 'The Impact of Migration on Women and the Family', Paper presented at the Non-Aligned Conference on Women and Development, Baghdad, May 1979.

6. Andrea Menefee Singh, 'Women in Cities: The Invisibility Factor and Urban Planning', Report prepared for the Population Council, New York, June 1979.

7. *World Development Report*, 1978 (Washington D.C.: The World Bank, August 1978); *Year Book of Labour Statistics, 1976* (Geneva: International Labour Office, 1976)

8. Town and Country Planning Organisation, *Jhuggi Jhonpri Settle-*

grammes often have the consequence of disrupting women's work-residence relationship far more than men's. A study of four resettlement colonies in Delhi in 1976 found that 25 per cent of the women had been thrown out of work because of the move compared to only 2 per cent of the men.[9] The *invisibility factor* continues to plague data collection processes, particularly in planning services and programmes which are not specifically 'women-oriented' (i.e., welfare-oriented). It is often assumed that a woman's position will improve if her husband's income increases because of the dependency assumption, an interesting variation of the now discarded theory of a 'trickle down effect' in the development process.

Although many men have begun to work with secondary data on women, their field research continues to be addressed primarily to men. Access to women's circles continues to be a problem for men in the highly sex-segregated societies of South Asia, though the problem is perhaps less in South India and Ceylon and tribal societies, than it is in North India, Pakistan, and Afghanistan where contact between women and male 'strangers' is more highly limited because of the normative strictures of *purdah* (seclusion). A related problem is access of highly educated urban researchers, both men and women, to the inner workings of the lower class rural and urban society. Few researchers in the region who have studied these groups have spent long periods of time actually living with the people, and research conducted during office hours is bound to miss very important aspects of community life. The social and cultural gap between these two classes is almost as difficult to bridge as the gap between the sexes.

Attitudinal research seems to be less prominent in the field of social change than it was previously, but it is worth mentioning some of the problems that have been and still are associated with this approach. First, it is often assumed that studies of changing attitudes among middle and upper class women reflect long-term trends which will eventually affect the poor majority

ments in Delhi: A Sociological Study of Low-Income Migrant Communities, Part II (New Delhi: Ministry of Works and Housing, 1975), mimeo.

9. K. Nischol, 'Resettlement Colonies of Delhi', Paper presented to the Delhi Development Authority, New Delhi. 1976, typescript.

since these women are trend setters and opinion leaders. While it is true that the higher classes are often emulated by the lower, the process is often long and indirect. As Bhatty[10] found, upper class Muslim women may be shedding their *burqa* while lower class women are donning it. Thus upper class women may not be the leaders of lower class opinion and behaviour, at least not directly.

Another assumption is that attitudes, especially those of young people, are a good measure of behaviour, both at present and later in life. It is unfortunate that there have been no major longitudinal studies of the groups which comprise the sample base for these studies, since other life factors change attitudes, often dramatically, as young people pass through different life stages. In a study of a middle class neighbourhood I found very few people who were willing to admit that caste would be an important consideration in arranging their children's marriages, yet genealogies showed that out of caste marriages were extremely rare.[11] Beteille[12] once wrote that younger village women in Tanjore District were starting to wear blouses and took this to be an indication of change. When I visited several villages in nearby Salem District in 1975, I also found younger women wearing blouses, and wondered why a few older women were not wearing them also if this was a process of change which had started at least ten years earlier. I was told that there was no point in trying to be modest after a woman reaches a certain age and has several children.

Attitudinal studies, for lack of accurate data on actual behaviour patterns in the past, also frequently assume that change can be measured by comparing present attitudes against some traditional ideal. Researchers are now becoming much more aware of the wide range of permissible deviation from the norm which has always occurred in the past, especially

---

10. See Zarina Bhatty, 'Women in Uttar Pradesh: Social Mobility and Directions of Change' in this volume.

11. Andrea Menefee Singh, *Neighbourhood and Social Networks in Urban India: Voluntary Associations of South Indians in Delhi* (New Delhi: Marwah, 1976).

12. Andre Beteille, *Caste, Class and Power* (Berkeley: University of California Press, 1965).

among lower status groups, but have not yet developed any appropriate measure of normative behaviour and attitudes in the past except for elite groups. This is a problem for other types of research as well. Kinship studies, for example, often assume that the great majority of women in North India have adhered to the ideal of village exogamy. Yet even in 1955, Cohn[13] presented genealogical evidence that showed that rural migration through affinal ties was frequent among lower caste groups at present as well as in the past, even in the North, and Gough[14] made similar observations about untouchable castes in the South in 1962. Both studies noted the importance of fluctuations in rural labour markets in influencing migration among landless groups. Too few studies of change, particularly those which focus on women, take into consideration the influence of wider economic and social factors such as the changes in the supply and demand of labour on such things as attitudes towards work or decisions to migrate. An important exception is Omvedt's[15] study of women's participation in peasant movements in which she finds it to be highest in areas where women have high rates of employment in agricultural labour. The fact that women's rates of employment as agricultural labourers in the last two decades[16] have increased dramatically may thus have important implications.

Studies of women as a category often do not include comparisons with male students, husbands of female students or working women, or males in similar occupations. An exception is the study of working mothers in white collar occupations in Madras where interviews with husbands of working and non-working mothers were held regarding both attitudes and actual

13. Bernard S. Cohn, 'The Changing Status of a Depressed Caste', in McKim Marriott (ed.), *Village India* (Chicago: University of Chicago Press, 1955).

14. Kathleen E. Gough, 'Caste in a Tanjore Village', in E.R. Leach (ed.), *Aspects of Caste in South India, Ceylon and North-West Pakistan* (Cambridge: Cambridge University Press, 1962).

15. Gail Omvedt, 'Women and Rural Revolt in India', *Journal of Peasant Studies* (1978).

16. *Toward Equality: Report of the Committee on the Status of Women in India* (New Delhi: Department of Social Welfare, Government of India, 1974).

practices.[17] In most studies, however, one is left without a clear sense of the differences and similarities between male and the female world view or of the mutual adjustments necessary between men and women in situations where women go beyond their traditional roles.

Finally, a word should be said about survey research where females are contrasted with males in terms of basic demographic characteristics. First, we find the inadequacy of existing categories arising from the data on which most development planning in India is based. Second, is the tendency to blindly adopt categories used in the more urban industrialised societies of the West. Such categories are not necessarily relevant to the Indian situation. For women, the catch-all category of housewife or non-worker seems inadequate for meaningful analysis in any society. The 1971 Census of India which emphasised the primary worker is known to have excluded large numbers of working women. There is also a great need to take notice of indigenous categories of work participation rates with regard to both males and females. Sometimes asking a woman what she does to get money yields more accurate information about her productive roles than asking her if she works.[18]

Studies based on this type of data are also conspicuous for their lack of qualitative data. Where correlations and trends are found to exist, caution must be exercised in accepting explanations which are based more on guess work than on solid empirical evidence. Correlations, after all, do not necessarily imply a casual relationship between two or more factors. Explanations must be based on more intensive research techniques. To give an example, it is widely known that females in India have an abnormally high mortality rate compared to males. The most common explanation for this discrepancy is that females in India, due to their lower status, are often more undernourished than males (therefore being more likely to die

17. Madras School of Social Work, *Working Mothers in White-Collar Occupations* (Madras: 1970).
18. Beverly Hackenberg, 'Migration and Mobility Among Women in the Philippines', Paper presented at Women in the Cities Working Group, East-West Population Institute, Honolulu, March 1979.

when ill), and that they are less likely to receive health care when ill.[19] While these explanations may be correct, it is possible that the explanation is far more complicated than this, especially if one considers the tremendous variation between male and female mortality rates in different regions of India, and even between different castes in the same region.[20]

Despite the many methodological problems which researchers have encountered in doing survey, research and studies of changing attitudes, they have served a useful purpose. Attitudinal studies give us a qualitative view of society which is difficult to achieve through other techniques. Survey research, of course, is tremendously useful in describing trends, in suggesting possible relationships between various factors and in generating hypotheses for further testing. But there is a need to continuously refine and redefine categories used. There is also a tremendous need for more indepth studies using qualitative techniques to test hypotheses that have already been generated.

Social and cultural factors

There are a number of social and cultural factors which make the position of women in South Asia somewhat different from that of their Western counterparts. Whereas the goals of equality, justice and peace in human development may be the same for all people, the fundamental problems and solutions are bound to be different in different societies.

While it is difficult, if not impossible, to isolate all of the variables which directly or indirectly affect the status of women in South Asia, it is possible to point to a few well-known factors which are of special relevance to the position of women in the South Asian situation. These include region, caste, religion, family structure and systems of kinship and marriage. One of the problems in studying any aspect of South Asian society, of course, is the complex interrelationship of all of

---

19. *Toward Equality*, op. cit.
20. Rural Health Research Centre, *Interactions of Nutrition and Infection*, Final Report to I.C.M.R. (Punjab: Narangwal, April 1972).

these factors. Although I shall discuss each of these factors separately, it should be remembered that none of these factors should be taken singly as the primary factor in determining the status of women.

Region

Karve writes:

The linguistic regions possess a certain homogeneity of culture, traits and kinship organisation. The common language makes communication easy, sets the limits of marital connections and confines kinship mostly within the language region. Common folk songs and common literature characterise such an area.[21]

Thus one might argue that the Bengali-speaking women of India have more in common with the Bengali-speaking women of Bangladesh than with the women in other linguistic regions of India,[22] and that Punjabi women in Pakistan have more in common with their Indian counterparts than with their non-Punjabi neighbours. A study of women in a large Karachi slum[23] found wide differences in women's work participation, use of household space, and felt needs and priorities that corresponded to both linguistic region and religion. Yalman[24] has argued that basic structural similarities exist between the people of Ceylon and the people of South India in their beliefs regarding women, and this he attributes to the similarities in language

21. Irawati Karve, *Kinship Organisation in India* (Bombay: Asia Publishing House, 1965), p. 4.
22. See T.N. Madan, 'The Dialectic of Ethnic and National Boundaries in the Evolution of Bangladesh', in Suren Navlakha (ed), *Studies in Asian Social Development*, No. 2 (Delhi: Vikas Publishing House, 1974).
23. Emmy Bos-Kunst, 'Women of Azam Basti: A Social Study Among Women of a Slum Area in Karachi, Pakistan', Report to the National Planning Commission of Pakistan, Karachi, 1970.
24. Nur Yalman, *Under the Bo Tree: Studies in Caste, Kinship and Marriage in the Interior of Ceylon* (Berkeley: University of California Press, 1967).

and the accompanying similarities in structure of thought. Kolenda, in a survey of literature on family structure, finds distinct differences in the statistical occurrence of joint family households in different regions of India which she attributes to the regional differences in a woman's control over certain means of rewarding or punishing her husband for his compliance or non-compliance with her wishes.[25]

There are many more studies which trace the social and cultural similarities and differences in regions of South Asia. I just wish to point out here that one must be careful to take regional differences into account when generalising about women in South Asian society, or even within a single country. It should also be remembered that most languages in India are part of a pan-regional cultural complex in some respects, but there are numerous cross-cutting factors which sometimes complicate the influence of regional and linguistic factors. Smartha Brahmins of Tamil and Kannada speaking areas, for example, might have more in common with each other in some respects than with non-Brahmins from their own village, but Brahmins of the South might have more in common in other respects with non-Brahmins of their own region than with the Brahmins of Uttar Pradesh. Thus the importance of regionalism depends very much on the purpose of the research, but it should certainly be taken into account when making generalisations about women in one country which are based on studies of women in particular regions.

Religion

Religion in South Asia, as has been widely acknowledged, plays an important role in defining the status of women, especially regarding beliefs about their inherent character structure, natural strengths and weaknesses, and their rights and obligations. The fact that the South Asian region hosts several major religions, each with very different myths, ideologies, beliefs and ritual practices, suggests that the status of women

---

25. Pauline M. Kolenda, op. cit.

would vary tremendously according to religion. These religions include Hinduism, Jainism, Buddhism, Sikhism, Christianity, Islam, Zoroastrianism and Judaism. Of these, Hinduism, Buddhism, Jainism and Sikhism originated in India, the latter three representing major breaks with Hindu ideology. It is generally acknowledged that Buddhism, Sikhism and Jainism support greater freedom for women than Brahminism.

In an interesting variation on this theme, Furer-Haimendorf suggests that the Buddhists' 'tolerant attitude to sexual laxity' might be related to the occurrence of polyandry among the Buddhists of Ceylon and the Himalayan regions.[26] He stops short of suggesting that Buddhist ideology is a causative factor in the development of polyandry, although he considers Buddhist morality to be 'permissive of a type of sexual arrangements unacceptable to the more puritan Hindu moralist'.[27]

In addition to broad ideological differences regarding the position of women in society, there are different religious streams within the major religions which should be taken into account. The *Bhakti* movement in Hinduism, for example, offered women a larger role in Hindu worship and greater freedom and equality than they had enjoyed previously. Unfortunately, however, we have very little empirical evidence to suggest how widely the effects of such movements were felt in society, or how they affected the status of women in their secular roles. In a study of South Indian migrants in a neighbourhood of Delhi, I found that four out of nine women who participated individually in voluntary associations attended female *bhajana* (devotional singing) associations.[28] These women, however, represented only a very small proportion of South Indian women in the neighbourhood and I found little evidence that participation in *bhajans* affected their status as women in a broader sense.

Another aspect of religion which may be of consider-

26. Christoph Von Furer-Haimendorf, *Caste and Kin in Nepal, India and Ceylon* (Bombay: Asia Publishing House, 1966), p. 8.
27. Ibid., p. 9.
28. Andrea Menefee Singh, *Neighbourhood and Social Networks in Urban India: South Indian Voluntary Associations in Delhi,* op. cit.

able importance in South Asian religions is the difference between popular religion and formal theology in their consequences for women. The tendency of those discussing religious ideology, beliefs and attitudes is to assume that the norms of what we might call the 'high religion' are equally applicable to all people. It is well known, however, that there has long been differential access to religious knowledge among Hindus with the Brahmins having an almost total monopoly over the texts and the right to interpret them. In popular Hinduism there is an emphasis on female dieties, spirit possession and supernatural cures which is quite different from the beliefs and practices of Brahmanical Hinduism. Wadley[29] has presented a fascinating analysis of women's participation in formal and popular Hindu ritual. Harper notes the high incidence of spirit possession among young married Brahmin women in a Mysore village and suggests that possession represents one means of coping with the tremendous strains inherent in their inferior structural position. (Other solutions include fasting and suicide.)[30] The consequences of popular beliefs and practices for women in the society deserve further exploration.

In the realm of ritual beliefs and practices, two other important topics have not received adequate attention. The first is the concept of pollution. Beliefs and practices regarding pollution in South Asia have received some attention by anthropologists, many of whom consider concepts of female susceptibility to pollution to be central to the structure of the whole society.[31] Another aspect of ritual which has received very little attention is the different roles played by males and females in ritual performances. It appears that in ritual performances, as in many other areas of social life, there is a dichotomy between male and female spheres of activity. La Brack suggests

29. Doranne Jacobson and Susan S. Wadley, *Women in India: Two Perspectives* (New Delhi: Manohar, 1977).

30. Edward B. Harper, 'Spirit Possession and Social Structure', in Bala Ratnam (ed.), *Anthropology on the March* (Madras: Social Science Association, 1963), pp. 165-177.

31. See Nur Yalman, op. cit., and Mary Douglas, *Purity and Danger* (New York: Praeger Publications, 1966).

that in Hinduism female ritual activity focuses around the domestic hearth, while male ritual activity involves a more public role.[32] This finding has been supported in my own work among low income women,[33] and again by Wadley.[34] In only a few ritual activities do men and women participate together, but even then they rarely share an equal ritual role.

The extent to which Hindu beliefs and practices have influenced other religions in the region is also not adequately understood. We know, for example, that caste is not limited to Hindus,[35] although caste is usually considered a purely Hindu structure. There is a need to know more about actual beliefs and practices and how they differ from religious ideology among the non-Hindu religions. This is important in trying to assess religious differences in the status of women when making cross-cultural comparisons.

Census figures and demographic surveys tell us that fertility rates, urban residence and income differ for the major religions in India, but as yet we do not know the causes of these differences nor their consequences for the status of women. In a study of working mothers in white collar occupations in Madras it was found that Christian women had a much higher rate of participation in white collar occupations than Hindu women and that Muslim women had a much lower rate.[36] The

32. Bruce La Brack, 'Male and Female Ritual Roles in Khalapur', Paper presented at the Fourth Annual Meeting of the Pacific Coast Association for Asian Studies, Los Angeles, June 21, 1971; Ursula Sharma, 'The Problem of Village Hinduism: Fragmentation and Integration', *Contributions to Indian Sociology* (New Series), IV (December, 1970), pp. 14-15, differentiates between individual and public ritual and notes the absence of women in the latter. See also Pauline Mahar Kolenda, 'Religious Anxiety and Hindu Fate', in Edward B. Harper (ed.), *Religion in South Asia* (Seattle: University of Washington Press, 1964), p. 78, for examples of female ritual concerns in Khalapur. La Brack's analysis was based on Kolenda's field notes.

33. Andrea Menefee Singh and Alfred de Souza, 'The Position of Women in Migrant Bastis in Delhi', Report prepared for the Department of Social Welfare, Government of India, October 1976.

34. Doranne Jacobson and Susan Wadley, op. cit.

35. Imtiaz Ahmad, (ed.), *Caste and Class among Muslims in India* (New Delhi: Manohar, 1975).

36. Madras School of Social Work, op. cit., p. 18.

authors suggest that Christians place fewer restrictions on the activities of women than other religions, and, therefore, Christian women have acquired more education and vocational training than women of other communities.[37] Hate found similar differences in rates of participation of working women according to religious identity in Bombay and Poona but offers a different explanation.[38] She claims that since there is no joint family system among the Christians, women work out of necessity or the expectation of the eventual need to be self-supporting.[39] Both studies attribute the low rates of participation of Muslim women to greater conservatism.[40] This question calls for more rigorous attention from researchers.

Too often the religious factor is left out altogether. Cormack, for example, who studied Indian women students at Columbia University, included Christian and Muslim women but titled her book *The Hindu Woman* and made no reference to religious differences among her subjects.[41] In her sample, in a study of marital adjustment among working women, Kapur includes non-Hindus in her sample but did not consider it relevant to marital adjustment.[42] In another study she says that she excluded non-Hindus 'In order to have a homogeneous group for study and also to delimit the scope of the study,'[43] but elsewhere she says she included Sikhs, Buddhists and Jains in her definition of Hindus since these religions come under the jurisdiction of the Hindu Marriage Act 1955.[44]

---

37. Ibid., p. 11.
38. Chandrakala A. Hate, *Changing Status of Women* (Bombay: Allied Publishers, 1969), pp. 36-37.
39. Ibid., p. 38
40. Madras School of Social Work, op. cit., p. 11; Hate, op. cit.
41. Margaret Cormack, *The Hindu Woman* (New York: Columbia University Press, 1953).
42. Promila Kapur, *Marriage and the Working Woman in India* (Delhi: Vikas Publications, 1970), p. 59.
43. Promila Kapur, (1973) op. cit., p. 15.
44. Ibid., p. 12.

Caste

There are a number of factors related to caste in India which clearly affect the position of women in society. Srinivas suggests that among the poor and low castes the relationship between men and women is more egalitarian than among the higher castes, and that when lower castes try to raise their status through Sanskritisation one of the consequences is lowering the status of women, making them subordinate to men in moral, economic and ritual terms.[45]

Other important caste-related factors are differences in kinship and marriage practices. A very interesting example of how these may differ within a particular region is the case of the Nayars and Namboodiris of Kerala. In a traditional society, Nayars maintained a matrilineal system of descent whereby status and property were inherited through the maternal line. They also practise natolocal residence where brothers and sisters stayed together with their mother's sisters and maternal uncles; husbands had visiting privileges only. Namboodiri Brahmins, on the other hand, maintained a strict patrilineal system with patrilocal residence where only the eldest son was allowed to marry and inherit property. Other sons were free to form alliances with Nayar women in marriage ceremonies which were considered legitimate by the Nayars, but not recognised by the Namboodiris. Among other things, this led to large numbers of Namboodiri women who were unable to marry. Thus there was a complimentary structural relationship between two castes in which the position of women was entirely different. While this is probably a unique case, there is little doubt that differences in kinship systems, marriage practices and patterns of residence among castes in other regions of India have very important consequences for the status of women.

We also find caste differences throughout most of India relating to the giving of dowry or bride price in marriage, both of which have very limiting consequences for women. The ease with which divorce may be achieved, the possibility of

---

45. M.N. Srinivas, *The Changing Position of Indian Women* (New Delhi: Oxford University Press, 1978).

remarriage for widows and divorcees, the extent to which women are allowed to move out of their houses or caste cluster, the possibility of working and what types of work are considered appropriate to the women of the caste—all these things are subject to normative limitations of caste, and are basic to the position of women in society. Of course, these factors may also be subject to the normative influence of religion or region. Nearly all castes in South India, for example, find cross-cousin marriage acceptable while hardly any North Indian castes would dream of such a marriage. As Kolenda points out, the incidence of bride price, divorce and remarriage varies in practice from region to region, despite differences in the ideal among castes within one region.[46]

Another interesting question regarding caste is the extent to which caste background affects the woman's self-image and influences her selection of a role model or reference group. As Srinivas points out, when the lower and middle castes imitate the Brahmins, the position of woman may be adversely affected.[47] But it is not at all certain that Brahmins provide the only or even the most common reference group for non-Brahmin women. It is possible that as the Brahmins are progressively stripped of their traditional powers, other important role models will emerge. In fact in North India Brahmins have long occupied a lower status in society than Brahmins in the South. Another important question is who provides the reference group for Brahmin women. It is interesting to note that both Goldstein[48] and Vreed-De Stuers,[49] in studies of changing attitudes among female college students, found that Brahmin women, who are a small minority of the total population, constituted the majority in their samples. Their findings are all the more interesting for what they tell us about Brahmin women in modern society, though this was not a consideration in either analysis. The dynamics of upward mobility for

46. Pauline M. Kolenda, 1967, op. cit.
47. M.N. Srinivas, op. cit.
48. Rhoda L. Goldstein, op. cit.
49. Cora Vreede-De Stuers, 'Attitudes of Jaipur Girl Students Towards Family Life', in Dhirendra Narain (ed.), op. cit., pp. 151-162.

females is certain to be more complex than most writers have assumed.

In the urban arena, caste continues to operate as an important factor. The caste system—i.e., inter-dependence of castes at the village level—may be largely irrelevant to the social life of the city, but caste continues to be a primary marker of social identity. In a study of middle class South Indians in Delhi, I found that caste was one of the most important factors in the formation of social networks and in organising voluntary associations.[50] It also appeared to be related to the types of occupations women pursue and whether they would work before marriage or after marriage. At the middle class level, however, only a small portion of women are employed. In a study of lower class migrants in Delhi,[51] I found a much higher proportion of women employed. Among some groups, nearly every able bodied woman was employed. Even at this level, however, caste and region play an important part in determining whether a woman will work or not and what type of employment she will take up if she does work. On the one hand, traditional caste occupation plays an important role in evaluating the suitability of different types of work and providing training and skills which might be adaptable to the urban situation; and, on the other hand, caste and village networks provide the mechanisms through which women are recruited to certain kinds of employment in the city. Bellwinkel has discussed these mechanisms with regard to Rajasthani contract labour in Delhi,[52] and Lubell notes a similar tendency for migrants from certain castes and regions to dominate specific areas of employment in Calcutta.[53] The relationship between caste and the employment of women in urban and rural areas needs more study. It is unfortunate that most studies dealing with occupational mobility, especially those that contrast tradi-

50. Andrea Menefee Singh, (1976), op. cit.
51. 'The Position of Women in Migrant Bastis in Delhi', op. cit.
52. Maren Bellwinkel, 'Rajasthani Contract Labour in Delhi: A Case Study of the Relationship between Company, Middlemen and Workers', *Sociological Bulletin*, 22 (March, 1973), pp. 78-79.
53. Harold Lubell, *Calcutta: Its Urban Development and Employment Prospects* (Geneva: International Labour Office, 1974), pp. 60-63.

tional village occupations with modern urban occupations, focus only on men.[54] The occupational mobility of women should be considered just as important.

Family structure

Studies of women in South Asia have sometimes assumed that changing attitudes towards the family and marriage provide an indicator of the changing position of women. It is assumed that the forces of modernisation and urbanisation lead to a decrease in the number of the joint families and an increase in the number of unarranged marriages (or at least a larger degree of choice in arranged marriages). Even if this is true, and there is some evidence it is not, it is necessary to consider whether a loss of traditional family support mechanisms is beneficial to the status of women or merely leads to greater exploitation.

To begin with, however, it is necessary to take a careful look at the assumption that joint families are on the decrease. A number of studies lead us to question this assumption. In a comparison of family structures in a village near Poona in 1819, 1958 and 1967, Kolenda found that the joint family was increasing, even after manipulating the data from 1819, to show the maximum number of possible joint families and the modern data to show the minimum number.[55] Singer notes that among the industrial elite in Madras city, the joint family is both structurally and functionally compatible with the requirements of modern industry and urban life.[56] Other authors have

54. See, for example, G.N. Ramu and Paul D. Wiebe, 'Occupational and Educational Mobility in Relation to Caste in India', *Sociology and Social Research*, 58 (n. 1. 1973), pp. 84-94, and Gene Kassebaum and N.E.C. Vidya Sagar, 'A Survey of Caste and Occupational Mobility in a Small City in India', *Man in India*, 54 (n. 4, Oct-Dec, 1974), pp. 253-269; Lubell, op. cit.

55. Pauline Mahar Kolenda, 'Family Structure in Village Lonikand, India: 1819, 1958 and 1967,' *Contributions to Indian Sociology* (New Series), IV (Dec. 1970), pp. 50-72.

56. Milton Singer, 'The Indian Joint Family in Modern Industry', in Milton Singer (ed.), *Structure and Change in Indian Society* (Chicago: Aldine Publishers Co., 1968).

found 'limited change' in the direction of nuclear families, but this seems to be conditioned by the extent to which occupation requires geographic mobility rather than purely urban residence.[57] A nuclear family living may be out of necessity or expediency rather than the result of changing attitudes or ideas. In Karol Bagh I found a higher incidence of joint families among long-time Punjabi residents, most of whom were self-employed businessmen, than among South Indian migrants, most of whom were in salaried white-collar occupations.[58] Even the South Indian migrants, however, maintained extensive kinship networks in the city, and a large proportion were extended families in composition, though not strictly joint by definition.

The next question is how these changes, when they do occur, affect the status of women, and how do changes in the traditional roles of women affect the stability of the joint family. Most researchers have assumed that changes in the attitudes and roles of women, especially those associated with higher education and employment, are related to the breaking down of the joint family. But the evidence of such a direct relationship can be questioned. While Kolenda found that a woman may exert a deciding influence in the break up of a joint family, she argues that her bargaining power must be

> institutionalised in such cultural practices as a wife's right to a legal divorce, bride-price negotiation of marriage, economic and social support to a couple from the wife's natal family or lineage.[59]

The key point is whether the husband gets economic or social support from the wife's kin that might modify or over-ride the advantages of joint family living. She also dismisses the argument that power derived from making an economic contri-

---

57. See, for example, M.S. Gore, *Urbanisation and Family Change* (Bombay: Popular Prakashan, 1968) and Sylvia Vatuk, *Kinship and Urbanisation: White Collar Migrants in North India* (Berkeley, Los Angeles: University of California Press, 1972).
58. Andrea Menefee Singh, (1976), op. cit.
59. Pauline M. Kolenda, 1967, op. cit., p. 216.

bution to the family income through working is related to jointness since there is a high incidence of joint families among castes whose women work in the fields in some regions and not in others.[60] One might add that working women do not necessarily maintain full control over their own incomes. Goldstein found that 77 per cent of the employed women in her sample of highly educated women turned over more than half their earnings to their families.[61] In fact, she found that the majority of her respondents, whether married or not, felt that education would *help* them fit into a joint family, that it 'will not cause them to challenge the traditional expectations of obedience to husbands and in-laws, but will enable them to handle role requirements better'.[62]

Whether or not a woman lives in a joint family may have important consequences for her position in society and the opportunities that are open to her. There is no doubt that in many cases joint family living restricts the freedom of women (especially younger women) with regard to movement outside the home, decision making in financial matters or running the household, and even in the dress they may wear. But the nuclear family has its own problems in India. When geographic mobility necessitates the establishment of a nuclear family, the joint family may continue to be the ideal, carrying with it obligations such as remittance of a significant part of the couple's income, participation in family ceremonies (sometimes at great cost if the distance is great), care for the aged or disabled, maintenance or supervision of family property, and so on. This, combined with the lack of other adult members in the family to share domestic chores and child-rearing responsibilities, or to provide adult company to alleviate the drudgery of household work, may be far more limiting in the end than joint family living.

It sometimes happens, in fact, that joint family living frees women for employment who would otherwise find it impossible to handle both an outside job and domestic and child-rearing

60. Ibid., p. 215.
61. Rhoda L. Goldstein, op. cit., p. 282.
62. Ibid., p. 284.

responsibilities. In the Madras study, it was found that half of the women who had once worked but withdrew from employment did so due to increased child care and household responsibilities at home.[63] At the lower class level, although it is common for female construction workers and domestic workers to carry at least their youngest children with them to work, joint family living may ease the domestic burdens of working women and increase the quality of child and household care. It is not just the younger female members of the joint family who may benefit; older women may also find greater freedom as Vatuk's study shows.[64] This type of sharing of female role responsibilities appears more acceptable and perhaps more realistic in the Indian setting than the Western alternative of shared responsibilities between husband and wife, although the Madras study has shown that even in India, husbands of working women participate in household tasks to a far greater extent than husbands of non-working women.[65] Of course it can be argued that as long as domestic and child-rearing chores are considered beneath the dignity of men, women cannot achieve equality. But we must also point out the alternatives of the joint family and, for middle and upper class women, of hiring full-time domestic workers (many of whom are men) in the Indian setting which are not usually realistic possibilities for women in the West.

I have touched here on only a few of the aspects of family structure which are of importance to the study of women in South Asia. It is clear that we need much more information than is presently available on the dynamics of family life in both rural and urban situations, and the consequences of family structures for women in society.

Kinship and marriage

I shall not go into detail here about the great variety of

63. Madras School of Social Work, op. cit., p. 34.
64. Sylvia Vatuk in this volume.
65. Madras School of Social Work, op. cit., p. 59; see also Hate,

systems of kinship and marriage found in South Asia since I have alluded to many of these differences above as they relate to region, religion and caste. Whether inheritance is matrilineal or patrilineal, whether dowry or bride price is given at the time of marriage (and who maintains control over these assets), whether cousin marriage is preferred or considered incestuous, whether the custom of levirate is practised, whether polygamy or polyandry are acceptable forms of marriage, whether hypergamous unions or marriages between men and women of equal status are preferred, where one draws the lines of endogamy and exogamy, and under what circumstances deviance from these norms are allowed—all of these things are clearly of immense importance to the understanding of the position of women in the society. In much of the general theory on kinship and marriage, women are treated as pawns in the system, being 'exchanged' or cementing 'alliances' between males in the system. Anthropologists have even gone to great lengths to explain how men in matrilineal systems continue to be the dominant force in the system. In South Asia one can find nearly every system of kinship and marriage which is described in the literature and it would seem to be an ideal setting for research into these systems from the female point of view.

One aspect of marriage which cuts across specific systems of kinship and marriage in India, and which has been widely discussed in studies of changing roles and attitudes of women, is the system of arranged marriages. Arranged marriages are practised by nearly all segments of the society, with the exception of tribals in most regions. Recent studies have not found much change in attitudes towards arranged marriage among college students: there is some evidence, in fact, that modern women are more in favour of arranged marriages than they were ten years ago.[66] This finding suggests that the system is not necessarily affected by the individual's level of education or the wider processes of urbanisation and modernisation.

op. cit., p. 86. Hate reports that many of her respondents would not have been able to work were it not for their living in a joint family.

66. Comment made by Promila Kapur in a panel discussion, 'The Problems of Working Mothers', India International Centre, August 13, 1974.

Higher education, however, may have the effect of limiting marital choices for women where it is considered imperative that the husband have equal, and preferably more, education than his wife.[67] Still, we cannot assume that this is a universal norm. Among the Punjabi business community in Delhi, for example, daughters often receive more education than sons, higher education for males being considered of no great importance in developing business skills and an early entrance into the business being deemed more important to their success in business than acquiring higher education. Parents of these young men, however, often seek out girls with B.As or M.As who, it is expected, will bring 'culture' to the household and will be better able to guide the children in their studies.[68]

We know, in fact, very little about the elements of personal preference which enter into the negotiations for marital matches, and how and why these are likely to vary. It is common to note trends in newspaper marriage advertisements, but it is not clear to what extent these changing preferences are representative of the wider population (most of whom arrange marriages without the help of classified ads) or just how relevant, for that matter, the stereotyped descriptions ('beautiful homely girl'; 'highly qualified boy') are to actual negotiations. The classified ads represent only an initial screening process for those unable to find suitable matches elsewhere or those wishing to broaden their choices. We need to know more about what happens after contact is made, whether through advertisements, paid marriage brokers or through more traditional channels.

The system of arranged marriage functions in many ways to limit life-chances and options of males as well as females in the society. It makes young people in South Asia highly dependent on their parents at a time when young people in the West are usually independent and in pursuit of their own careers and life styles. It prevents them from trying out new roles and experiences which their elders believe would harm their marriage

67. Rhoda L. Goldstein, op. cit., p. 272.
68. K.R. Unni also noted this tendency among businessmen in Old Delhi (private communication with the author, October 1969).

chances, creating pressure for conformity to traditional roles and expectations. At the same time it reinforces and supports the persistence of caste and ethnic groups within the wider society by eliminating marriage contact across these boundaries.

Many people seem to believe that dowry and bride price can be eliminated without changes in the system of arranged marriages, but despite legislation this has not occurred. One could argue that as long as marriages are arranged in a highly limited and competitive market through negotiations between elders (who, it may be assumed, have their own interests to look after in addition to whatever considerations they may have for the preferences of their children), dowry and bride price are bound to enter into the negotiations. It is interesting to note that the Chinese, in the Marriage Law of 1950, abolished arranged marriages along with wife-buying, polygamy, infanticide and child marriage, and legalised divorce and widow remarriage, in the belief that all of these practices were inextricably linked.[69] The result has not been the emergence of a western-type system where marriage is based primarily on romantic love, apparently, but a situation where young couples agree to marriage on the basis of both traditional and modern Chinese values, keeping in mind their parents' preferences and advice.[70]

The system of arranged marriages is not without its benefits for women. First, a dowry which usually includes moveable property of some value such as furniture, saris and jewellery, provides a certain basic security (to the extent that the girl can maintain control over these assets) that she can fall back on under adverse conditions. Second, it is quite possible that parents, where their daughter's happiness is their over-riding consideration, because of their long experience in marriage and their intimate knowledge of their daughter's strengths and weaknesses, may be able to make a far wiser choice of a life-long mate for their daughter than if she were left to make the choice wholly on her own. An important consideration is often the other family members and kin of the prospective groom

---

69. Carol Tavris, 'Women in China: The Speak-Bitterness Revolution', *Psychology Today*, 7 (n. 12, 1974), p. 49.
70. Ibid.

because of the intensity of these relationships, their hierarchical pattern, and the large degree of sex segregation in the family and society. Third, it is possible that the modern Indian girl is free to pursue higher education and career opportunities single-mindedly since she can take comfort in the knowledge that her parents will take up the time consuming task of finding her a satisfactory mate when the time is right.

The system of arranged marriages appears to be at the core of the society's ability to sustain traditional images and roles for women, despite the revolutionary changes in the economic and political spheres of the wider society. Regionalism, caste, religion, and, to some extent even the joint family, find reinforcement through this practice. The complex interrelationship of all these factors deserves the special attention of those interested in the study of women in the South Asian region.

Research issues

While it is important to keep social and cultural variables in mind when assessing the status of women and changing patterns in the South Asia region, a number of more general issues of special relevance to the policy making process have emerged which merit the special attention of researchers. Because of the invisibility factor in official data sources, researchers can make a special contribution to building a better data base on which planning and policy decisions can be made. These research priorities tend to cut across cultural and national boundaries and, to the extent such research can be stimulated and encouraged, could provide valuable insights and data on which policies aimed at improving the status of women might be formulated.

First, there is a clear need to develop better macrolevel data on the migration patterns of women and their patterns of change. This is true of rural as well as urban migration. In India, for example, the largest volume of migration (69 per cent) is rural migration, and 77 per cent of all rural migrants are female. It has long been assumed that this migration is basically marriage migration, but practically nothing is known about the volume of other types of female rural migration. The Committee on the Status of Women in India found large numbers of women seeking casual employment during slack agricultural seasons in irrigation, road and other construction work,[71] but we still lack accurate statistics on the magnitude of this type of migration or on regional variations in its scope. In some regions, e.g., Punjab and West Bengal, it is known that migrant female labourers from other districts or states are hired during planting, weeding, and harvest seasons; in some districts of Andhra Pradesh, women and children comprise an important part of the migrant labour force in the tobacco industry.[72] The impact of this type of migration on women and the family is in need of clarification in terms of volume, the special needs of women which arise out of such migration, and the relationship between population growth, regional disparities in rural development, and the resulting patterns of female population movements. This type of migration could be of considerable magnitude in those countries in the region which have low levels of urbanisation and a tradition of female agricultural labour (e.g., India, Nepal and Sri Lanka).

Rural-urban migration of women is also in need of further study. By World Bank estimates, in 1975 more than 20 per cent of the total population of Pakistan (27 per cent), Sri Lanka (24 per cent), and India (22 per cent) lived in urban areas, and by the turn of the century it is likely that at least a third of the population of these countries will be urban.[73] In India the volume of female rural-urban migration has been increasing more rapidly than that of males for the last several decades,[74] though the reasons for this trend are not adequately understood. One consequence is that while the sex ratio of rural population has registered a steady decline, that of urban areas has increased. The increasing urban sex ratio, however, is not entirely due to

71. *Toward Equality*, op. cit., p 35.
72. M.S.A. Rao, 'Tobacco Development and the Labour Migration: Planning for Labour Welfare and Development', *Economic and Political Weekly*, 13 (n. 29, 1978).
73. World Development Report, 1978, op. cit., p. 104.
74. Andrea Menefee Singh, 'Women in Cities', op. cit.

increasing sex ratios in migration streams, as Joshi points out,[75] but also due to a decreasing tendency to marry girls back into villages, and the snowballing demographic effect of more women in the cities having children. These trends need to be closely monitored, and their implications brought out for the planning and design of urban services.

Because of the dependency assumption, we have very little understanding of the economic and other important determinants of female migration. As mentioned earlier, job opportunities for women, however lowly in status and pay, may be an important consideration in whether they come to the city or stay back in the village, and they may also be an important drawing card for women who are the primary or sole supporters of their family. Research on the determinants of female migration also needs to go beyond the individual level to include familial considerations at both the place of origin and the place of destination. A woman's kinship ties in an urban area may be as important a resource as those of a man; and the better health and educational facilities available for children in urban areas may be another important consideration. Differences in *perceived* opportunity structures in rural and urban areas may play an important role in decisions to migrate for both men and women. Societies with a highly unequal distribution of wealth or resources often experience a high rate of migration among the most structurally disadvantaged groups.

There is some evidence that the disparities in the distribution of income is increasing in many countries in the South Asia region, and it will be important to know how this will affect the propensity of women to migrate among the lower income groups. Since these are the women who have always had the highest work participation rates, changing patterns of migration could have profound implications for the urban opportunity structure, particularly in the unorganised sector where the majority of these women find work.

Another important subject in need of more research is differences between men and women in the disposition of income.

---

75. Heather Joshi, 'Prospects and Case for Employment of Women in Indian Cities', *Economic and Political Weekly*, XI (n. 31,32,33, Special Number, 1976), pp. 1303-1308.

The fact that women usually earn less than men does not necessarily mean that their contribution towards the basic needs of the family is also less. Chatterjee,[76] for example, found that among sweepers in Lucknow where a high proportion of women were employed and earning the same amount of income as their husbands, it was customary to set aside a certain proportion of family income as spending money for husbands and sons, but not for women and daughters. I have also found that employed women in squatter settlements spend about 95 per cent of their income on food and other basic necessities of the family.[77] It was mentioned earlier that a large number of married women are primary or sole supporters of the family due to the irresponsible spending patterns of their husbands. This information could be of considerable value to evaluating the affordability of housing and other basic services such as health and education in both rural and urban areas. It could also provide insight on the link between household income and the nutrition of family members.[78]

The role of women in the unorganised sector is still badly in need of clarification. According to one estimate, nearly 50 per cent of the small retailers, vendors and food service providers in Hyderabad are women;[79] elsewhere in India women comprise an important part of unskilled construction workers, and the majority of domestic workers. In Calcutta, Banerjee[80] suggests that the displacement of women from the organised sector, especially in manufacturing and industry, has forced large num-

76. Mary Chatterjee 'Conjugal Roles and Social Networks in an Indian Urban Sweeper Locality', *Journal of Marriage and the Family* (February, 1977).

77. Andrea Menefee Singh, 'Women and the Family: Coping with Poverty in the Bastis of Delhi', in Alfred de Souza (ed.), *The Indian City: Poverty, Ecology and Urban Development* (New Delhi: Manohar, 1977).

78. The World Development Report, 1978, op. cit., pp. 34-35, suggests that increasing the income of the poor will be the most effective strategy for eliminating malnutrition in low-income countries, but does not consider the possibility that this might be more true of women's income than of men's. The report also credits Sri Lanka's large-scale public food distribution system with 'dramatic improvements in nutrition and life expectancy'.

79. Andrea Menefee Singh, 'Women in Cities', op. cit.

80. Nirmala Banerjee, 'Women Workers and Development', *Social Scientist*, 6 (March 1978), pp. 3-15.

bers into piecework and self-employment which yields less than a subsistence income. In rural India, while the number of women classified as cultivators (i.e., those who work on their own land) declined sharply between 1961 and 1971, their numbers increased even more dramatically among agricultural labourers.[81] While it may be difficult for governments to enforce minimum wage and other labour legislation in the unorganised sector, an understanding of the distribution and needs of women in this sector is essential for the design and delivery of needed social services (e.g., credit, child care, and health programmes).

An important area of enquiry which as yet has been the subject of very little research in the South Asia region is the impact of trans-national corporations and export oriented industries on women's employment. In most developing countries of Southeast Asia and Latin America, the export oriented textile and garment manufacturing industries have traditionally given preference to young unmarried women in employment.[82] Because they have a fairly high rate of turnover due to marriage, the industry can continue to hire at the lowest possible wages without incurring long-term expenses such as increments and payment of pensions. Similar patterns are observed in the manufacture of electronic components.[83] In India, however, women have not been given preference in garment manufacturing, although they have found expanding opportunities in pharmaceutical industries. In textile industries their numbers have steadily declined due to mechanisation and the adverse impact of protective legislation. These patterns need to be monitored and the reasons for them explored if effective regulations are to be formulated at the national level.

All of the above research could also be useful in the identification of important disadvantaged female constituencies as target

---

81. See Gail Omvedt, op. cit.
82. See Helen Safa, 'Women Textile Workers in New Jersey and Brazil', Paper presented at the Xth International Congress of Anthropological and Ethnological Sciences, New Delhi, December 1978.
83. Robert Snow, Research on Transnational Corporations and Women', Paper prepared for Women in the Cities Working Group, East-West Population Institute, Honolulu, Hawaii, March 1979.

groups for regulation, legislation, and the design of social services to meet their most presssing needs. The invisibility factor obscures the important contribution these women make to rural and urban economies as well as to the household economy. The social service needs of women will obviously vary according to a number of factors such as age, marital status, occupation, and type of migration (e.g., seasonal or permanent). They will also vary according to stage of economic development, and national goals and priorities. While these considerations must help shape the recommendations which emerge from research on women, it is also important to try to assess the needs and priorities expressed by the women themselves. Too often the perceived needs and priorities of middle class researchers, planners and policy makers provide the basis for planning and programme design. Housing is often given highest priority when in fact more or better employment may be the first priority of low-income women. Institutionalised child care often holds little interest to women who have always depended on informal family structures of support to meet their child care needs.

There is a great need for more research on successful and innovative programmes for low-income women in both rural and urban areas. The expansion of basic services to low-income populations has been found to have an indirect effect of the redistribution of income, and in many countries or regions, including Sri Lanka and Kerala, have been associated with rapidly declining levels of fertility.[84] The social, economic and political circumstances under which programmes can thrive tend to differ from one country to another, and for this reason it is important to build up the knowledge about successful programmes at the country level in so far as this is possible. Economic programmes for women in particular are in need of better models. The Mother's Club programme in Bangladesh and Korea has apparently met with high levels of success, whereas productive programmes in India have done little to expand

---

84. David R. Francis, 'Fewer Births, a Better Life', *Sunday Star Bulletin and Advertiser* (Honolulu, Hawaii, March 11, 1979). In this article Francis describes the findings of demographer Ribert Repetto of Harvard University's School of Public Health.

employment or provide more than subsistence level income for women in India.[85] In India, on the other hand, programmes which provide ready access to credit for self-employed women have met with spectacular success in generating both income and employment, especially for women engaged in small scale retail or service activities.[86] We need to develop a much greater pool of information about successful strategies for improving the status of women and their access to resources. Important considerations in such evaluations are the possibility of replication and cost recovery. Welfare oriented programmes may require a high degree of subsidisation, but economic and development programmes should not. Other types of programmes in need of identification and description include health and family planning, low-income housing, women's cooperatives, and child care.[87] The case study approach to programme design and evaluation could provide a pragmatic link between the theoretical background and skills of trained social science researchers, and the needs of policy makers and planners.

Finally, researchers can play a useful role by examining the impact of current policies and planning processes on the status of women.[88] Low-income housing policies, for example, often disrupt the woman's work-residence relationship more seriously than the man's, and this results in a subsequent decline in the real income of the family. Credit and employment programmes are often aimed only at a male constituency, while rural development strategies tend to generate income only for landowners who in the vast majority of cases are men. The negative impact of such policics on the status and opportunities of women need to be brought out and, if possible, supported by statistical

85. Andrea Menefee Singh, 'Women in Cities', op. cit.
86. Ibid., Bhatt, op. cit.; Seshagiri Rao, 'A Case Study on the Functioning of A.P. Women's Cooperative Finance Corporation Limited and Impact of Assistance Extended by it', Report prepared for the Indian Council of Social Science Research, New Delhi, 1979.
87. Ruth B. Dixon, *Women's Cooperatives and Rural Development: A Policy Proposal* (Resources for the Future, Inc., Washington D.C.)
88. See Judith Bruce, 'Urban Policy Makers and Women: Arranging a Meeting', Paper prepared for the Working Group on Women in Cities, East-West Population Institute, Honolulu, Hawaii, Marh 1979.

measures, in order to promote more equal strategies. On the other hand, most countries in the region have explicit national goals which shape their policies and can be used as a rationale for promoting public policy which is supportive of women. These include increasing equality of opportunity and access to scarce resources of disadvantaged groups, redistribution of wealth and property, promoting economic self-sufficiency, and increasing the standard of living of the poorest sections of society.

3 Trends and Structure of Female Labour Force Participation in Rural and Urban Pakistan*

Nasra M Shah
Makhdoom A Shah

This paper has three main objectives. Firstly, to analyse the trends of female labour force participation in rural and urban areas of Pakistan. This is done by analysing data from as many sources as possible. The accuracy of trends obtained from Census data is cross validated with household sample surveys of women. Secondly, the structural composition of the labour force in terms of occupation, employment status and place of work is examined. Changes in the occupational structure over time are discussed. Finally, questions about the correlates of female work participation have been raised and analysed with the help of a recent survey. The paper is organised on the basis of these three themes, in the same order.

Data sources and limitations

Because of its trend analysis dimension, data from three Censuses of Pakistan (1951, 1961 and 1972) and the Labour Force Surveys have been used. Labour force data for the 1972 Census of Pakistan were collected in a Housing, Economic and

*The authors appreciate the helpful comments of Philip M. Hauser, Alfred de Souza, Robert Retherford and Dee Chapon on an earlier draft. Gayle Uechi provided valuable computer programming assistance.

Demographic (HED) survey in 1973. Also, data from two household level KAP (Knowledge, Attitude and Practice) demographic surveys have been used. These surveys are the NIS (National Impact Survey, 1968) and the PFS (Pakistan Fertility Survey, 1975).[1] Analysis of the current status of labour force structure and correlates of work is restricted largely to an examination of the PFS data.

A word about the data limitations, particularly in terms of their comparability, would be in order. Methodologically, the Census data differ from data in household surveys. They have used different definitions.[2] The reference period used in the

1. Training, Research and Evaluation Center, *National Impact Survey Report* (Lahore, Pakistan: TREC, n.d.); Population Planning Council of Pakistan, *Pakistan Fertility Survey* (Islamabad: PPC, 1976).

2. The 1951 Census defined the economically active population to consist of all persons who were 12 years of age or more and were self-supporting, partly self-supporting or were seeking work. Reference period of one month was used for the question. In the 1961 Census the age limit was lowered to 10 years and any person working for profit, wage or salary or helping any family member in trade or profession or those who were looking for work during the week prior to the Census enumeration were classified as being in the civilian labour force. The reference period of one week was used only for non-agricultural workers. See Home Affairs Division, Government of Pakistan, *Population of Pakistan, 1961* (Karachi, Pakistan: Manager of Publications, 1964).

For the series of Labour Force Surveys, the civilian labour force was defined as non-institutional civilian population of age 10 and above who were either working for pay or profit in cash or kind, including unpaid family helpers (who had worked at least 15 hours during the reference week) or had a job but did not work. The unemployed component of the civilian labour force was defined to include all persons who, during the reference week, were either looking for work, or temporarily laid off, or assured of a job but did not start work and the persons who were not looking for work because they believed a job was not available.

The HED (1973) survey used the same definition as the Labour Force Surveys, except that the words 'in cash or kind' were dropped from the definition of employed person.

The National Impact Survey enquired from women, 'Have you ever done any work other than housekeeping?' If yes, 'Did you do any work other than housekeeping during the last week?' The economic activity question asked for their husbands was, 'Has your husband worked at any time?' If yes, 'Has your husband worked at any time during the last week?'

The Pakistan Fertility Survey (1975) enquired from ever married women

Censuses and Labour Force Surveys has generally been in terms of 'last week'. The household surveys have asked about work in terms of a broader time dimension, along with current work (during the last week). The quality of enumerators in the two sources has been very different. Similarly the quality of training, supervision and data processing has probably been better in the household surveys than inthe Censuses. Finally, the Censuses and Labour Force Surveys have interviewed any adult male member of the household, while in the KAP demographic surveys the eligible woman herself provided information on her labour force participation. It might be noted here that the various surveys (HED, Labour Force and KAP) have different samples (coverage) and very different sample sizes. Assuming the random-stratified nature of all the samples, this aspect should not be a ground for making the various samples non-comparable. The difference in sample size, however, does affect the amount of detail that a researcher can explore in the data without running into a problem of small cell sizes.

Keeping all these methodological and other differences in mind, comparisons between the various sources should be made and interpreted with caution. We have made an attempt to eliminate biases which could be generated by age, marital status and other factors, wherever possible.

Trends in labour force participation

The proportion of adult females that is economically active has been recorded to be traditionally low in Pakistan. The main source on which this finding has been based are the Census data, or the Labour Force Surveys which used roughly the same kinds of measurement techniques and methodology as the Censuses. The figure that has been reported in these sources, for women ten and over, has varied between 6.3 and 10.5 per cent for different years from 1961 to 1975 (Table 1). The two

'As you know many women work . . . I mean aside from doing their own housework. Some take up jobs for which they are paid in cash or kind. Others sell things or have a small business. Are you doing any such work at the present time?'

TABLE 1: Trends in Labour Force Participation Rates by Sex and Rural/Urban Areas.
1951-1975

Year/Sources	Male Total	Male Rural	Male Urban	Female Total	Female Rural	Female Urban
1951 Census of Pakistan (a)	79.4**	—	—	3.1**	—	—
1961 Census of Pakistan (b)	80.8	83.9*	72.2*	9.3	10.9*	4.1*
1961 Census of Pakistan (a-I)	83.9**	—	—	9.6**	—	—
1966-67 PLFP (i) (b)	86.3	89.0	88.2	10.28	11.34	7.04
1967-68 PLFP (b)	86.7	89.7	77.8	10.54	11.62	7.04
1968-69 LFS (ii) (b)	79.0	82.1	70.0	6.6	7.22	4.0
1968-69 National Impact Survey (c) (Currently Married Women age 15-49)						
Currently Working	—	—	—	18.7	22.3	9.0
Ever-worked	—	—	—	23.0	27.1	13.0
1969-70 LFS	80.0	83.1	71.0	8.1	9.5	3.7
1970-71 LFS (b)	78.6	81.6	69.8	8.0	9.4	3.9
1971-72 LFS (b)						
1973 HED Survey (iii) Women 10+ in the labour force	77.6	70.5	80.3	9.0	8.6	9.1

Currently Married Women 15-49 currently working					
1974-75 LFS (b)	76.7	79.8	6.34	7.54	3.54
1975 PFS (women 15-49) (d)		69.5			2.6
Ever-Married, ever-worked	—	—	19.1	21.2	23.3
Currently Married, ever-worked	—	—	21.7	21.4	22.5
Ever-Married, currently working	—	—	17.2	17.8	15.6
Currently Married, currently working	—	—	17.5	18.1	15.6

Source :

* R.A. Karwanski, *Projection of Labour Force for Pakistan and Provinces, 1960-1990*, Appendix II, Manpower Section, Planning Division, Islamabad, 1969.

** Ghazi M. Farooq, *Dimensions and Structure of Labour Force in Relation to Economic Development*, (Table II-6), Pakistan Institute of Development Economics, Islamabad, 1975.

(i) PLFP—Population and Labour Force in Pakistan. (CSO) Tables 28, 29, 30.

(ii) LFS—Labour Force Surveys (Statistics Division), Tabulation No. 5, 5(A), 5(B).

(iii) H.E.D. Survey: Housing, Economic and Demographic Survey, Tabulation No. 16. Persons 10+ in the civilian labour force.

(a) All persons of age 12 and above.

(a-1) All persons of age 12 and above (adjusted figures for the 1961 Census of Pakistan).

(b) All persons of age 10 and above.

(c) National Impact Survey data (1968-69).

(d) Pakistan Fertility Survey data, 1975.

rather glaring exceptions to this uniformly low participation rate are provided by the National Impact Survey (NIS) and Pakistan Fertility Survey (PFS). These surveys render estimates of labour force participation that are almost twice as high as those of the Censuses and Labour Force Surveys. Nineteen per cent of the currently married women aged 15-49 reported to be currently working in the NIS, while 23 per cent reported that they ever-worked. The corresponding proportions reported by the PFS women were somewhat smaller (18 and 22 per cent) but still significantly higher than other sources.

One might argue that the observed differences between the Census (and LFSs) and the two KAP demographic surveys are present mainly because of the difference in the age and marital status of the samples in the two sets of sources. That is, the Census figures include women of all marital statuses, including single women who are ten years of age and above. The KAP demographic surveys include either currently married or ever married women in the reproductive ages (15-49). While some of the observed differences may be present due to the factors identified above, we feel that such differences cannot account for a very large part of the variation in rates for the following reasons: Firstly, the age specific activity rates of women in Pakistan have a fairly flat pattern.[3] The 1961 Census showed that from 5 per cent in the youngest (10-14) age groups the proportion of working women rose to 12 per cent for women 45-54; and declined to 7 per cent for oldest (65+) women. The age pattern of activity reported in the HED survey was even more flat than the 1961 distribution (Appendix Table 1). Given this relatively even distribution of work participation by age, exclusion of the very young (<15) and older (50+) women from

3. Lee L. Bean, 'Utilisation of Human Resources: The Case of Women in Pakistan', *International Labour Review*, 97 (n.4, 1968). For studies on the trends and structure of labour force participation in Pakistan up to 1961, see Ghazi M. Farooq, 'Labour Force Participation Rates in Pakistan: Urban 1961', *Pakistan Development Review*, VIII (n. 1, 1968); Lee L. Bean, D.M. Farooq and Masihur Rehman Khan, 'The Labour Force of Pakistan: A Note on the 1961 Census', *Pakistan Development Review*, VI (n. 4, 1966); and for international age-sex patterns see Ettore Denti, 'Sex-Age Patterns of Labour Force Participation by Urban and Rural Populations', *International Labour Review*, 98 (n. 6, 1968).

the KAP demographic surveys, should not make a substantial difference for the overall activity rate.[4] Secondly, participation rates among the single women and currently married women were low and close (0.7 and 1.4 per cent respectively) while the rates for the widowed and divorced women were much higher (6 and 12 per cent) in 1961. The same trend seems to be true from the HED data.[5] Given this pattern, the exclusion of the single, widowed and divorced women from the NIS, we feel, would not have led to an 'artificial' increase in the participation rate. If anything, the rates obtained in the NIS might have been still higher if widowed and divorced women had been included.[6] Although the activity rates of widowed and divorced women in the PFS were lower compared to currently married women, the overall activity rates in the PFS were much higher compared to the Census and HED. We are, therefore, inclined to believe that the activity rates as reported in the KAP demographic surveys are closer to the 'true' rates.

Assuming that the higher rates obtained in the two KAP demographic surveys are true rates, what are some of the reasons which may account for such wide variations (between sources) in economic activity of females in Pakistan? Apart from factors like definition of work, reference periods, season of interview which may have a serious impact on the measurement of female work participation, one factor which we feel is of crucial importance in measurement is the individual who is asked the

---

4. The rate for the 1961 Census was recalculated, using women 15-44 only. The rate came to 10.0 per cent which is very close to the rate for women 10+ shown in Table 1.

5. In the HED, the participation rates for single as well as married women were 5 per cent each, in the rural areas, and about twice as high for widowed and divorced women. In the urban areas, the participation rates for single, married, widowed and divorced women were 5, 3, 14 and 12 per cent respectively. The PFS, however, showed fewer widowed and divorced women to be in the labour force as compared to currently married women. (Appendix Table 2.)

6. Support for this last argument is found in the HED Survey figures for participation of all women 10+ in economic activity compared to currently married women aged 15-49, in the urban areas. Four per cent of all urban women were economically active in the week prior to interview while 2.6 per cent of the currently married women aged 15-49 were economically active.

labour force participation questions.[7] In Census type situations where the enumerators are usually male, questions are asked from any male member of the household, often times the household head. This can lead to a considerable under-reporting of economic activities, particularly if (i), the male member does not recognise the woman's activity as anything beyond her housework or (ii), if the societal norms prescribe her activity as being anything close to 'undesirable'. In the first case he would under-report her activities involuntarily. In the second case he might under-report her activities voluntarily. In the two KAP demographic surveys which rendered higher activity rates the woman herself was the respondent. Even though the woman herself may in some (or many) cases be embarrassed at reporting to an outsider (the interviewer) that she has to work in order to supplement the household income, we feel that the relative under-reporting in her case would be smaller. A conclusive statement about the extent of such under-reporting is however not possible in the absence of well designed methodological studies which should be conducted in order to answer many of the questions in the measurement of female work participation.

Researchers in the past have attributed the traditionally low participation rates to religious attitudes in Muslim countries, as pointed out by Farooq (1975, p. 29-32). Farooq, while questioning the validity of what he terms the 'Hypothesis of Islamism', offers several alternative hypotheses, inadequate measurement being one of them.[8] Data from the recent KAP

7. For detailed discussion of these and other problems in the measurement of female labour force participation in Pakistan see Nasra M. Shah, Makhdoom A. Shah and Tauseef Ahmed, 'Labour Force, Employment, and Underemployment Statistics in Pakistan', *Manpower and Employment Statistics in Pakistan*, Proceedings of a National Seminar (Islamabad: Pakistan Manpower Institute, 1977); Nasra M. Shah, 'Problems in Measurement of Female Labour Force Participation and Its Relation with Fertility', a Paper presented at the Ninth Summer Seminar in Population, East-West Population Institute, Honolulu.

8. This hypothesis states that the rate of female labour force participation is lower in Muslim countries due to the Muslim values, such as those relating to women's movement outside the house, segregation of sexes, etc. See Ghazi M. Farooq, *Dimensions and Structure of Labour Force in Rela-*

demographic survey show that female activity rates in Pakistan are indeed higher than have been stated in the past. Accurate estimates of activity rates, we feel, are difficult to be obtained from Census type surveys. What is needed for providing more accurate estimates are specially designed studies which can try various alterations of techniques of measurement and are directed to the working female herself.[9]

Narrowing of rural-urban gap in female work participation

Consistently higher participation rates had traditionally been reported in rural as compared to urban areas in Censuses and in Labour Force Surveys. In the 1968 NIS also, more than twice the women in rural areas were reported to be currently in the labour force compared to urban areas (22 and 9 per cent respectively). This trend of higher participation in rural areas seems to have narrowed, or even reversed. Both in the 1973 HED and 1975 PFS surveys, almost the same percentage of women in rural and urban areas was reported to be active in the labour force. Nine per cent of both rural and urban women were reported to be in the civilian labour force in the 1973 HED survey. The corresponding figures for the rural and urban women, currently in the labour force, in the PFS were 18 and 16 per cent respectively. If the total work experience rather than current work of the PFS currently married women is considered, the rural-urban differential is reversed i.e., more urban women (23 per cent) reported to have ever been economically active than rural women (21 per cent). Although the absolute proportion of women reported to be in the labour force was much higher in the PFS, the relative differences between the rural and urban areas were very small in both the sources.

The higher participation rate of women in urban areas as compared to the past could be the result of actually expanding

tion to Economic Development (Islamabad: Pakistan Institute of Development Economics, 1975).

9. A reasonable quality of training and supervision of field and office staff, adequate translation of the instrument, a good quality of data processing are, of course, assumed.

TABLE 2: Changes in the Occupational Structure from 1961-1975, Rural and Urban Females in Pakistan
(Percentages)

Occupational Structure	1961 Census [a,b] Non-agricultural labour force	NIS, 1968 R	NIS, 1968 U	HED, 1973 [c,d] R	HED, 1973 [c,d] U	PFS, 1975 R	PFS, 1975 U
Nurses, teachers	10.1	0.6	10.2	1.8	25.8	1.2	8.2
Technical, sales, admin., clerical	2.5	1.0	2.6	4.9	19.5	2.1	2.1
Farm workers—agric. labourers, fishermen	1.5	49.1	7.7	82.1	7.1	37.7	1.8
Housekeepers, domestic servants, caretakers	28.8[4]	3.2	13.5	4.4[2]	27.8[2]	6.7	14.8
Spinners, weavers	32.0[1]	3.4	14.7	1.2	3.2	14.7	18.4
Tailors		7.0	26.3	1.2	6.4	25.5	40.0
Other skilled	16.0	5.7	7.7	2.2	7.6	7.3	11.5
Unskilled, labourers	9.0[3]	12.1	16.7	1.4[3]	2.6[3]	4.8	3.0
Unpaid family help	—	17.9	0.6	—	—	—	—
N	299,550	470	156	490,760	129,070	565	330

Sources: PFS, NIS, HED data and *Census of Pakistan, 1961*, Vol. 6, Part 1, Table 2, pp. 24-29.

¹Textiles, textile goods and weaving apparel.
²Housekeepers and other service workers.
³Labourers and street vendors, stall holders.
⁴Domestic service workers and caretakers.

ᵃExcludes workers not classified by occupation and those who were not employed but were looking for work.
ᵇA breakdown by occupations for rural and urban areas is not available from the 1961 Census. These data are restricted to all women (10+) who were in non-agricultural occupations.
ᶜExcludes workers not classified by occupation.
ᵈHED figures are only for women 15-65 years of age, for all marital statuses.

job opportunities for women in urban areas, coupled with an increase in the women's skill levels and education. On the other hand, the higher participation might simply be an artifact of better reporting of female economic activity in the urban areas in recent years. It is possible that the extent of under-reporting of female economic activity in the urban areas might have been higher during the earlier surveys due to certain normative constraints which might have changed in the 1970s. The validity of these alternatives cannot be tested in the present study. A partial examination of the changes in rural-urban participation is made by analysing the changes in occupational structure over time.

Rural urban occupational structures

Urban Structure

Of all women employed in the non-agricultural labour force whose occupation was reported in 1961, 60 per cent were classified as spinners or weavers and domestic servants (Table 2).[10] A similarly high proportion (55 per cent) of working women in urban areas, were reported to be in these occupations in 1968 NIS. By 1975, the proportion of women engaged in these occupations had increased to 73 per cent—which perhaps lends support to the argument of expanding job opportunities in urban areas. The 1973 HED survey provided a somewhat different picture, with only 38 per cent of women working as domestic servants or weavers or tailors. The heavy concentration of urban women in just two or three occupations is probably an indication of the continued limitation of opportunities in other sectors that women are faced with. The spinning and tailoring occupations do not, however, require the woman to leave her house for work. She can bring the work home. Also, we feel that such occupations are generally regarded as more 'acceptable' (respectable) occupations compared to working as a street vendor or a labourer where a woman is faced with relatively more vulnerable situa-

---

10. The reader may be reminded here that it was some adult male member of the family and not the woman who reported her occupation.

tions and has to be in more frequent contact with males who might be strangers.[11]

Looking at the category of domestic servants only, the proportion of women reported as domestic servants was twice as high in the 1961 census and HED survey than the two KAP demographic surveys (roughly 28 and 14 per cent respectively). Since similar coding schemes were used for coding this occupational category in the different surveys, it is possible that the differences resulted from a differential reporting bias in the various sets of data. The woman herself might be regarding domestic service as less prestigious than being a tailor or a weaver. Thus, she might be mis-reporting her occupation, particularly if she is engaged in more than one job, in the two KAP demographic surveys. Nothing conclusive can, however, be stated about the directions of such mis reporting by different groups of women unless we can assess the prestige-ranking that they attach to being employed in a given job.

Professional women have constituted about one-tenth of the labour force, in the non-agricultural or urban setting in Pakistan (calculated as a proportion of all women employed in non-agricultural occupations). We have presented in Table 2 the proportion of nurses and teachers as a separate group because these professions have dominated the 'professional' group. The proportion of nurses and teachers remained steady between 1961 Census and 1968 NIS, at 10 per cent, and declined to 8 per cent in the PFS. The HED Survey reported many more (26 per cent) women to be employed as teachers and nurses. Of these 22 per cent were teachers. Although it might be a welcome change in the female occupational structure, the high HED figures for teachers seem implausible given the rate at which the number of female teachers has been growing as a

---

11. For other studies and factors related to variable perceptions of occupational desirability, see Hanna Papanek, 'Purdah in Pakistan: Seclusion and Modern Occupations for Women', *Journal of Marriage and the Family*, 33 (n. 3, 1971); Carroll McC. Pastner, 'Accommodations to Purdah: A Female Perspective', *Journal of Marriage and the Family*, 36 (n. 2, 1974); Kishwar Saeed, *Rural Women's Participation in Farm Operation* (Lyallpur: West Pakistan Agricultural University Press, 1966).

proportion of all teachers.[12]

It might be pointed out here that the occupational concentration of females is much higher compared to males, and has remained so during the last one and a half decades. Also, the proportion of males in 'professional' occupations was lower compared to females in 1961 (4 and 10 per cent respectively), and has remained so. The corresponding figures for males and females in the HED survey were 5 and 10 per cent for the country as a whole.[13] This differential is a result largely of the sex segregated educational facilities and the strict preference for female doctors and nurses. The proportion of female teachers at the primary and secondary level has increased steadily since the late 1950s and early 1960s, and the trend is likely to continue with expanding educational facilities for females.

Rural structure[14]

Within the rural areas, the proportion of working women who are reported to be employed in agricultural occupations varies drastically between the different sources. The HED survey showed 82 per cent women to be engaged in agricultural work while PFS reported only 38 per cent women to be engaged in such activities. The NIS figure (49 per cent) was closer to the PFS. This rather striking difference between the activity rates reported in the two KAP demographic surveys and the HED survey may essentially be attributed to the different measurement

---

12. The proportion of female teachers, as a per cent of the total, increased by about 11 per cent for primary and secondary school teachers from 1961 to 1975 from 19 to 30 per cent. Nasra M. Shah, 'Female Participation in Selected Occupations Within the Organised Sector: Pakistan', *Sub-Regional Seminar on Status and Role of Women in the Organised Sector* (Geneva: ILO, 1977). Thus, the proportional increase in female teachers reported in the HED survey seems unreasonable.

13. The HED figures for urban areas were 30 per cent and 8 per cent for professional females and males.

14. Data on the occupational structure for 1961 is not available separately for rural and urban areas. The comparison here is, therefore, restricted to NIS, HED survey and PFS.

TABLE 3: Occupation by Place of Work and Working Status, Urban and Rural Currently Married Women, Age 15-49 PFS, 1975

Occupation*	Urban (Percentages)					Rural (Percentages)				
	Work at home		Work Outside		N	Work at home		Work Outside		N
	Employee	Self Employed	Employee	Self Employed		Employee	Self Employed	Employee	Self Employed	
Nurses, teachers	—	11.1	81.5	7.4	27	—	—	71.4	28.6	7
Clerical, adm., sales	—	71.4	14.2	14.2	7	8.3	41.7	—	50.0	12
Farm workers	—	16.6	83.3	—	6	—	0.5	75.6	23.9	213
Housekeepers, domestic servants	—	2.0	93.9	4.1	49	5.3	—	84.2	10.5	38
Spinners, weavers	26.2	68.9	4.9	—	61	7.2	91.6	—	1.2	83
Tailors	6.8	90.9	2.3	—	132	11.1	81.9	2.8	4.2	144
Other skilled	2.6	60.5	34.2	2.6	38	4.9	73.2	7.3	14.6	41
Unskilled	30.0	10.0	50.0	10.0	10	—	14.8	40.7	44.4	27
Total	29	196	98	7	330	27	234	216	88	565

*Percentages have been calculated on the basis of the occupation that a woman was engaged in.

technique used in the HED survey, namely, a male reporting the activities of the females. The enumerators, who were males, (probably) have a predisposition to assume that if a woman, in the rural areas, is reported to be working then she must be working in agricultural or related occupations. In other words, the enumerators might have tended to not to probe for specifying the occupation.

The proportion of employed rural women engaged in professional occupations was much smaller (1-2 per cent) than the urban women and was reported to be consistently small by all the three sources. A significantly larger proportion (40 per cent) of women were reported to be in the spinning and tailoring occupations in the PFS compared to NIS (10 per cent) and HED Survey (2 per cent). Assuming that the large proportion of spinners and tailors in the PFS is based on accurate reports, part of the reason for such increase might be the growth of cottage industry (industrialisation) in the country side. In recent years, a growing number of entrepreneurs has been known to have brought to the villages the art and business of embroidery and carpet weaving.[15] The women can finish these jobs within their homes and get cash payment for their services. Hence, the increase in the proportion of rural women working as spinners, weavers and tailors.

Occupational structure by place of work and employment status

As discussed in the preceding section, female participation in the labour force is highly concentrated in two or three occupations—in both rural and urban areas. In this section we have analysed the relationship between occupational structure and employment status and place of work.[16] Table 3 shows very clearly that participation in certain occupations is highly correlated with both place of work and employment status. A

---

15. Personal observations, experience and communication with other researchers. Also increase in export of such goods.

16. PFS is the first survey which has ever provided data on the place of work for women. Such tabulation is not possible from the previous surveys.

very large proportion—82 per cent urban and 71 per cent rural—of all nurses and teachers were employees working outside the house. Similarly, large proportions of women who were employed as farmers (83 per cent urban and 76 per cent rural) or domestic servants (94 per cent urban and 84 per cent rural) were employees who worked outside the house.

On the other hand, the three groups of skilled workers, namely spinners, tailors and other skilled workers, were constituted of predominantly self-employed working at home. Of all the tailors, for example, 91 per cent in urban and 82 per cent in rural areas were self-employed and worked at home. The two groups which exhibited relatively more variations were those of unskilled labourers and the 'residual' group of administrative, clerical and sales workers. This last group had relatively few cases and cannot, therefore, be discussed in any detail. The labourers seem to be a more diverse group. Most (85 per cent) of the labourer women in rural areas, for example, were working outside the house, but about half of these were employees while the rest were self-employed workers.

The foregoing findings have two implications. Firstly, the argument relating to the concentrated and homogeneous nature of occupations that working women are engaged in is further strengthened. More than two-thirds (68 per cent) of the urban and about half (46 per cent) of the rural women were engaged in occupations which they pursued within the home largely on their own.[17] Thus, most of the urban women were engaged in sheltered, protected occupations where they could work at home and probably did not have to come in contact with urban employers, who in many cases would be likely to be men. The relatively unchanging (or even increasing) proportion of women engaged in cottage-industry type occupations indicates that opportunities for women to work in other jobs—outside the house or for employers—are still limited. This is probably a result both of lack of skills that the women have and the availability of such jobs to women. The cultural definitions pertaining to whether a job is regarded to be desirable or not are of

17. We do not have information on whether these self employed women were paid in cash or kind for their work.

course present, but the relative constraint that such values place on participation cannot be evaluated unless jobs are made available and women are provided the skills to take part in such jobs.[18]

Secondly, the very close association between place of work and employment status indicates that we can easily use one variable as a substitute for the other without much loss of information. This finding implies that the data on employment status which the Censuses and Labour Force Surveys have traditionally provided, as an aspect of the structure of the labour

TABLE 4: Characteristics of Currently Married Working and Non-Working Women, Urban and Rural Pakistan, PFS, 1975

Characteristics	Urban Working	Urban Non-Working	Rural Working	Rural Non-Working
$\bar{X}$ Age (yrs.)	30.5	30.6	29.9	30.5
$\bar{X}$ Age at marriage	16.4	16.8	16.1	16.4
Wife's education % literate	23.7	27.3	4.4	5.4
Husband's education % literate	53.4	62.5	35.0	35.0
$\bar{X}$ CEB*	4.4	4.4	4.1	4.2
$\bar{X}$ Living children	3.4	3.5	3.1	3.2
$\bar{X}$ Children last 5 yrs.	1.1	1.1	1.0	1.1
$\bar{X}$ Children Desired	3.9	3.9	4.5	4.3
% know F.P. person	34.5	40.2	23.1	26.3
% know F.P. methods	82.6	82.7	70.4	73.4
% know F.P. place	50.1	56.0	22.2	26.8
% ever used method	18.6	22.7	6.3	6.3
% currently using	9.9	12.9	2.8	2.7
% want more children	33.8	35.6	51.1	45.1
No additional children wanted	.99	.97	1.4	1.3
Total	323	1406	558	2271

*CEB=Children Ever Born.

18. Our personal experience leads us to believe that as more women get educated to higher levels of education, the norm relating to work in the formal sector changes. Working becomes not only permissible, but desirable also. This phenomenon, however, manifests itself in an extremely small subgroup of the urban population and at relatively high levels of education (B.A. to Masters).

force, are sufficient and do not need to be supplemented by place of work information. Accuracy of Census data on various aspects of the female labour force, however, have to be evaluated by comparison with other studies focusing especially on women.

Why do Pakistani women work?

After describing the nature of jobs women are engaged in, and seeing that 80-90 per cent are engaged in low-paid jobs requiring limited skills, but at the same time demanding considerable time and effort, one is impelled to ask: Why do some Pakistani women opt to work while others don't? An attempt is made in the following section to answer this question by analysing data from the PFS, 1975.[19] Firstly, working women have been compared with non-working women in order to find any characteristics on which the two groups might differ. Secondly, various factors which could have effects on work participation, as indicated by past research, have been used as predictors in a multivariate model.[20]

The first thing that strikes the eye is the rather high degree of similarity between the working and non-working women in Table 4. In the urban areas, both the working and non-working

---

19. One of the problems with using PFS data is that this survey represents a sample of ever-married women in their reproductive ages. If the motivations/correlates of work for single women differ significantly from those of ever-married or currently married women, we cannot analyse this from the PFS data. The basic reason for selection of the PFS for this section is that this is the most recent national survey which provides data on several socio-economic and demographic factors that can be used for such an analysis. Also, the data in this survey might have greater reliability and validity because of its close supervision and adequate training (of various field and office personnel) components.

20. The technique used for this analysis is Multiple Classification Analysis or MCA. This is a multiple regression technique designed to examine the interrelationships between several predictor variables and a dependent variable within the context of an additive model (Frank Andrews, James Morgan and John Sonquist, *Multiple Classification Analysis* (Ann Arbor, Michigan: Institute of Social Research, University of Michigan, 1971).

women were of the same age, had borne the same number of children in their lives and the same number of children in the five years prior to interview, and had the same number of desired children. The only variable on which there was a noticeable difference between the two groups was the husband's education. A smaller proportion of the husbands of working women were literate (53 per cent) compared to husbands of non-working women (63 per cent). A similar kind of differential, though smaller, was present for the wife's education—24 per cent of the working and 27 per cent of the non-working wives being literate. Some of the other variables which showed a noticeable difference between the working and non-working groups in urban areas were related with family planning knowledge and use (Table 4). Consistently larger proportions of non-working (or the more literate groups) women reported knowledge of the personnel and clinics of family planning as compared to working women. Also, 23 per cent of the non-working women had ever-used a method compared to 19 per cent of the working women. This differential in family planning knowledge and use might, however, be largely attributable to the higher literacy of the non-working wives and their husbands.

Within the rural areas also, the differences in the demographic characteristics of the working and non-working women were rather small. There was, however, no difference in the literacy status of the husbands of working and non-working women. Slightly more of the non-working women were literate compared to the working women (5 and 4 per cent respectively). Somewhat larger proportions of non-working wives had knowledge of family planning personnel and clinics than working wives, but the use rates for the two groups were practically the same.

The effect of some of the factors examined in Table 4 was further analysed by controlling for the effects of several variables which have been known to have direct or indirect influence on work participation. The results are presented in Table 5. As already indicated by the data in Table 4, the only variable which had a strong negative effect on work participation, in urban areas, was the husband's education. This negative effect remained unchanged after adjusting for demographic factors like age of wife and number of living children etc. Twenty-two per cent of women with illiterate husbands, in urban areas, were engaged in some activity (apart from household work) compared with 18 per cent of women whose husbands had 5-9 grades of education and 13 per cent of women whose husbands had ten or more grades of education. The differential in rural areas was much smaller. Participation rates were smaller only for women whose husbands had ten or more grades of education. The wife's own education did not have any clear relationship with work participation. One reason for this might be our inability to divide the sample so that we could observe women at the higher educational levels i.e., above matric or perhaps even B.A.[21]

It was found in an earlier study based on the NIS data that some of the socio-economic variables like husband's education, perceived adequacy of living, ownership of land and durable items all had significant effects on work participation in both rural and urban areas.[22] Also, observance of *purdah* (veiling of women), which was positively associated with socio-economic status, was found to have a strong negative effect on work participation. The PFS data do not provide information on any of these variables except husband's education. If husband's education can be used as a proxy for the family's socio-economic level, then we can conclude that the negative effect of belonging to a high socio-economic level (on work participation) which was present during the late 60s is still persisting, at least in urban areas.

In the earlier study, there was some indication that older women at higher levels of parity were more likely to work, particularly if we examined the subgroup of other-employed

---

21. Such regrouping was not considered appropriate in view of the small sample size for women at the higher levels of education. Matriculation is equal to ten grades of education, while B.A. refers to Bachelor of Arts or 14 grades of schooling.

22. Nasra M. Shah, 'Work Participation of Currently Married Women in Pakistan: Influence of Socio-Economic and Demographic Factors', *The Pakistan Development Review*, XIV (n. 4, 1975). It must be noted that the earlier study was based on a bivariate analysis of the data and findings from that are hence comparable only to the unadjusted proportions in Table 5.

TABLE 5: Factors Related with Work Participation of Females, Urban and Rural Pakistan, PFS, 1975
(Percentage of Women in Labour Force)

Characteristics	Urban Unadjusted %	Urban Adjusted[1] %	Urban N	Rural Unadjusted %	Rural Adjusted[1] %	Rural N
Age of Wife	(F=.33 N.S.)**			(F=1.6 N.S.)		
15-24	18.6	18.6	520	21.4	22.2	908
25-34	17.6	17.8	694	18.7	19.1	1053
35+	19.2	19.1	660	18.4	17.3	1083
No. of Living Children	(F=.092 N.S.)			(F=.55 N.S.)		
0	17.7	18.9	300	21.1	19.9	492
1-2	18.6	19.1	478	18.3	17.2	895
3-4	19.1	18.9	450	19.6	20.2	786
5+	18.3	17.5	646	19.3	20.6	871
Age at Marriage	(F=1.8 N.S.)			(F=3.8*)		
10-14	21.1	20.8	486	21.5	21.3	867
15-16	18.9	18.5	574	20.8	20.5	1014
17-19	15.4	15.7	486	15.4	15.4	735
20+	17.9	19.1	328	18.7	19.8	428
Marital Status	(F=.50 N.S.)			(F=3.4 N.S.)		
Currently Married	18.6	18.7	1767	19.7	19.7	2866
Widowed/Divorced/Separated	15.9	14.4	107	14.0	14.6	178

Wife's Education		(F=1.3 N.S.)		(F=.46 N.S.)
Illiterate	18.9	1378	19.5	2886
1-4 grades	21.0	128	16.2	74
5+ grades	15.8	368	16.7	84
Husband's Education	(F=4.7*)		(F=.79 N.S.)	
Illiterate	21.6	739	19.3	1997
1-4 grades	21.4	154	20.9	273
5-9 grades	17.7	485	20.3	577
10+ grades	13.5	496	15.7	197
Births last 5 yrs.	(F=.30 N.S.)		(F=1.8 N.S.)	
0	18.2	865	19.3	1324
1	20.0	320	21.7	663
2+	18.1	689	17.9	1057
R^2 (adjusted)	31.1		37.2	
N	1874		3044	
Grand mean	18.5		19.4	

[1]The adjusted percentages are calculated after controlling for the effects of the variables included in this table.

Note: The F values in the table represent a measure of association between the predictor in question and the dependent variable, without controlling for the effect of any of the other variables included in the table.
*Significant at p=.05.
**N.S. means Not Significant.

women.[23] Such a trend is not apparent from our analysis of all working women in Table 5.[24] In fact, the variation by wife's age, number of living children, age at marriage and births in last five years (recent fertility) is generally small and insignificant. It was argued in the earlier study that larger family size constituted a demographic pressure (for the other-employed women) which pushed women into the labour force. Such a phenomenon is not visible for all employed women in the PFS, 1975. It is nevertheless the relatively illiterate women with relatively more illiterate husbands who are in the labour force. Such participation is rooted probably in the following reasons. First, the lower SES women probably have a greater economic need to work than the higher SES women. Second, work is socially more permissible for the lower SES women—both as the women perceive the situation and as the community (including the peer group) and society defines the situation for them.

As mentioned earlier, one finding which is contrary to the 1961 Census and 1973 HED Survey is the smaller proportion of widowed and divorced women who reported themselves to be in the labour force in the PFS, 1975. Sixteen per cent of the urban and 14 per cent of the rural widowed and divorced women were in the labour force compared to 19 and 20 per cent of urban and rural currently married women (Table 5). It might be recalled that both the 1961 Census and the 1973 HED Survey had shown considerably higher participation rates for widowed and divorced women as compared to currently married women (see Appendix Table 2). This contradiction in activity rates for the groups of currently married as opposed to widowed and divorced women is puzzling, and needs further investigation.[25]

Summary and discussion

The three themes that were pursued in this paper consisted

23. Other-employed refers to women who were employees rather than own-account workers.
24. It is possible that we might get similar findings if we analysed the groups of self-employed and other-employed women separately.
25. This differential may partly be explained by the relatively more

of: (i) examining the trends in female labour force participation rates from 1951 to the latest available survey in 1975; (ii) analysing trends in the occupational structure and (iii) studying the correlates of female work participation in rural and urban Pakistan. Several sources of labour force data, including Censuses and Sample Surveys, were used for the analysis. Some of the major differences (methodological and others) among the various sources have been listed and taken into account while making comparative conclusions.

Contrary to the earlier findings which reported a consistently low participation rate varying from roughly 6-10 per cent among women age ten and over, data from two national KAP demographic surveys show that the participation rates reported by the women (themselves) are about twice as high. Nineteen per cent of the currently married women in the NIS and 18 per cent in the PFS reported that they were economically active at the time of the interview. These higher participation rates, it has been argued, are closer to the 'true' rates of work participation in Pakistan. The 'true' rate might be even higher. An accurate estimate of the actual participation rates for females cannot be obtained from the Census and Labour Force Surveys, largely because of the relatively greater underreporting of female activities that is likely to occur when a male respondent reports on female economic activity. There is an urgent need for specially designed methodological studies aimed at assessing the quantum of female participation in various activities in order to undertake effective human resource planning, development and utilisation.

The gap between rural and urban participation rates seems to be closing, as seen from two recent surveys (HED and PFS). Significantly more urban women have been reported to be in the labour force in the 1970s as compared to the 1960s. Such an increase in activity rates for urban females perhaps provides an indication of expanding work opportunities for women. Such opportunities, if they have actually expanded, continue to be concentrated in the traditional occupations like spinning,

accurate reporting of economic activity for the currently married women in the PFS as compared to earlier sources (1961 Census and HED Survey).

tailoring and domestic service. Almost three-fourths of all employed urban women were engaged in these three occupations in 1975. Also, a significantly larger proportion (40 per cent) of the rural women was engaged in spinning and tailoring occupations than reported in earlier surveys (10 per cent in NIS and 2 per cent in HED). The proportion of urban professional women does not seem to have increased over the years, and stands at about 8 per cent in 1975, with nurses and teachers continuing to form the bulk of professional women.[26]

The persistent higher participation of urban women, and the growing proportion of rural women, in cottage-industry occupations which can be performed in the home indicate both a preference for, and availability of such jobs. It is reasonable to conclude that more women would be willing to work in such occupations (which could be pursued within the home) if they are provided the skills and additional jobs are made available. As the female labour force gets educated and acquires more varied skills, a diversification of the occupational structure would be expected. Planning for such diversification, however, must take into account the cultural constraints attached to the permissibility of female work. The trends in the structure of the female labour force lead us to believe that there is at present a demand for jobs related to the cottage industry in both rural and urban areas, and more women would participate in such activities if the opportunity were provided. One other area in which it might be possible to expand job opportunities for women is that of primary school teachers in boys' schools. This would be socially permissible, but might be feasible only if the female teachers are not displacing male teachers who do not have alternate job opportunities.

The question relating to the correlates of female work was examined in order to understand some of the motivations behind work participation. Analysis of the 1975 PFS showed that the single factor which exerts a strong (negative) influence on work participation of urban women is the family's socio-economic level, as measured by husband's education. In other

26. The exceptionally high figures for professional women provided by the 1973 HED Survey have been discussed earlier.

words, women who do not have an economic need to work don't work. The picture is, however, not so simple since larger proportions of women in urban areas are now working. Demand for work cannot be viewed as a homogeneous entity since demand might vary under different conditions. We offer the following hypothetical framework for future validation. Given the relatively homogeneously low socio-economic levels in the rural areas, we feel that the response to opportunities in rural areas would be larger in magnitude. In the urban areas the response would be more diverse. At one end of the scale are the relatively more illiterate (poorer) women who work out of sheer necessity. In the middle there is a sizeable group of women whose husbands have reasonable education (Matric to B.A.) which can enable them (husbands) to get relatively low-paid clerical and administrative jobs. This group seems to define female work in more negative terms than the low SES group. At the other end of the scale, there is a small group of highly educated (M.A. and above) women with educated husbands, if married. We believe that the innate demand for jobs is relatively higher in this group.

This kind of curvilinear relationship is pointed out by Farooq.[27] Also, evidence of a greater demand for jobs by educated women is provided in a study by Korson.[28] He shows that even though a large proportion of the female university graduates said that their parents would allow them to work only under *purdah* conditions many of these graduates were employed, not necessarily in occupations offering such conditions, or were looking for work. Eighty five per cent of the graduates in Karachi and 65 per cent in Lahore were employed or were looking for work.[29] The proportion of unemployed women was particularly high in Lahore—32 per cent. One reason for the higher employment of Lahore graduates could be the non-availability of jobs that would provide *purdah* conditions—jobs that their parents would define as being permissible.

27. Ghazi M. Farooq (see footnote 8 on page 102).
28. J. Henry Korson, 'Career Constraints Among Women Graduate Students in a Developing Society: West Pakistan', *Journal of Comparative Family Studies*, 1 (n. 1 autumn 1970).
29. J. Henry Korson, op. cit., Table 5.

On the other hand, almost two-thirds of the Lahore graduates had been trained in the humanities disciplines which offer relatively fewer job opportunities. Thus it seems that the type of skills as well as cultural constraints related to skill acquirement and utilisation can act as barriers in limiting the potential contribution of females to the labour force. This is particularly true in societies where sex segregation is a positive value.

APPENDIX

TABLE 1: Activity Rates by Age of Women, 1961 Census and 1973 HED Survey

Age	1961 Census[1] Rural	1961 Census[1] Urban	1961 Census[1] Total	1973 HED Survey[2] Rural	1973 HED Survey[2] Urban
10-14	6.0	1.3	4.7	3.2	1.1
15-19	9.4	2.4	7.6	4.1	2.1
20-24	11.6	4.0	9.6	5.4	4.2
25-29	12.8	5.1	10.6	5.8	4.2
30-34	12.8	5.1	10.6	5.9	4.2
35-39	12.8	5.1	11.7	5.8	3.9
40-44	12.8	5.1	11.7	5.9	4.2
45-49	13.1	6.7	11.8	5.3	4.0
50-54	13.1	6.7	11.8		
55-59	11.4	5.4	10.8	4.3**	4.4**
60-64	8.7*	4.6*	10.8	4.3**	4.4**
65+			8.8		

[1]From Karwanski, 1970, Appendix I-II

[2]Activity rates for women who were currently working the week prior to survey.

*Rate for women age 60+

**Rate for age 50+

TABLE 2: Percentage of Employed Women by Age and Marital Status, Rural and Urban Pakistan

Marital Status	1961 Census % of Married Women 10 *	1973 HED Survey Women 15-49 R	1973 HED Survey Women 15-49 U	1973 HED Survey Women 50-65 R	1973 HED Survey Women 50-65 U	1973 HED Survey Women 15+ R	1973 HED Survey Women 15+ U	1975 PFS Women 45-49 R	1975 PFS Women 45-49 U
Single	0.7	5.2	5.3	22.5	19.1	5.6	5.5	—	—
Married	1.4	5.3	2.6	4.4	2.8	5.1	2.7	19.7	18.6
Widowed	6.1	11.0	14.2	4.6	7.1	6.7	9.5	14.0	15.9
Divorced	12.1	9.8	11.6	5.6	11.4		11.6		

*Pertains only to women 10+ in non-agricultural labour force. Similar figures for women in the agricultural labour force were not available.
Sources: *Population Census of Pakistan*, 1961, Vol. 4 Table 4, and Vol. 3, Table 13 HED Survey and PFS data.

4 Family Status and Female Work Participation

Victor S. D'Souza

The study of participation of women in the working force is beset with many difficulties. First of all the problems of measuring the extent of their participation in gainful employment has not yet been solved. Attempts at refining the definition of the working force affected the measures of female work participation the most as in the 1961 and 1971 censuses. However, distortions brought about in the rate of female work participation by changes in the definition of the working force apart, there are certain clearly discernible trends about female work participation which are quite puzzling.

A careful examination of the census figures shows that while the rate of male work participation is more or less uniform, that of female work participation fluctuates very highly from region to region. The percentage of women workers in the total working force as well as their percentage in the total female population have been declining. Underlying the overall trend there are certain structural features and the changes in these features which can be gleaned from the census data as well as the various city surveys conducted recently. While the majority of both male and female workers are illiterate, the percentage of illiterate workers among females is much larger than among males. When occupations are divided into different prestige grades the proportion of workers in the lower prestige grades is much larger among females than among males. The rate of female work participation declines from rural to urban and from smaller to larger communities.[1]

Two hypotheses

It is possible to explain these trends with the help of a theoretical model using generalisations of an economic nature, as I did in my earlier study.[2] The model is based on two hypotheses. First, the main reason why most women work is the low income of their menfolk. When the husband's income is not adequate for the support of the family, the wife also is compelled to work. This hypothesis agrees with the fact that the vast majority of women are employed at lower occupational prestige levels and it can be presumed that their husbands are also employed in correspondingly lower prestige occupations with very low incomes. The hypothesis is further corroborated by the data pertaining to rural agricultural labour families which show that the higher the wage rate for men the lower is the number of women per family in the working force.[3]

The second hypothesis of the model is that with the socio-economic growth of a society the proportions of occupations of higher prestige are, on the whole, increasing at the cost of occupation of lower prestige. This has been clearly demonstrated in the case of the U.S.A.[4] and I have indicated that a similar trend is visible in our country also.

By relating these two hypotheses it is possible to derive some implications for trends in female work participation. It is obvious that the occupational structures of rural and urban communities are different. In the urban communities there are relatively lower proportions of occupations in the lower prestige

1. Victor S. D'Souza, *Social Structure of a Planned City: Chandigarh* (New Delhi: Orient Longman Ltd, 1968), pp. 241-242; Kamla Nath, 'Women in the Work Force in India', *Economic and Political Weekly*, III (August 3, 1968), pp. 1205-1213.
2. Victor S. D'Souza, 'Implications of Occupational Prestige for Employment Policy in India', *Artha Vijnana*, 1 (n. 3, 1959), pp. 233-274.
3. Ibid., pp. 239-240.
4. Nelson N. Foote and Paul K. Hatt, 'Social Mobility and Economic Advancement', *American Economic Review*, XLII (1953).

levels. So also there are lower proportions of occupations of lower prestige in larger communities as compared to smaller ones. Since in the urban areas as compared to the rural ones and in larger communities as compared to smaller ones, there are higher proportions of men in higher prestige and hence higher income occupations, lesser proportions of women will have need for employment. Hence the differential female work participation rate. In the country as a whole it is evident that the proportion of urban population has been increasing in the recent decades and so is the proportion of people living in larger cities. There is also continuous socio-economic growth. These trends account for a diminution in the rate of female work participation.

It is on the basis of this analysis that I predicted that the proportion of women workers in the working force would come down as long as the proportion of occupations at the lower prestige level keep on diminishing as a result of socio-economic growth.[5] Nath's analysis of the female working force in the 1971 census lends support to my prediction.[6]

But there is another important trend in female work participation which, although I noticed in my study referred to above, I did not take into account in the analysis because it was then of a small magnitude. The trend is that while at the lower levels of education, say below Matriculation, with increasing education of women the rate of female work participation declines (which is consistent with my theoretical framework), at higher educational levels the rate goes on increasing (which is inconsistent). This trend was relatively more prominent in the 1961 census.[7] If it is assumed that at higher educational levels the husbands or fathers of working women are also working in higher prestige and higher income occupations, there is no ostensible reason for the women to work. Therefore, the hypothesis that the low income of their menfolk is the main reason why some women work, which is an important assumption of my theoretical framework, stands unsupported. It has, therefore, become necessary for me to re-examine the model.

5. D'Souza, see footnote 2 on page 126.
6. Nath, see footnote 1 on page 126.
7. Nath, ibid., pp. 1206-1207.

The contradictory evidence shows that I had given too narrow an interpretation to the factor of economic motive by regarding it as a need to make both ends meet—for mere subsistence. It would, however, appear that the economic motive is almost universal; if one has enough income for raising one's standard of living; and even if one has enough wealth for a comfortable living one would still desire more money for the power and prestige which wealth brings. If the economic motive for women to work is a universal one, it obviously cannot account for the fact that some women work while others do not.

Curvilinear relationship

The revised theoretical framework has to reconcile two apparently irreconcilable trends: (a) in the lower educational levels the rate of female work participation declines with the increase in education, and (b) in higher educational levels the rate increases with increase in education. The two trends together represent a curvilinear relationship between the rate of female work participation and the education of women. It would appear that the change from the linear to the curvilinear relationship between these variables is a relatively recent one which has been brought about by the growth of education.

One of the important assumptions of the earlier theoretical framework is that work participation on the part of women is related to the type of employment of their male relatives like husbands and fathers. A major dimension of occupations which is relevant for studying the relationship between the occupation of women and their male relatives, say, husbands, is their prestige. But the earlier observation was that with the increase in the occupational prestige of husbands the rate of work participation on the part of wives declined in a linear relationship.

The observation of the more recent trend of the curvilinear relationship between the education of women and their work participation led to a re-examination of the relationship between the rate of work participation of women and the occupational prestige of their husbands with reference to more recent information. The relevant data from the study of Chandigarh[8] are presented in Table 1 according to the percentage of working wives in the various occupational prestige categories of husbands who are heads of households. The occupations are classified into seven prestige categories, from the highest to the lowest, according to an objective scale of occupational prestige devised for that study.[9] It can be seen that in the lower prestige levels of husbands, i.e., from category VII to category V the percentage of working wives goes on diminishing with the increase in prestige. But from category V onwards, by and large, it goes on increasing. Thus the variation in the rate of participation in work by wives at different prestige levels of husbands' occupations is more or less similar to the rate of female work participation at different educational levels. As in the case of educational levels we have two contradictory trends: (1) at lower prestige levels of husbands' occupations the rate of work participation by wives goes on diminishing with increase in occupational prestige and (2) at higher prestige levels the rate goes on increasing with increase in occupational prestige.

TABLE 1: Percentage of Working Wives in the Occupational Prestige Categories of Husbands

Occupational prestige categories of husbands	No. of working wives	Total no. of wives	Percentage of working wives to total
I	3	65	4.6
II	12	185	6.5
III	8	307	2.6
IV	24	644	3.7
V	0	143	0
VI	5	213	2.4
VII	11	45	24.4
Total	63	1602	3.9

Source: Victor D'Souza, *Social Structure of a Planned City: Chandigarh* (New Delhi: Orient Longman Limited, 1968).

D'Souza, see footnote on page 126.
D'Souza, ibid., pp. 379-383.

Occupational prestige of wives and husbands

Another important element in the relationship between the employment of wives and their husbands is the relationship between their occupational prestige. This is given in Table 2 in respect of a sample of married working women in Chandigarh taken from a field study conducted by Kulwant Anand.[10] As in the case of the Chandigarh study referred to above the occupations in this case are also classified into seven prestige categories in a descending order using the same occupational prestige scale.

There is a remarkable association between the occupational prestige of wives and husbands. Out of 168 cases for which complete information is available, 79 women (47 per cent) are in the same occupational categories as those of their husbands. In another 45 cases (27 per cent) the occupational prestige categories of the wives are just one step lower than those of their husbands. The general trend is for wives to have occupations either of the same prestige levels or of levels one step lower than those of their husbands. It may, however, be pointed out that in the occupational prestige category III of wives quite a substantial number of women have occupations one step higher in prestige as compared to that of their husbands. This apparent discrepancy is due to the coarseness of the scale for occupational classification. The women in question are mostly primary school teachers who, along with secondary school teachers, are included in prestige category III, whereas their husbands who are mainly clerical workers are included in prestige category IV. If primary school teachers are equated in prestige with clerical workers, these women would mostly have the same occupational prestige as that of their husbands. Thus the evidence on the whole confirms the statement that when both husband and wife work, the wife follows an occupation either of the same or slightly lower prestige as compared to the occupational prestige of her husband. The prevalence of wide disparity between the occupational prestige

10. Kulwant Anand, 'Impact of Changing Status of Women on Population Growth' (Chandigarh: Unpublished Ph.D. dissertation, Punjab University, 1970).

of husband and wife, and also cases in which the wife has higher occupational prestige, are very rare. These findings are supported by the evidence reported in another study of the same community but using a different sample.[11]

TABLE 2: Occupational Prestige of Wives and Husbands

Occupational prestige categories of wives ↓ \ Occupational prestige categories of husbands →	I	II	III	IV	V	VI	VII		Total
I	15	4	2	2					23
II	5	12						1	18
III	3	25	5	15				3	51
IV		1	3	5				2	11
V			1	8	8	4		3	19
VI					3	4		6	14
VII				1		1	35	2	39
Total	23	42	12	30	6	9	36	17	175

Source: Kulwant Anand, 'Impact of Changing Status of Women on Population Growth' (Unpublished Ph. D. dissertation, Panjab University, 1970).

In addition to the two empirical generalisations noted above this evidence provides a third generalisation stemming from the relationship between the employment of husbands and wives. This may be stated as follows. There is an association between the occupational prestige of husbands and wives, the wives' occupational prestige on the whole being slightly lower than that of their husbands.

While the first two generalisations indicate contrary trends in the work participation of women at different prestige levels, the third generalisation points to a uniform pattern in the association between the occupational prestige of husbands and wives at all levels. It, therefore, suggests the possibility of finding a larger generalisation which can explain all the three different trends.

11. D'Souza, *Social Structure of a Planned City: Chandigarh*, p. 80.

Family status consistency

In the three empirical generalisations just discussed the unit of analysis is the husband and wife pair and the major variable considered is occupational prestige. It would, therefore, occur to one that for a logical explanation of the phenomena under study one should consider the family and its status as important elements in one's analytical framework. In sociological literature the family is usually taken as a status unit meaning thereby that the husband and wife who constitute integral members of a family have the same status. To be more specific, in most of the societies including that of India which are male dominated, the wife occupies a slightly lower status in the family as compared to the husband. Therefore, for consistency in family status husband and wife should have near equal status, the husband being slightly superior to his wife. Family status consistency is necessary for an efficient functioning of the family, and since the family is an integral unit of society it can be assumed that there is always a tendency for the family to maintain a consistent status system.

On the other hand, the status of a person is usually derived from his occupational prestige. Generally, it is the man who is considered to be the natural breadwinner in the family, and the various members of the family including his wife derive their status from his occupational prestige. So long as only the man in the family is working there is no ambiguity about the status of different members in the family. If the wife is also working, this raises problems for family status consistency. For consistency the wife should follow an occupation which is almost equal in prestige to the husband's occupation or slightly inferior to it. If the wife is not able to fulfil this condition she does not participate in work.

Three factors

The above reasoning gives rise to a fourth more general hypothesis, namely, the work participation of wives or female work participation is a function of family status consistency.

This hypothesis is in conformity with the third generalisation noted above that the occupational prestige of women is either the same or slightly less than that of their husbands, which provides positive evidence of concomitant variation in support of the former. To substantiate the fourth generalisation more fully it is also necessary to adduce negative evidence of concomitant variation. It would consist in showing that if the wife is not working it is because she is unable to secure an occupation at the level of family status consistency. Since occupational prestige and educational level are interrelated, it would mean that in the case of working wives their education is almost equal to that of their husbands, as a consequence of which they have succeeded in securing occupations at consistent levels; on the other hand, in the case of non-working wives there is a wider disparity between their education and that of their husbands because of which they are unable to secure occupations at consistent levels.

The above hypothesis can be tested from data taken from the study of Kulwant Anand, referred to already, which consists of two samples, one of working married women and the other of non-working married women, but derived from the same community, namely, Chandigarh. In Table 3 the samples of working and non-working women are classified according to their own educational levels and those of their husbands. It can be seen that in the case of working wives there is a great similarity between their levels of education and those of their husbands, whereas in the case of non-working wives there are wide disparities; while 117 out of 169 (67 per cent) working wives are at the same educational levels the corresponding number among the non-working wives is only 26 out of 150 (17 per cent). This confirms the hypothesis that if the wives are not working, it is because they are unable to secure occupations at consistent levels.

Now it can be explained why at the lower educational levels of women and at the lower prestige levels of husbands the rate of female work participation decreases and at higher levels it increases. The explanation has to take into account several factors: (a) first of all, for participation in work a woman's education should be more or less equal to that of her husband;

TABLE 3: Sample of Working (N=169) and Non-Working (N=150) Married Women in Chandigarh According to Education of the Subjects and their Husbands

Education of Husbands → Education of Wives ↓	Working women							Non-working women						
	Illiterate	Below Matric	Matric	Graduate	Post-Graduate & Professional	Total		Illiterate	Below Matric	Matric	Graduate	Post-Graduate & Professional	Total
Illiterate	43	6	1			50		3	6	4	7	7	20
Below Matric	2	10	9			21			3	26	19	7	55
Matric	1		9	11	3	24			2	10	20	16	48
Graduate			1	13	11	25					2	15	17
Post-Graduate & Professional	1		1	5	42	49					2	8	10
Total	47	16	21	22	56	169		3	11	40	50	46	150

Source: Kulwant Anand, op. cit.

(b) a second factor is the requirement that the wife should be subordinate to the husband. Because of this a man usually marries a woman younger to him in age and also less educated than he. If we look at Table 3 we find that it is only rarely that the wife's education is higher than that of her husband. Among working women such cases are only 11 out of 169 and among non-working women they are 4 out of 150. Then again in 12 out of the total of 15 aberrant cases the difference between the wife's and husband's educational levels is only one step. It is also possible that in such cases what is lacking in the quantity of the education of the husband is made up by its quality, as, for instance, in the case of a husband who is a first class graduate married to a third class postgraduate wife; (c) A third factor in the explanation is that hitherto the education of women has been more neglected than that of men so that at every level of education there are relatively more men than women.

From an analysis of these three factors it becomes evident why the variation in the rate of female work participation in different educational categories follows a curvilinear pattern. According to factor (b) at one extreme, all illiterate men have to marry only illiterate women and at the opposite extreme all highly educated women have to marry only highly educated men. Therefore, because of factor (c) the chances of husbands and wives having equal educational background are the greatest in the case of wives who are either illiterate or highly educated. Hence by factor (a) the rate of work participation on the part of women is greater when they are illiterate or when they are highly educated.

Some applications

Because of the intimate relationship between educational levels and occupational prestige, the above reasoning can also be employed to explain the curvilinear relationship between the variation in the rate of female work participation and occupational prestige levels of husbands.

The preceding analytical framework can also be used to show why there is a marked decline in the rate of female work participation from the rural to urban communities and from smaller to larger communities. In the rural areas the overwhelming majority of men and women are illiterate and, consequently, most of the husband-wife pairs have equal education, making it possible for relatively more women to take to gainful employment. In the urban communities, because of the growth of education the disparity in the education of husband and wife occurs in a greater proportion of husband-wife pairs and, consequently, a relatively lower proportion of women is able to secure occupations at consistent levels. Larger the community, the greater the development of education, the greater the proportion of husband-wife pairs with educational imbalance and so smaller the rate of female work participation.

The tendency for the rate of female work participation to decline in the urban communities, however, is not an indefinite one. In these communities, while the chances for husbands and wives to have equal education at lower levels diminish, such chances increase at higher levels The net decrease or increase in the rate would depend upon the magnitude of these two opposite trends. To begin with, the decline in the rate at the lower educational level would be greater than its increase at the higher level, but eventually, its increase at the higher level would more than offset the decrease at the lower level and on the whole the rate would increase. I have discussed this phenomenon elsewhere.[12]

Thus, I have demonstrated in this paper that through a system of logically interrelated propositions it is possible to explain the different features of the female work participation. It may be pointed out that social causation is a highly complex phenomenon involving a large number of factors making up the casual nexus. For a satisfactory solution of a problem all the relevant factors have to be identified and the nature of their relationship should be specified and this has to be accomplished in a theoretical framework. I should admit that in the present case I have not taken into account all the factors,

---

12. Victor S. D'Souza, 'Changing Socio-Economic Conditions and Employment of Women', in *Trends of Socio-Economic Change in India 1871-1961* (Transactions, Vol. 7: Simla: Indian Institute of Advanced Study, 1969), pp. 443-457.

but indicated some of the important ones.

For instance, while the consistent educational background is an important factor in a wife's participation in work, by itself it may not be sufficient; in addition, it is necessary that suitable occupation should be available and also that it should be conveniently located so that her customary residence with her husband is not disturbed. The type of occupational structure of the community is also an important variable. Factors like these should be taken into account in formulating a theoretical framework for the actual solution of a given problem about female work participation. It should also be borne in mind that the propositions put forward may not be adequate for explaining problems of all kinds in the field under consideration. For instance, one may use the generalisation that female work participation is determined by family status consistency to explain changes in the rate of female work participation in a given region and over a period of time, but it cannot provide an explanation of the variation in the rate among different regions, without taking into account important historical and cultural factors.

In discussions about the economic independence of women and their right to work, the economic and legal issues, such as, equal employment opportunities and equal wages for equal work at par with men, usually come to the fore. Such issues can also be legislated upon. One may, therefore, get away with the impression that the constitutional right of women to work could be secured through legal means alone. This paper, however, has focused attention upon some important social structural factors which also underlie the participation of women in work. Not all these factors are susceptible to legal manipulation but can only respond to broad social changes and social movements.

Among the relevant publications which have come to my notice since my article was first written, two papers, one by Ritter and Hargens[13] and the other by Valerie Kincade

---

13. Kathleen V. Ritter and Lowell L. Hargens, 'Occupational Positions and Class Identifications of Married Working Women: A Test of the Asymmetry Hypothesis', *American Journal of Sociology*, 80 (n. 4, 1975), pp. 934-948.

Oppenheimer,[14] deserve special attention. The conclusions reached by these authors about the economic role of women in the American society are akin to my explanation about the participation of women in the working force in India. However, their approaches and mine are different.

Although the scientific method involves both induction and deduction, in actual practice one may adopt either of the following two procedures: (1) Deduction followed with induction, and (2) Induction followed with deduction, and again with induction. My study has followed the second course. The point at issue in my study is why some women work whereas others do not. Starting the study with deduction would have meant the formulation of a theoretical model so that the selection of the problem would have come as a hypothesis deduced from this model. As I was unable to do this to begin with, I started my investigation with empirical observation and arrived at a series of empirical generalisations through induction. The insights drawn from these generalisations have served as a basis for formulating a theoretical model as the second major step in my study. The solution of the problem that the female work participation is related to the requirements of family status consistency, has been deduced from this model. The hypothesis has been tested through the method of induction once again.

Ritter and Oppenheimer have followed the first of the above two procedures, which starts with deduction. Their objectives are to test some of the hypotheses about women's economic role, which can be deduced from the theory about the American nuclear family put forward by Talcott Parsons. Some of the relevant formulations of Parsons are that the American nuclear family is a unit of diffuse solidarity and as a result, the members of a given family must share a common status in the overall system of stratification; that the primary determinant of the family's status is the occupational position of the husband; that because of the possibility of disruptive status competition between husband and wife, the society and the members of the family ignore the occupational status of the wife (if she is

---

14. Valerie K. Oppenheimer, 'The Sociology of Women's Economic Role in the Family', *American Sociological Review*, 42 (n. 3, 1977), pp. 387-406.

employed) and perceive only the husband's occupational position as giving status ranking to the family.[15]

The theory of Parsons about the nuclear family gives rise to the following hypotheses among others: (1) Even when the wife is working, her status will be derived entirely from the occupational status of her husband and not from that of her own occupation; (2) For the reasons of avoiding status competition with her husband, the wife, if employed, will play only a marginal economic role by following an occupation of a much lower status in comparison to her husband (Oppenheimer).

After deducing these and other related hypotheses from the theoretical formulations of Parsons, Ritter and Hargens, and Oppenheimer in their respective studies examine the empirical evidence on the occupational status of wives in relation to that of their husbands. Their conclusions are that the above hypotheses are invalid. The status of a working women is as much influenced by her own occupational status as by that of her husband. So also, rather than a wife's taking up an occupation much lower in status than that of her husbands' occupation, the tendency is for the wife to equalise her occupational status with that of her husband. Parsons' assumption that the family as a whole constitutes a single unit of status is substantiated but his other assumption that the status of this unit is solely determined by the occupational status of the husband, turns out to be untrue. The occupational status of the wife also is aimed at maximising the status of her family and in doing so an effort is made at achieving consistency or compatability between the roles of husband and wife and at avoiding competition.

The conclusions drawn by these authors in the process of testing the theory of Parsons about the American nuclear family thus agree with my theoretical model partially explaining the reasons why some women work whereas others do not, although our objectives and approaches have been different. Ritter's and Oppenheimer's studies along with mine indicate that work participation of women in the USA and India follow certain broad patterns which are similar.

15. Ritter and Hargens, op. cit.

5 Women in Bangladesh: Food-for-Work and Socio-Economic Change

Marty Chen
Ruby Ghuznavi

Saleha and her daughter walk down the lane that leads from their village onto a well-packed mud road shaded by overhanging bamboo. Some three miles further the road suddenly ends. Saleha and her daughter climb down a gentle slope and up onto a newly-raised extension. Alongside lies a deep water channel, now dry. The earth at the bottom of the channel looks hard and packed. A few women have begun digging a pit deeper still. A rampway of earth runs alongside the pit. Certain other women are carrying baskets brigade-style up the slope.

Saleha and her daughter join the ranks of the basket carriers who move steadily in a slow pattern. Each woman carries a basket of earth the distance of ten feet (if on the slope) or fifteen feet (if on the level) and transfers the heavy basket from her hip to the hip of the next woman. She then picks up the empty basket dropped by that woman and returns to her starting point to receive a freshly loaded basket. The motion of hips and backs as they transfer baskets is fascinating. The women have perfected the transfer. Their motion is graceful but the load is heavy. Each woman wears a rag of quilt on her left hip to cushion the weight of the filled baskets. The last in the chain of basket carriers dumps the earth onto the extension.

Saleha is the leader of the gang of female labourers from her own village. Her daughter is a member of the gang.

During a mid-morning break, Saleha sits hunched under the shade of a tree and begins her story:

> I was the only child of my parents. They died when I was just a baby. So my maternal uncle, *mama*, raised me. He was like a father to me—kind and loving. He died only recently. He was always a reasonably prosperous man and owned 20 naukhas (boats) when he died. His four sons were like brothers to me. My childhood was a happy one.

Saleha's *mama* arranged her marriage. Her husband was the only surviving child of his parents. He tilled the 5 *pakhis* of land belonging to his family. But this land was gradually eaten away by the Barol river. 'My daughters never saw our fields', sighs Saleha. After the birth of their fourth daughter, Saleha's husband alone could not support the large family. Her *mama*, who maintained a kind relationship (bringing her home for visits; presenting her gifts of clothing, etc.) could not be expected to help them out in any substantial, steady way.

Saleha began to work in other people's homes. She would receive 5 annas for a day's work: husking, cooking, house-repair, whatever in other households. Her *mama* was furious, 'You should not work for other people'. There was much unpleasantness and many quarrels between Saleha and her *mama*. He offered to look after Saleha and her children if she returned to his house. The village community sided with the *mama*. 'But how could I abandon my husband and his family?' protests Saleha. She resisted her relatives' and the village community demands. She would not beg, she would not steal, she would not abandon her husband. She would work and prove how hard she could work.

Saleha was embarrassed, at first, to work in the open. 'I worked in the fields at night, by moonlight, or at times when there was the least likelihood of being seen. I did any kind of work I could find—resurfacing houses with mud and dung, planting *khejur* (date palm) and other fruit trees, paddy husking, harvesting'. As she grew accustomed to the work, the criticism also died down. Survival of the family became particularly difficult during the flood of 1954. Saleha's husband sold their house for

Tk. 50 (about US $ 6.00 at the time) to a distant relative—without Saleha's consent or knowledge. They were allowed to continue living in the same house. But Saleha is still resentful, 'We could have scraped through without that Tk. 50 and own something today'.

> My husband is a day labourer (*kamla*). For three months of the year, during harvest, he takes our young son (12 years or so) to work with him in other districts. I have two married daughters who live in other villages. Their in-laws are good. Their husbands are also day labourers, but my daughters do not need to work. And their husbands will not let them work. My third daughter was divorced by her husband, who returned to his first wife. They had no children. She now lives and works with me. My youngest daughter worked alongside me at food-for-work last year. She was married recently to a young man she met at the work site. So now we are four persons at home.

Many of the Pachbarol gang are widowed or deserted. The husbands of the rest, if not weak and disabled, are day labourers dependent on seasonal work. Like Saleha, the women have been forced to seek odd jobs: processing rice and repairing the houses of wealthier village neighbours or working as bond servants in a nearby town. Last year they formed a gang to seek work as earth-cutters. Saleha was their leader.

Saleha is one of 303 female labourers interviewed for a recent study sponsored by the World Food Programme, Bangladesh. Although Saleha and others like her have done odd jobs outside their villages before, the participation of women in rural works schemes is a new phenomenon. How can one explain this phenomenon? Who are the women who participate? Why do they participate? This paper, which is based on the study report, 'Women in Food-for-Work: The Bangladesh Experience', attempts to answer some of these questions. But before turning to these answers, let us look for the moment at Saleha's village.

When traditions persist

Saleha's village, Pachbarol, is typical of the rice-growing delta of Bangladesh. The houses and roads are built on raised ground surrounded by watery fields. A lane lined by date-palms winds through the fields linking individual *baris* (compounds of related households). The houses are built variously of mud, jute straw, or woven cane matting attached to bamboo frames with thatched or tin roofs. Smaller structures for sheltering animals, storing grain, housing the ricehusker and the indoor mud stove are scattered about. The houses face inward on the central courtyard whose hard-packed mud surface serves as a drying floor for straw, paddy or fish (whatever the season dictates) and as the outdoor cooking area. Most houses are backed by small vegetable and fruit tree gardens.

The Bangladeshi village woman is busy from before sunrise until after dark. She rises early to wash the previous night's dinner dishes and to prepare and serve breakfast. After breakfast, she must care for the milch animals and poultry, fetch water, and clean the house and kitchen. There are spices to be ground, fruit trees and vegetables to be tended, clothes to be washed. Some part of each day is spent processing rice. Threshed paddy must be parboiled and then spread on a bamboo mat in the open air to dry. The parboiled paddy must then be husked and winnowed before being cooked and eaten. At least one half day a week goes into husking the family's weekly paddy requirements. At harvest time, the village woman must also thresh, winnow, dry and store large quantities of rice. She prepares the rice storage bins, separates some paddy for seed. The village woman stores and sprouts the seed (not only for paddy but also for wheat, pulse, and oil seed crops). She collects fuel and water, makes implements (including the mud stove on which she cooks), cleans and repairs the house and kitchen. In weaving and fishing communities, village women contribute substantially to the work load by making nets and spinning thread.

Early on young village girls, if not in school, are kept busy working at home tending to younger siblings and sharing in household chores. The female literacy rate is very low (27.9 per cent) especially in the villages (10.9 per cent) of Bangladesh. Marriage is almost universal for Bangladeshi women. Most village girls leave their parental homes between the age of 13 and 16 to marry husbands chosen by their parents. The responsibility for their protection is transferred from the father or guardian to the husband and his family. The young bride must now keep her husband and more so her mother-in-law happy. She is broken into her new social and economic roles by her mother-in-law. With the birth of her first son, the bride's status is enhanced. The average Bangladeshi woman undergoes 8 pregnancies and bears 6 live-born children. The older or widowed woman is, traditionally, supported by her sons. If she had no sons, a woman will turn first to her husband's family and then to her own for support. But this support is not guaranteed.

Bangladeshi rural women are conditioned to be dependent both economically and socially. Rural women's work is usually unpaid and unrecognised. Their social roles (whether as daughter, sister, wife, or mother) are defined in relation to their male supporters. The village woman is known chiefly by the kin terms related to her roles, as so-and-so's *bou* (wife), *maa* (mother), or *bhabi* (brother's wife), rather than by her given name. Village women carry little social status as individuals.

Bangladesh is the world's eighth most populous country with nearly 80 million people crammed into a little over 55,000 square miles. Approximately 90 per cent of these people live in the rural sector. The nation's economy is primarily agricultural. Bangladesh agriculture is predominantly subsistence; that is, more production goes for self-consumption than to markets. Rice is the principal food crop. The cash crops include jute, edible oil, tea, tobacco, and sugarcane. Farm holdings are very small and fragmented, and an increasing proportion (perhaps 40 per cent) of the total agriculture labour force comprises landless labourers.

Subsistence farming in Bangladesh involves a partnership with a division of labour by sex. Roles are complementary and well understood within the village. But to the urban visitor or planner, the rural woman remains often 'invisible'. The man's economic role as paddy grower in the fields is 'seen' the woman's role as rice processor in the *bari* is not. Although what the rural woman does is not 'seen', the value added of her work is substantial. Over 15 million women in Bangladesh support themselves by agriculture either as self-employed labourers in their own homesteads or as hired labourers in others'. But for the women who participate in food-for-work the traditional patterns of production, the division of labour by sex, the prevailing cultural influences, and kinship support systems no longer pertain. Let us try to understand what is happening to these women.

As traditions break down

The female labourers in food-for-work projects represent a sub-set of the rural poor of Bangladesh. Women's participation in food-for-work activities is a new phenomenon. The female labourers have not gone unnoticed. Many epithets have been used for these women. They are referred to variously as 'marginal', 'destitute', 'drifting', 'vagrant', 'vulnerable'; and, more elaborately, as 'wretched strugglers for survival on the fringes of farm and city'.

But who, in fact, are these women? A profile of female landless labourers has been drawn from the data on the 303 women interviewed in the study. Women of every age group participate in food-for-work activities in Bangladesh. Most women are between 20 and 50, but about 17 per cent are under 20 years of age. A third of the women are married. But their husbands are day labourers, often unemployed. Another third are widowed. The remaining third are either unmarried, divorced, or deserted. Just under half of the women are the chief income earners for their families. These women average 3.7 dependants each. Although not all are absolutely 'destitutes' in the strictest sense of being divorced or deserted, all are 'destitute' in the sense of being in a condition of extreme need. In better times, these women were sustained by the subsistence economy. But these women can no longer fully depend on their fathers, husbands, sons or their possessions and land.

What then has happened to these women? What are the features of the subculture in which they live?

Most have known better times

The living standard of most of these women has declined during recent years. This decline is accredited by some to the Malthusian principles of population explosion or to laws of inheritance (whereby land becomes increasingly fragmented); others analyse the trend in Marxian terms. The women themselves explain this decline in simpler more concrete terms.

Porishkar (Widow, Manikganj)—There was enough land for my father-in-law and my husband to cultivate and keep the family free of any kind of want or anxiety. There was always plenty for everyone and always enough saved for the future. With their death all this changed. Not being accustomed to earning a living, I lost all our savings and assets and was reduced to total poverty within two years.

These women are roughly one generation away from economic and social security, however marginal. They look back fondly to their days in a subsistence farm household. To those for whom there is no paddy to be husked, no cow to be milked, no food to be cooked, subsistence-level tasks centred in the *bari* are a thing of the past. In looking at these women and their dependants, one is looking at what, years ago, was a subsistence level family. The female landless labourers of today were the subsistence farm labourers of yesterday.

Most have been dependent

Women in rural Bangladesh are conditioned to be dependants. They are dependent, in turn, on fathers, husbands, and sons. They are dependent on the subsistence economy which provides them unpaid agricultural and household employment. Some of the female labourers in food-for-work are still dependent but have taken to supplementing the income of their male supporters. Their family units have fallen below subsistence, their possessions, land and traditional occupations no longer sustain them. Disaster conditions (both man-made and natural), chronic unemployment, coupled with landlessness have brought increasing impoverishment to these family units. As families get poorer all members try as best they can to find small jobs.

Some are now independent

The interdependence of the family unit often breaks down. Male members of the family are the first to seek employment outside the village. Too many times they do not return. Increasing numbers of women are becoming the sole income earners for their dependants. These women have fallen out of the traditional social web into a state of enforced independence. When the subsistence society and economy no longer support women, they enter a frightening independence. Nothing in their unbringing or the rural economy prepares them for this independence or to be sole supporters. All that was the norm is taken away.

These female heads of households become significantly dependent on wage earnings. The most impoverished always fear unemployment. These women could be reduced to beggary or prostitution, in order to provide for their own support and that of their dependants. These women suffer from hunger and exposure. They have no leisure to ask 'why' ? Their only cry is for work. If these women are not allowed to enter the rural wage economy they might drift to the already overburdened towns and cities.

Saleha Begum (Widowed, Barisal)—Since I have come out of my village in search of work, work I shall. If educated women can find work, why can't we? We may not be able to do paperwork but we can cope with any other work, no matter how difficult it is.

All face economic necessity

These women all need work—whether to supplement others' meagre earnings or to eke out their own survival. They face the constant threat of unemployment, of hunger. Work opportunities are upmost in their minds. They will work anywhere. When economic need arises, whenever there is work, these women will go. Traditional work opportunities—agricultural and household—do not argue strongly for these women. They are relatively freed from these responsibilities. They have no paddy to be husked, no cow to be tended, often no rice to be cooked. The rural wage economy is not ready for these women—either economically or socially. There is an imbalance between the demand and the opportunities for rural employment. Moreover, society has not adjusted to offering women equal access to available opportunities. The woman in search of work faces a double obstacle.

Many have paid a social price

Women working in the open fields and roads is a new phenomenon. The rural society in Bangladesh is not ready for these social and economic pioneers. But to these women, economic need argues more strongly than social stigma.

Atika Begum (30, Deserted, Sylhet)—When I first started working to support myself people had much to say against it. I knew that no one would give me a meal, so why would I care about their opinions? They said the world had become a hell, with women working in the fields and roads. I paid no heed to them. People with empty stomachs do not have to worry about social norms. If begging does not hamper my self-respect, why should hard work erode my dignity.

Here are women, below subsistence, who must generate an income whatever the social price.

Social change and economic aspirations

What will become of these women? Obviously, their future is largely being determined by their own resourcefulness. The women themselves will manoeuvre the social transitions required by their economic aspirations. But these economic aspirations must be met. To date, these women are not migrant labourers or vagrants. They still have roots—however tenuous—in their own or their in-laws' village. Employment opportunities must be provided to ensure these roots hold. Food-for-work programmes can guarantee that food aid reaches these women, the poorest of the poor. Food-for-work programmes can address, in part, the women's need for work. The recognition accorded the female participants in food-for-work activities has raised several basic questions. Are there continuing options for these women in the rural wage economy? If not, what will happen to these women in search of work? Food-for-work activities are one answer, but others must be found.

Profiles of women in food-for-work

Porishkar (Widow, Dholai)

Childhood. Now at 30, Porishkar found it difficult to recall the happy, contented days of her childhood. Her father had been a subsistence farmer with three *pakhis* of land, enough to easily support his family of two sons and four daughters. Her mother only took care of the family, never needing to step out of her secure home for anything. Porishkar was the eldest child and a favourite one. To pamper, and marry off with a generous dowry to an affluent boy from the village of Gusta. She was barely 6 years old then (having just lost her first tooth) and her husband, a playful boy of 9 years or so. For the first three years, she was only taken on visits by her father and mother-in-law. She was showered with gifts of clothes and jewellery and plied with special food, so that she would acquire a stronger attachment for them and get to know her husband gradually. When she was 10 years old, she moved into her husband's home permanently.

Early married life. Her husband was the only surviving child of a family of eight children. There was enough land for her father-in-law and her husband to cultivate and keep the family free of any kind of want or anxiety. There was always plenty to go around, plenty put aside for the following years, or so it seemed. Porishkar reciprocated the affection lavished on her both by her in-laws and her husband. She recalled those times tenderly. 'He always bought me little gifts, a new sari, some coloured bangles, some scented hair oil . . . even after the children were born, he would tease me by saying no one in the world cared for me more than he did'.

Her in-laws died when the third child, a daughter, was only a baby. The son and daughter born earlier had both died in their infancy. The $2\frac{1}{2}$ *pakhis* of land which they owned was eroded by the river Barol; to this day she holds the legal documents which will entitle her to claim any 'char' land that may come up during her lifetime. So far, there has been no sign of it.

Widowhood. About 4 years ago when she was expecting her young son, her husband got ill with cholera. In spite of all medical care, he died on the fourth day. 'He left me without any warning. I could never had done that to him'. Not being accustomed to earning a living, she soon worked through her meagre possessions and had to retun to her father's home in Dholai within two years. The prospect of supporting a daughter with two young children did not seem an easy task to her father. He made it very clear that she could stay only if she gave up her children. Or simply remarried. To Porishkar neither of the alternative was acceptable—she could not imagine remarrying, much less abandoning her children. 'I will die with my children clutched to my breast, rather than marry again (*Bachcha muke korey morum kintu beye boshum na*). My father was willing to give a second dowry but not our food.' For deing 'unreasonable' she was forced to leave home within the next months. In the beginning, the neighbours took pity and allowed her to stay in the sheds, the outhouses, or simply under the trees in their compounds (*bhita*). She began supporting herself by collecting grain left in the fields after harvesting. Then she worked at the house repairing, cooking, cleaning, husking paddy, harvesting of turmeric and vegetables, etc. In exchange, she received only food. Soon people tired of having her children around—it meant giving her a little extra food for them. Sometimes, it meant simply the leftovers, sometimes the rice starch (*phen*), both of which would in any case be thrown away. Realising that Porishkar could support herself and the children, her father allowed her to live in his house, on the clear understanding that she would not expect anything else. Very calmly she added, 'And I would not want it otherwise. There will never be any confusion about where his obligations ended, and mine began. But for my children it will not be so. I will educate them both, my son and my daughter, and they can always return to me for help, for love. Their life will be very different from mine'.

The daily pattern of work in the homes, both in her village or in the neighbouring ones, was a set one. She went to work before daylight, cleaning the compound, giving the animals their food and collecting cow dung to make fuel. Washing of the utensils and clothes would be completed before the household awakened. Then she would cook the day's big meal. After everyone had eaten, she would have something to eat depending on what she received. In the afternoon she would do the husking, the plastering of the house (with mud and dung) and other repair jobs. Finally, she would cook the evening's meal, and go home with her share of the food, which was her only payment. Sometimes people were kind enough to give her enough; sometimes not, so that it meant she would be able to feed the children but go hungry herself. During the day, her mother or sister kept an eye on the children but they ate the food put aside by Porishkar, before she left for work every morning.

The present. Two years ago, she and some of her friends approached 'an uncle' to find out whether they could join the earthwork that was going on under a Food-for-work project.

They were told they could and that 20 of them could come from the next day. Sixty turned up, and worked right through the season. The problem of social constraints did not enter the matter—'Nor would it have made any difference to any of us, if people had been critical about our work. We did not beg or steal. Why should we have been ashamed of working?'

She realised that if she did not save a little from her earnings, she would never rise above her oppressive conditions. She bought clothes for the children, a sari for herself, and still had a little saved. At this time, BRAC organised some credit facilities for them with which this group of women decided to do paddy husking during the following months. She and her sister received a loan of Tk. 210 to buy paddy and together they earned enough for her to repay her loan to BRAC, live through to the next work season and also save Tk. 60. For extra earnings, she and her friends also made puffed rice (*muri*) to sell locally. On moonlight nights she made mats from date (*khejur*) leaves to sell for Tk. 6 each.

Unfortunately, both Porishkar and her little son got very ill last winter and although she did not want to waste her savings on medication for herself, she spent more than Tk. 40 of it on her son. Her son survived but where is she to get the kind of food that is needed to nurse him back to his healthy self? She missed part of the earthwork season due to her illness, so that after her great hopes of last year, she was now run down both physically and in spirit.

The future. Now her earnest hope is that she can participate in some agricultural programme, like another group of women in Manikganj, till the next FFW season. 'If I can put some grain in the loft, there will be peace' (*Manchai dhan uthate pari, ta holey shanti*). If the women can get a loan of Tk. 300 they can lease one *pakhi* and harvest 5 or 6 maunds of paddy. They can also do multiple cropping. If they can get this minimal amount of credit, she can answer her 7 year old daughter's painful question, 'Ma we do not have paddy, so can we never eat rice?'

Amirjan (widow, Manikganj)

Pots and pans, two pairs of rubber sandals, patches of an old quilt, and a broom are piled under a jackfruit tree. Nearby is the plinth—now overgrown with pumpkin vines and moss—where a house once stood. This still life in poverty is Amirjan's 'home'. She is called 'Samed Khaner *bou*' (Samed Khan's wife)—although Samed Khan died fifteen years ago.

One daughter, Razia Khanum, arrives. She was married ten years, has one young son and has came home on *nayor* (annual visit to one's parents' house). Her husband promised to send money for food and clothing, but all that she received was the news that her husband had deserted her and their son. She stands on the overgrown plinth to change her sari as if four imaginary walls offer her privacy.

Another daughter—Shamila—arrives carrying a basket of vegetables. She is the youngest child of Amirjan. She was one month old when her father died. Shamila worked last year at food-for-work but her health began to deteriorate. She began coughing up blood. She speaks with a husky voice which belies her youthful, however tired, body and face. She is now more or less bed-ridden with T.B., but she has no bed. She rests where there were once steps leading into their house.

Amirjan arrives She has a soft, moon-shaped face. Her teeth, slightly bucked and separated, are stained with betel juice. She wears an amulet around her neck. This is her story:

Brief childhood. Amirjan was the only child of a cultivator who died when she was still very young. She received some religious schooling. 'I learned *namaz* (prayers) but not the Quran', says Amirjan. When she was seven, her mother remarried.

First marriage. Amirjan's mother married Amirjan to her new stepson in order to ensure her hold on her new husband's property. Amirjan was only seven. As she explains with a laugh, 'I lost my first tooth after marriage'. Her husband, apparently not much older, used to thrash her for not doing housework. One day Amirjan's maternal uncle, *mama*, found Amirjan weeping after a thrashing. Amirjan's *mama* rescued her, took her home, and obtained a divorce for the child bride.

Second marriage. Amirjan's *mama* soon found her another husband. A smile covers Amirjan's face, 'He was older than I and very kind and loving'. Her second husband was the eldest of four sons and a daughter of an affluent man, a village *matabor* (elder) with a flourishing milk business. After the father-in-law died, much of his property and assets was lost in litigation. What remained was divided between the brothers, each of whom got a small portion.

Amirjan and Samed Khan lived the life of the subsistence level farm family. All went well and life was good until Amirjan's husband died 15 years ago.

Widowhood. Samed Khan was the eldest of four brothers. Saber and Maqbal Khan are subsistence level farmers. Saber Khan is comparatively wealthy. He is a member of the Union Parishad and owns 20 *bighas* of land. The three brothers live is one extended compound. They all have large families. The brothers-in-law are unable, or unwilling, to help Amirjan—except when she becomes desperate.

With the death of her husband, Amirjan began working in neighbour's homes to support her family—repairing houses with mud and dung, husking paddy, cooking, cleaning, anything. Five years after the death of her husband, Amirjan sold part of the land she inherited. Three years ago, she sold another 2½ *pakhis* of land. She still owned 3½ decimals of household land and a house. That is, until a storm swept her house away. She cooks now under her jackfruit tree. She and her daughters are allowed to sleep inside the houses of her brothers-in-law.

The children. Three daughters live with Amirjan. Two had once been married. Her eldest daughter was married to a young man of Dhautia village, but he had an affair, married again secretly and, despite the protests of the village elders, divorced Amirjan's daughter. Amirjan's second daughter—Razia Khanum—was recently deserted. The youngest daughter—Shamila—is weakened by T.B. A third daughter, recently married to a tubewell mechanic, lives in a rented house in nearby Manikganj town. Amirjan announces proudly, 'Sometimes I bathe at my third daughter's house in Manikganj, using her soap and oil'.

Survival. Amirjan has a remarkable gift for hanging on, for eking out small wages from odd jobs. She and her three daughters participated in food-for-work activities during the spring, 1976. Paid two seers wheat daily each, they were able to save, four months' wheat earnings lasting them seven months. But a fierce storm in June, 1976, blew their house away and with it many seers of saved, processed wheat. With the monsoon rains of July, 1976, Amirjan was forced to move into Manikganj town where she rented a room for Tk. 30 per month. She and one daughter found jobs as bond servants in a home, but they returned to their village, Dhautia, 'before the elections' of January, 1977.

Back in Dhautia, Amirjan and her daughters sought whatever employment they could find: harvesting *kolai* (lentil) from a 1½ *pakhi* field for Tk. 25; harvesting *payra* from 6-12 noon for Tk. 20; harvesting potatoes from 1-4 p.m., earning 5 seers of potatoes for each maund picked. In the spring of 1977, they did seven days of road building but received a total of only Tk. 7. Amirjan moved on to a food-for-work project and did FFW every morning (6-12 noon) for three months. She harvested and processed tobacco for Tk. 3 per day, once back in Dhautia. Somehow by May, Amirjan had saved enough to build herself a new straw house. The thatch cost her Tk. 120; the jute sticks Tk. 50; another Tk. 100 for bamboos, and, finally, Tk. 60 for the labour charges. Amirjan went into debt for Tk. 50 for her house. But she now has a home. Meanwhile, Shamila's health has improved as she has seen a doctor and is on medication for her T.B.

But not everything is looking up in Amirjan's life. Her third daughter had just returned home from Manikganj town. Her husband had received word from his parents in Barisal district that their house had blown down in a storm. He dispatched a note from his office to his wife saying, 'I have left for Barisal. I will not be able to return until I have made sure that my parents are no longer in need of my presence'. Amirjan has hope, 'I think his intentions are good, I think he will come back'. Meanwhile, no luxury of soap and oil, only an additional mouth to feed. Amirjan has watched times change. 'Marriage in my time was different. I got love and respect from my husband although I came from a modest background. My daughters have been divorced and deserted because I have no money to buy the radios and watches demanded by my sons-in-law. They expect dowries and have no sense of moral obligations. The sons-in-law, if they cannot get anything material out of you, do not stay with your daughters. Marriages have become very unstable'.

Motia (Young girl, Dinajpur)

Motia worked in the Ghagra Canal Re-excavation Project in Dinajpur. This smiling 14 year old informed us that she has become an expert at doing earthwork and would be happy to do it for ever. Behind the smile lay a story of courage, determination and hope.

'My grandfather was a big doctor in Gaibandha. He had educated his only son well and married him to my mother, who was from a well-to-do businessman's family. My father moved to Dinajpur permanently and became a successful construction contractor. He did very well and we were never in any kind of need. In fact, he often helped the poor people of the neighbourhood.

'We three sisters and my little brother had everything we needed. My sisters and I went to school regularly, never thinking life could be any other way. But this did not last. Suddenly my father acquired some eye problem and in spite of all efforts and medication, he lost his sight.

'My mother took over the task of supporting the family and in spite of her initial sense of despair and fear, she managed to fulfil her obligations quite adequately. She could make some herbal medicines and treat common ailments, with which she managed to make ends meet. At no point, did she consider discontinuing our schooling. She believed that if the older two could be educated, we would, in turn, take over the responsibility of bringing up the younger children. But this dream of hers could not be fulfilled. Five years ago, my mother got ill and died. No one could tell from what. I had just finished Class V . . . if she had been alive I would have finished my schooling today.

'After the death of my mother I took on the task of supporting my blind father and my small brother and sisters. I had known a lot of the bricklayers who had worked for my father; I went along with them and joined work, no matter how far from my house it was. I only made sure that I was home before dark, otherwise my brother and sisters would be lonely and afraid. Since then I have worked continuously at earthwork or as a bricklayer's helper.

'What I earn is enough for us but my father who thought he was a burden on me, an extra mouth to fed, moved into the local mosque where he receives his food free. I like earthwork very much because I earn enough for the whole family; also I have become an expert in cutting and carrying earth. This project site is close to my house, so I have no problems getting home early, there is nothing to be afraid of. When I do this kind of earthwork, my worries fall away. I can earn regularly and no longer have to go from place to place looking for work. If I did food-for-work for the whole year I would not be exhausted. In fact, I would be most happy'. Motia's face lights up when she talks about her work.

Ullashini (Non-working husband, Jessore)

Ullashini has been supporting her invalid husband and children for five years now. Yet she still finds it difficult to believe that she is actually coping with it successfully. Her background did not prepare her for such a possibility and it is not without a certain amount of pride that she recounted the story of her life.

'As an only daughter of my parents I was pampered and spoilt, not only by them but also my older brothers, uncles, aunts ... everyone. My father cultivated his own land, my mother looked after the family. I went to school and spent the rest of the time visiting our many relations. Work was not meant for me. My father was reluctant to get me married in case I had to move far away from him. In the end he did manage to find a very good, kind hearted man for me, from our own village.

'My husband's family was quite well off too. My husband was the only one who was not educated, so he had learnt to be a fine weaver. His brothers were teachers and service holders. There was enough for everyone and more. There was peace and harmony as I don't seem to come across in anyone's life today, let alone mine.

'With the death of my father-in-law, the property was divided, giving us all our homes and cultivable land. In the Liberation War we lost a great deal of it but I was grateful to God for sparing our lives. My husband worked harder than ever and managed to keep our family in comfort. We may not have had as much as before but the quality of life had not diminished to any great extent.

'One day, five years ago my husband returned home with a high fever, which continued unabated for six days, in spite of medication. After that he became bloated and doctors could not do anything to ease the condition. For the first time in my life, I knew what real fear was. I did all I could to get him the best medical care. I looked after him day and night but he did not get better. Today, he is still an invalid.

'I was overwhelmed by my problem; I sold all our possessions to get my husband cured but it was not to be. We were faced with an impossible situation. My children were always hungry, there was never enough for them or for me and my husband. I tried to get help from my brothers but by then no one's financial condition allowed them to offer any real help and I needed far too much.

'So I decided that I would take the only recourse left to me. I would find work and support my family. And so I did. I accepted any kind of work I could find just so long as it helped us to survive. I have not been able to send my children to schools as before but there was nothing I could do about that. Today I deeply regret not having learnt to weave from my husband. I could have had a profession to see me through these difficult days—without always dreading whether I will have work tomorrow or will my children be crying in hunger?

'When I first heard of earthwork I was hesitant about going for it. I was not sure I would be able to do those long hours of arduous work. Look at me today. I can not only do it but do it well. I earn enough wheat for my family's consumption. I even manage to save a little. It is not work that I am afraid of but the lack of it.'

Food-for-work: with new opportunities

At the request of the Ministry of Relief and Rehabilitation, Bangladesh, for advice on the integration of women into food-for-work activities, World Food Programme, Dacca, consulted a number of women involved in different women's programmes. An Advisory Committee on Women's Participation in Food-for-Work was formed in March, 1976, to advise the World Food Programme, Dacca, on appropriate and effective means to integrate women into food-for-work activities.

Two members of the Advisory Committee undertook the current research into the socio-economic implications of food-for work for female labourers. The objectives of the research were: (1) to identify, socially and economically, the women who participate in food-for-work activities in Bangladesh; (2) to examine the socio economic implications of food-for-work participation for these women and their families; (3) to quantify a work norm for female labourers in food-for-work; and (4) to derive policy and project recommendations that would ensure women's interest and rights in food-for-work and other development activities in Bangladesh.

Findings in Bangladesh

The food-for-work season comes at the end of the dry, winter months in Bangladesh. Dust hangs in the air. At some projects—pits and tanks—labourers have to lift earth a great height. Other projects—roads and embankments—run on for miles with gangs of workers strung out along each side, digging from small wells of earth. Female labourers do the same work as male labours: that is, gross, physical earth moving. Where women work in mixed gangs men dig the earth and women carry and dump the earth. When they work in female gangs, women dig, lift, carry and dump earth.

There are many channels for recruitment of female labourers to food-for-work activities. Some women, either individuals or in an organised group, request employment from a known gang leader, project supervisor, or local government official. Other are recruited by experienced gang leaders or the local officials incharge of food-for-work activities. The channels for recruitment are various and informal. Most women come from villages within a radius of three miles of a given site. Some women are known to walk more than six miles each way daily.

There are many factors which effect the participation level of women in food-for-work in Bangladesh. The attitudes of officials responsible for implementing food-for-work activities are important. The responsive and supportive official can make all the difference in guaranteeing the recruitment and rights of women in food-for-work activities. Many officials are already favourable and supportive to the employment of women. For some, the employment of women in food-for-work is a new idea. A few officials are obstructionist. One local official, responsible for recruitment, contacted women from other villages but not his own, protesting. 'Women in my village are not needy'. But the needy women from his village organised to request work through another official.

Economic need usually outweighs negative official attitudes and/or social barriers. Economic need argues more strongly than social stigma to these women. When asked why other needy women known to them were not participating in food-for-work, very few women cited social barriers as the obstacle. Most said other needy women found no food-for-work openings. The acutal number of food-for-work opportunities available and/or offered to women is the major constraint to their employment. The actual number of food-for-work opportunities offered to women relates directly to whether officials favour recruitment of women.

Participants in food-for-work are expected to contribute 70 cubic feet of earth-moving daily (the average for the Bangladeshi male) in return for a payment of 3 seers (2.8 kilos) of wheat (the minimal daily requirement for a family of five). Women usually are not able to perform at this level of physical work, in part because of biological differences and in part because of other demands on women's time. Moreover, women, unlike men, have special nutritional needs, over and above the need for physical work. The simplistic response to this work differential was to adjust downwards the wheat payment to women according to their performance by male standards. Numbers of dependants, health and nutritional needs and other socio-economic factors affecting well-being were not taken into account.

Three studies at separate sites indicated that women average 44 5 cft. of earth moved and 2 seers of wheat as payment daily. Part of the difference reflects the fact that women cannot work as many hours a day as men because they have household responsibilities, which include the care of men and children. Male labourers often work a double shift. All female labourers report working a single shift. The female labourers face a double day: earthwork in the morning; processing and cooking wheat, caring for children etc. in the afternoon.

The policy of concession for extraordinary working conditions (e.g. difficult soil conditions, lift, lead, etc), officially called 'payments for allied work', enables male labourers to earn their nutritional requirements even though they may be moving less than the prescribed 70 cft. of earth. An adjusted work norm for women (perhaps equal pay for equal hours) would be consistent with this practice of concessions.

Where the future lies

Saleha's story has a happy ending. Last seen she and her group of co-workers were transplanting paddy. Working alongside them in the same field, were five male daily labourers the women had hired. Not only had these women been reabsorbed into the agricultural sector, but they had overturned the traditional division of labour and dependency pattern. How did this come about? Let us go back to Saleha first seen engaged in food-for-work.

That was during the 1976 food-for-work season, the first year Saleha and her co-workers sought employment in food-for-work schemes. Since then the Pachbarol group with loans from a local rural development agency formed the Pachbarol Destitute Women's Cooperative. Together they have husked paddy for sale and cultivated potatoes and sugar cane on leased land. Most recently they leased four acres of land and purchased several beds of transplant paddy seedlings. They contracted two male relatives (including Saleha's husband) as their 'technical experts'. These men are teaching the women to broadcast and transplant paddy. The two men work alongside and share equally with the women members of the cooperative. As the water receded after the monsoon rains and the rate of transplanting had to be stepped up, the cooperative also hired five male day labourers on a daily wage basis.

Saleha has a pock-marked face. Her eyes are bright. Her cheek bones high and wide. There is a soft smile at all times on her lips. She wears a pair of old, silver bracelets on each arm. She keeps a few Takas and pins and her *paan* (beetle nut) tied in the end of her sari. She has a habit of looking off into the distance—as if remembering something pleasing. But when she speaks of the Pachbarol Cooperative, she talks with a great nodding of her head and sweeping gestures of her hands: 'If we can handle the livestock, surely we can transplant seedlings. Next year we will be able to perform all the agricultural tasks—including ploughing'.

But not all the stories have a happy ending. Since last seen, Porishkar's youngest son has died. Amirjan's third daughter has been deserted. Amirjan and her daughters heard about a rainy season food-for-work scheme (clearing of water hyacinth) but were refused employment by the local Union Council members. As Amirjan says, 'There are 25-30 of us women. We feel we can do the water hyacinth clearing by drawing the hyacinth with a bamboo to the shore and then lifting them to one side. Why should we be refused work'?

What happened to the Pachbarol women has not happened for most other female labourers. The Pachbarol women were identified through food-for-work and supported by a local non-government development agency. They were able to receive cash and kind loans to finance their long-term cooperative activities.

The issues outlined above are not unique to food-for-work projects, but relate to all development programmes in Bangladesh. Food-for-work is simply illustrative of certain basic, larger issues. The central fact is that certain rural women in Bangladesh want paid job opportunities. These women can and want to participate in food-for-work and other wage sector employment opportunities. Food-for-work programmes are positive food aid because the aid is earned, reaches the poorest (by the very nature of the work), and helps women assume new roles. Through food-for-work programmes, which have provided some women entry into the paid labour force, these women have become 'visible'. These women are completely or very significantly dependent on wage earnings, but food-for-work is seasonal and they need year-round employment.

The central problem is the imbalance between demand for and opportunity for rural employment. Women face the additional problem of access to opportunities. These women who need them must be provided opportunities in the wage sector of the rural economy. If they are not so provided, these women might well join the migration to the already overburdened towns and cities. If female landless labourers are to have equal access, as male landless labourers, to any and all employment opportunities in the rural economy, a sustained effort will have to be made to involve them in long-term development activities or full-time wage employment.

6 Women and the Law: Constitutional Rights and Continuing Inequalities

Joseph Minattur

'Our women have more rights than women of other countries, but there are large areas wherein women are suffering, where, maybe they are not conscious of their rights,' said Indira Gandhi, the Prime Minister of India, in April 1975.[1] Her reference here may have been to certain provisions in the Constitution of India relating to equality of the sexes and universal adult suffrage. The Preamble to the Constitution speaks of securing to all citizens of India equality of status and of opportunity as well as justice—social, economic and political. One of the directive principles of state policy prescribes that the state should direct its policy towards securing equal pay for equal work for both men and women. Although the directive principles are fundamental in the governance of the country and are to be applied in enacting legislation, they are not judicially enforceable. In this context, one of the provisions of the Constitution is of special significance. After having laid down that the state shall not discriminate against any citizen on grounds of sex, among other things, it provides that nothing in this article shall prevent the state from making any special provision for women and children.[2] So there is a constitutional

---

1. Gulshan Ewing, 'Indira Gandhi Talks About Women and International Women's Year', *Eve's Weekly* (May 10, 1975), p. 8.
2. Article 15 (3).

provision in India permitting the state to discriminate in favour of women, if such discrimination is found necessary.

Women claim to be the largest minority in India with a variety of social and economic disabilities which prevent them from exercising their human rights and freedoms in society. Child marriage, especially of the female infant, was common; widow marriage was prohibited. Even if she succeeded in escaping from the funeral pyre of her deceased husband where she was expected to be burnt alive, a divorce was generally looked down upon and her remarriage was socially disapproved. If some of these attitudes still persist it is not because legislation has lagged behind, but because law has not succeeded in playing its role of social engineering and changing certain deeply rooted social attitudes. During the last two decades a number of laws were adopted with a view to ensuring equality of status and opportunity for women. But it appears that in practice this equally eludes the Indian woman's grasp.

In what follows an attempt is made to examine some of the more important legislation enacted by the Central legislature[3] in India to ameliorate certain unhappy conditions in which women, particularly Hindu women, found themselves. Occasionally, there is talk about ameliorating the conditions of Muslim women, but political considerations stand in the way of doing anything substantial towards that end. Muslim personal laws are considered to be part of the religion of Islam and government generally considers it necessary not to interfere directly in matters regarded as religious.

Marriage and divorce

With a view to preventing child marriages, especially the giving away of infant girls in marriage, the Child Marriage Restraint Act was passed in 1929 declaring it an offence for a man to marry a girl under fifteen years of age. As amended in 1978,

---

3. Various state legislatures also adopted certain legislative measures; see, for instance, prevention of prostitution enactments and suppression of immoral traffic acts passed in Bihar, Uttar Pradesh and West Bengal.

any person who performs a marriage where the bridegroom is below 21 years or the bride below 18 years commits an offence, as also parents or guardians of the bridegroom or the bride. This socially motivated legislation has been made relatively ineffective by stating that a marriage celebrated in violation of the stipulation regarding age would nevertheless be valid. The same restrictions regarding marriageable age are found in the Hindu Marriage Act, 1955. There is a Dowry Prohibition Act (1961) also in the Indian statute book which prohibits the giving and taking of dowry. But this again is ineffective in practice mainly because any dowry given may be construed as 'presents' which are not prohibited by law if made at the time of marriage. In the case of both these statutes, the teeth of the legislation are practically blunted both by loopholes within the law and by the resistance of social structures and attitudes to change. Certain conservative sections of the community regard child marriage as a good, if not a proper, thing and would prefer to pay a fine rather than keep their infant sons and daughters unmarried. A large number of young men and their parents consider dowry a legitimate stepping stone to higher rungs in the social ladder, and possibly a passport to domestic comfort, if not, happiness.

Two years before the adoption of the Hindu Marriage Act, which *inter alia* provided for divorce, the Special Marriage Act, 1954 was enacted. There is a provision in the Special Marriage Act for obtaining a decree of divorce by mutual consent, provided the parties have lived separately for a year and at least a year has elapsed since the date of marriage. Apart from the common grounds on which either party to the marriage may obtain dissolution of a marriage performed or registered under the Act, the wife may sue the husband for divorce on the ground that he has committed rape, sodomy or bestiality. Persons married under other forms may obtain registration of their marriage under the Act with the result that they would now be governed by its provisions. Those who marry under the Act or whose marriages are registered under it are, in matters of inheritance, governed by the Indian Succession Act, 1925. When a man to whom the Indian Succession Act applies dies leaving a widow and lineal descendants, the widow is entitled to one-third of the property of the deceased and the lineal descendants to two-thirds. Under the Act, in the case of Christians other than Indian Christians, a widow in the absence of lineal descendants will get the entire property of the husband provided its values does not exceed Rs. 5,000. If it does, she will receive Rs. 5,000 and a share in what remains along with the kindred of the deceased according to the specific rules laid down in the Act. Some persons, especially women, prefer to be married under the Special Marriage Act because of its beneficial provisions regarding divorce and intestate succession. We shall advert to this later.

It may be said in general that the right of a wife to obtain a divorce in India is much more restricted than that of the husband under customary law; however, in certain Hindu communities, as also among most tribal groups, it is possible for the husband and the wife to obtain divorce without recourse to court. They are only required to follow some customary practice, like making a declaration before the elders of the community[4] or the headman of the tribe that they no longer desire their marital relationship to continue. It is well known that among Muslims, while the husband can unilaterally and without assigning any reason divorce his wife by pronouncing *talaq* (that is by uttering the words, 'I divorce you') three times, the wife has to get a judicial pronouncement of divorce on specified grounds.

It is, however, possible for the wife to have the power of divorce delegated to her by the husband at the time of entering into the marriage contract. For instance, it may be stipulated that if he takes a second wife, she should have the option of repudiating her marriage. Such delegation is, however, uncommon. Considering the fact that the Constitution makes provision for equality of the sexes, it may be desirable to give judicial recognition to *fasaq* by means of which a Muslim wife may unilaterally repudiate her marriage. An opportunity for such recognition was lost when the Kerala High Court in 1975[5]

---

4. See Sujata Manohar, 'Token Concessions or Legal Rights', *Eve's Weekly* (May 10, 1975), p. 12.

5. Moyin v. Nafeesa, 1972. *Kerala Law Times*, 785. A.R. Kutty reports that in the Laccadives, under certain circumstances, a Muslim woman 'enjoys the legal right to sever a marital relationship. The procedure is

ruled that the right of Muslim women to obtain divorce is exclusively governed by the Dissolution of Muslim Marriages Act, 1939 and that it is not permissible to go beyond it.

The divorce provisions of the Hindu Marriage Act, 1955 maintain equality of the sexes in the matter of grounds for divorce. The Act applies to Hindus, Buddhists, Jains and Sikhs. Under the provisions of an amending Act adopted in 1976 it is now possible for a couple married under the Hindu Marriage Act to obtain a decree of divorce by mutual consent. The parties have to present a joint petition stating that they have been living separately for a period of one year or more, that they have not been able to live together and that they have mutually agreed that the marriage should be dissolved. On a motion made not earlier than six months and not later than eighteen months after the date of the presentation of the petition, the court, if satisfied that the averments in the petition are true, will pass a decree of divorce.[6] The amending Act also provides that, in general, no petition for divorce may be presented before the expiry of a year since the date of marriage. In the provisions of the Indian Divorce Act 1869 which applies to Christians there is some discrimination between the sexes in the matter of grounds for divorce. A single isolated act of adultery on the part of the wife is a valid ground for granting a divorce on the petition of the husband but, if a wife has to be successful in her petition for divorce, she has generally to prove against her husband not only adultery, but also an additional ground such as desertion or cruelty. Commission of rape, sodomy or bestiality by the husband can also be ground for obtaining a decree of divorce.

This Act was modelled after English enactments for matrimonial reliefs adopted about the middle of the last century. Over a hundred years later the United Kingdom prescribed by

---

known as *Fasaq*; in it the woman utters the formula of divorce dictated by the Kazi'. A.R. Kutty, *Marriage and Kinship in an Island Society* (Delhi: National, 1972), p. 184; Leela Dube also refers to the same legal right enjoyed by Muslim women in the Islands. See Leela Dube, *Matriliny and Islam* (Delhi: National, 1969), p. 72.

6. Section 13B of the Hindu Marriage Act, inserted by the Marriage Laws (Amendment) Act, 1976.

legislation a single valid ground for divorce, that is, irretrievable breakdown of marriage. If in 1869 the idea was that Indian Christians would do well to follow in the footsteps of the British in obtaining matrimonial reliefs, is there any valid reason to assume that they should be governed by rules different from those applicable to the British after the passage of a century. If irretrievable breakdown of marriage is made the only ground for judicial declaration of divorce applicable to all communities and religious groups in India there will be equality of treatment not only between men and women but also between various religious groups. Perhaps one has to wait for the adoption of a uniform civil code for such unification of laws. In the meantime the Indian Divorce Act could be amended making grounds for divorce identical for both men and women, preferably adopting the provision regarding irretrievable breakdown of marriage as the *sole* ground of divorce as laid down in the (British) Divorce Reform Act, 1969.

During the pendency of a suit under the Indian Divorce Act, a wife may apply for alimony and the court may grant an amount not exceeding one-fifth of the husband's average net income. While passing a decree for divorce or judicial separation, the court may order the husband to pay a lump sum or make periodical payments for life to the wife, taking into account her fortune, the means of the husband and the conduct of the parties. There are similar provisions for the benefit of the wife in the Parsi Marriage and Divorce Act, 1936. The spirit of equality envisaged in the Constitution finds clear expression in the Hindu Marriage Act, 1955. It makes provision for the grant of expenses of matrimonial suits and a monthly allowance for the support of either spouse during the pendency of legal proceedings, provided the spouse applying for the expenses and allowances has not sufficient income to support herself or himself. The Act also has a provision for making an order for permanent alimony or maintenance in favour of either of the spouses. On remarriage the spouse loses his or her right to maintenance. Further, if the recipient of the alimony is the wife, she is required to remain chaste; if maintenance is granted to the husband, he is enjoined from having sexual relations with any other woman.

In spite of the provisions for divorce in the Act of 1955, it is not often that recourse is had to them; this is because Hindu social values in general are opposed to the concept of divorce. As Kapadia puts it, 'the principle of divorce is alien to the social pattern' with the result that 'the norm accepted by law has not been accepted in practice'.[7] Whereas prior to 1955, divorce was considered absolute anathema by women of the higher castes, after the passing of the Act it is the women of the upper classes and higher castes as well as the rich and the educated in urban areas who petition the courts for divorce. Probably, the illiterate women in the rural areas do not even know that there are legal provisions for divorce apart from those enshrined in the customary law of certain communities or tribes.

Succession

We have already seen that marriage under the Special Marriage Act has the effect of making the provisions of the Indian Succession Act applicable to the parties. These provisions were more beneficial to women, be they Hindus, Muslims, Indian Christians of Pondicherry or Indian Christians in those areas of Kerala which formerly comprised the princely states of Travancore and Cochin, provided they were not governed by matrilineal customs. Before the adoption of the Hindu Succession Act in 1956, when a woman succeeded to the divided property of a deceased Hindu male, she took only a limited interest. A woman was denied legal capacity to be a coparcener in a Hindu joint family. The Hindu Succession Act, 1956 which applies to Hindus, Buddhists, Jains and Sikhs determines the heir on the basis of consanguinity or affinity without any discrimination on the ground of sex. It gives a woman full ownership in the property inherited or acquired by her. The widow, the mother and the daughter now not only inherit property along with the son but also take

7. Quoted in A.J. Barot, 'The Divorced Woman and her Options', *Eve's Weekly* (May 10, 1975), p. 31.

an equal share with him. A Parsi woman takes only half the share that her brother gets in their father's property. A similar half share is the lot of Muslim women as well.

Though the Indian Succession Act is generally applicable to Christians there are various regions in the country where the Act is not applied. There are also certain Christian communities to which it is not applicable. Certain tribal Christian communities and those who follow matriliny are outside the purview of the Act.

In the erstwhile princely states of Travancore and Cochin, there are in operation local enactments relating to succession among Christians which appear to discriminate against women. Under the Travancore Christian Succession Regulation, 1916, the share of the widow in the estate of the husband is a life interest, terminable on her death or remarriage, except where she gets the whole estate in the absence of certain specified relatives of her deceased husband. Under the Cochin Christian Succession Act, 1921, the widow gets a share equal to two-third of the share of a son if the deceased is survived by a son or lineal descendants of a son. The Travancore Regulation seems to discriminate against daughters who can take only one-fourth of the value of the share of a son or Rs 5,000 whichever is less. The Regulation does not apply to the small body of Indian Christians in the taluk of Neyyattinkara of the erstwhile princely state who follow *marumakkathayam* (matrilineal descent). The Roman Catholic Christians of the Latin rite and certain non-Catholic Christians living in a few southern taluks of Travancore follow their customary usage, and among them male and female heirs of an intestate share equally in his property. Under the Travancore Regulation, the maternal relatives are excluded from succeeding to the intestate if there are paternal relatives surviving him, whereas in Cochin Act no maternal relatives are included among the heirs.

The areas where these two enactments are still in force are remarkable for a high female literacy rate and a large number of highly educated women. Nevertheless the fact remains that these women, if they happen to be Christians to whom these enactments apply, have a right to only a quarter of the share of a brother in the property of their deceased father. Would these educated women and their literate sisters think of reverting to matriliny which was once prevalent in these areas? At the moment they do not appear to be eager to effect any change.

Adoption

The Hindu Minority and Guardianship Act, 1956 also bestowed a few additional rights on Hindu women.[8] It provides that though the father may appoint by will a guardian for his minor children, any such appointment will not take effect during the lifetime of the mother if she survives the father. It will take effect only on her death, provided she has not appointed a guardian by her own will. A Hindu mother is entitled to act as the natural guardian of her minor children if the father ceases to be a Hindu or renounces the world by becoming a hermit or ascetic. The Hindu widow and the Hindu mother, entitled to act as the natural guardian of her minor children are empowered under the Act to appoint guardians for them by will.

In 1956 substantial changes were effected in the law of adoption applicable to Hindus.[9] The Hindu Adoption and Maintenance Act, 1956 has invested the Hindu woman with certain rights of adoption which she had not enjoyed before. Previously an adoption could only be to a male but, under the Act, a woman is competent to adopt to herself a son or a daughter. Again, under the Act, a married man cannot, except under certain special circumstances, make an adoption without the consent of his wife. Under the earlier law her consent was immaterial but under the present law, her consent is unnecessary only when she has renounced the world or has ceased to be a Hindu or has been judicially declared to be of unsound mind. A Hindu woman who is not of unsound mind and who is not a

---

8. These enactments which are considered parts of a Hindu code, apply to Hindus, Buddhists, Sikhs and Jains, so that a reference to Hindu women in this context includes Buddhist, Sikh and Jain women as well.

9. Adoption as a legal institution exists only among Hindus in India. See J.D.M. Derrett, *Introduction to Modern Law* (Bombay: Oxford University Press, 1963), p. 92. Though a bill has been introduced in Parliament, no general legislation relating to adoption has yet been passed into law.

minor is now competent to adopt a son as well as a daughter, provided she is a spinster, divorcee, or widow or one whose husband has finally renounced the world or has ceased to be a Hindu or has been judicially declared to be of unsound mind. In general, during coverture it is only the husband who can adopt. If the woman wants to adopt a son, she should not have a Hindu son, son's son or son's son's son living at the time of the adoption, and the boy to be adopted should be younger to her by at least twenty-one years. If she intends adopting a daughter, an essential condition is that she should have no Hindu daughter or son's daughter living at the time of the adoption. Corresponding requirements have also to be observed by the man who wishes to adopt a son or daughter.

The wife has a right to maintenance for life. She may not forfeit this right even if she lives separately from her husband on certain specific grounds such as the husband's cruelty, desertion, keeping a concubine or having another wife, his suffering from a violent form of leprosy, his conversion to another religion or any other cause justifying her living separately. She, however, forfeits her right to maintenance if she is unchaste or ceases to be a Hindu.

Employment and education

The Factories Act, 1948 empowers state governments to prohibit employment of women in dangerous operations. A few enactments lay down the general rule that women should not be permitted to work between 7 P.M. and 6 A.M., but this rule is relaxable to certain circumstances.[10] Provisions for maternity benefits for women have been incorporated in the Employees State Insurance Act, 1948 and a number of state enactments. While maternity benefit in coal mines is governed by the Maternity Benefit Act, 1961 women workers in factories and plantations are entitled to maternity leave according to the maternity benefit enactments of different states. Both the Factories Act,

10. See K.N. Vaid, *Labour Welfare in India* (New Delhi: Shri Ram Centre for Industrial Relations and Human Resources, 1970), p. 301.

1948 and the Plantations Labour Act, 1951 make is obligatory for factories and plantations employing not less than fifty women to provide creches.

In spite of these statutory benefits and the constitutional directive regarding equal pay for equal work, women agricultural labourers generally get 10 to 60 per cent less in wages than men for the same work. It is not infrequent that, when the husband becomes a 'bonded labourer' for the landlord or the labour contractor, the wife also become similarly 'bonded' with the not unusual result that she is made vulnerable to exploitation including trafficking for immoral purposes.[11] The formal abolition of 'bonded labour' does not appear to have made any substantial change in the situation.

Only 13 per cent of Indian women, according to the 1971 Census, may be regarded as workers, i.e., those who are engaged in some form of economic activity. About 80 per cent of these working women are engaged in agriculture. Only 12 per cent of the total employees in central and state administrative services and public sector undertakings are women. This may not be unrelated to their education or lack of it. Only 18 per cent of Indian women are literate. Though one of the directive principles of the Constitution requires the state to provide free and compulsory education for all children under 14 years of age the directive is generally followed with callous disregard of its spirit and its significance for the country. Coupled with the general apathy to women's education, this indifference to put in practice a constitutional directive results in greater social and economic deprivation for girls than for boys.

At the primary school level while 97 out of 100 boys attend school, the corresponding figure for girls is 62. Further, out of 100 girls who enter the first grade only 26 go up to the fifth grade. It is only about 2 per cent of women who are able to benefit by the opportunities provided for higher education.[12] In

---

11. Kamla Mankekar, 'Employment Among Women in India', *Eve's Weekly* (May 10, 1975), p. 65. See also V. Dhagamwar, *Law, Power and Justice* (Bombay: N.M. Tripathi, 1974), p. 183 and Appendices.

12. See *Women in India: Selected Statistics* (New Delhi: Department of Social Welfare, Ministry of Education and Social Welfare, 1975), mimeo.

1971-72, 36 girls only were under instruction at various levels of education compared to a hundred boys.[13] If in 1971 about 18 per cent of women were literate this may appear to compare well with only 8 per cent literacy for women on the eve of Independence in 1947, but an increase of 10 per cent in the not too short span of about three decades is hardly something that should make us complacent.

Abortion

There are certain other types of social legislation which seek to protect interests and benefits that are of special concern to women. The Suppression of Immoral Traffic in Women and Girls Act, 1956, as its title indicates, is intended to protect helpless women and girls from a typical mode of exploitation not altogether unknown in the country. The same year saw the enactment of another piece of social legislation: the Women's and Children's Institutions (Licensing) Act, 1956. This was later on superseded by the Orphanages and Other Charitable Homes (Supervision and Control) Act, 1960. The object of the enactment was to regulate the activities of these institutions and to prescribe a proper standard to which the treatment and the training of the inmates should conform. Such a measure was found necessary because, while there are many good and properly managed charitable institutions, there are many others run with the objective of exploitation as their main and sustaining inspiration.

The Medical Termination of Pregnancy Act, 1971 may also be mentioned in the context of social legislation relative to women. The enactment seeks, among other things, to protect women's interests. It has a few provisions which, it is clear, were enacted with the sufferings of women in the legislator's mind. It provides that a pregnancy may be terminated where the length of the pregnancy does not exceed twenty weeks, if two medical practitioners are of the opinion that the continuance of the pregnancy would involve a risk to the life of the pregnant

---

13. Kamla Mankekar, op. cit., p. 35.

woman or of grave injury to her physical or mental health. Two explanations are offered in the enactment itself of what constitutes grave injury to the mental health of the pregnant woman. The first explanation reads:

> When any pregnancy is alleged by the pregnant woman to have been caused by rape, the anguish caused by such pregnancy shall be presumed to constitute a grave injury to the mental health of the pregnant woman.

In this case the 'anguish' is perhaps palpable. The second explanation is more intriguing in that 'anguish' is given an extended application. It states:

> Where a pregnancy occurs as a result of failure of any device used by any married woman or her husband for the purpose of limiting the number of children, the anguish caused by such unwanted pregnancy may be presumed to constitute a grave injury to the mental health of the pregnant woman.

Though the promotional slant of the government's family planning programme may be perceptible in this explanation, it is evident that Parliament cannot be blamed for any lack of solicitude for the largest minority in the country. This solicitude may be even more evident in another provision of the Act which stipulates that in determining whether the continuance of a pregnancy would involve grave risk to the health of the pregnant woman, account may be taken of her actual or reasonably foreseeable environment. This enactment has been hailed as 'a major landmark in India's social legislation', and 'a far-reaching measure assuring the women of India freedom from undesirable and unwanted pregnancies'.[14]

It is generally assumed that the Act was envisaged by the government partly as a family planning measure and some of the rules framed by the government appear to strengthen the

---

14. S. Chandrasekhar, *Abortion in a Crowded World* (London: Allen and Unwin, 1974), p. 106.

basis of this assumption.[15] In this context it may be interesting to hear what the government has to say about abortion. Mrs Gandhi said: 'Unless the girl's life is in danger, there should be no abortion. No, I definitely think...I would not like abortion to be easy'.[16] In fact, it has been made easy by legislation. If the then Prime Minister's concept of social value trails quite a few steps behind the law adopted by her government could one blame the illiterate village woman if she does not take kindly to permissive legislation relating to widow remarriage or divorce, or medical termination of pregnancy which is the accepted euphemism for abortion?

Conclusion

From a study of the ameliorative legal provisions relating to women and the actual situation in which they find themselves, it is clear that something more than legislation is required. Perhaps the first thing to be attempted is to make women aware of their rights, however this is done. It is also necessary to change the attitudes of both men and women, of society in general, to social objectives sought to be achieved by legislation. A radical change in the attitudes of women induced by an awareness of their rights which are constitutionally guaranteed and legally protected will be the first step in the complex process of transforming the social structure so that women may enjoy full equality with men in every sphere of life.

---

15. See J. Minattur, 'Medical Termination of Pregnancy and Conscientious Objection', *Journal of the Indian Law Institute*, 16 (October-December, 1975), p. 705.

16. Gulshan Ewing, op. cit., p. 11.

7 Women and Religion: The Status and Image of Women in Some Major Religious Traditions

Ursula King

Religious beliefs and practices have been a universal feature of human life. Thus, it is not surprising that women have always had a place in religious activities, however much the degree of their participation may have varied. Of great importance are the explicit teachings about women which the major religious traditions have propounded. On one hand, these teachings reflect the actual position held by women in society at different times in history; on the other, the teachings have in turn contributed to determining such positions by upholding a particular image or ideal of womanhood.

What is the nature of woman? What is her particular role in the family, her position in society at large, her situation in the general scheme of salvation? All religions have to some extent provided answers to these questions, however inadequate they may be for us today. In the higher religions, we find the great philosophical and theological teaching about the essential sameness of human nature, of the intrinsic worth of all human beings as everyone, woman just as much as man, is endowed with a soul, a divine spark, or is part of the same *atman*. This lofty ideal is often of very little practical consequence, however; in actual practice, much of the ethical teaching and the religious counsels reflect the social position of women in a particular environment. As a result, we also possess many sacred texts which relegate women's place to a lower or secondary rank to man. Such texts are frequently quoted as the scriptural basis for the legitimation of women's low status through the ages; they are the sacred authority which teaches that woman's status has to be low and unequal to that of man. In addition, we have the paradoxical situation that in some religious teachings an idealised exaltation of woman in her role as mother and wife occurs; in some instances, an ideal of woman in her eternal essence is projected when in actual social life subjugation is woman's common lot.

Today, with an altogether different situation in society, the religions are faced with an entirely new challenge. Since the social, economic and political emancipation of women has become widely accepted, new pressures from the social environment are affecting all the religious traditions, and the inadequacy of their traditional teaching regarding the general status or image of woman is being fundamentally questioned. How do different religions respond to this new and challenging situation? Before discussing this important question, we have to look more closely at the situation in the past.

Women and the history of religions

It has been rightly pointed out that the various attempts to write a comprehensive history of women through the ages and variety of cultures, have all proved to be failures. The conditions of life and local traditions have been too disparate, the gaps in our historical knowledge too great. Any attempt to write a continuous history of women, including their role in primitive cultures, ancient civilisations and modern societies has to be abandoned. All one can aim for is an investigation limited to a certain time and space.[1] The remark applies equally well to the relationship of women and religion. We can hope to possess a complete picture of the situation through the ages and varieties of religious teachings and practices. No uniform development can be traced through the general history of religions, nor

---

1. Cf. the entry 'Women, Status of' in Encyclopaedia Britannica, *Macropaedia*, Vol. 19, pp. 906-916.

through the history of one particular religion as great discrepancies have occurred at different times.

It may be stimulating, however, to reflect upon a few random data provided by the history of religion.[2] Women have not always and everywhere been excluded from religious rites and relegated to an inferior status. Certain writers have, in fact, maintained that early matriarchy and mother-right preceded patriarchy and male dominance in the development of human societies. However that may be, there is no doubt that the status of women in early agricultural societies was relatively high. Women were not only creators of life, providers of food, and helpmates of men, they were also the supreme symbols of fertility itself. Thus we find a widespread worship of the mother-goddess in the form of many powerful deities in the civilisations of Babylonia, Egypt, Phrygia and Phoenicia from where it spread to Greece and Rome, paradoxically coexisting there with a legal position of women's complete subordination to the authority of either father or husband. We also know of the presence of the mother goddess in the Indus Valley Civilisation, possibly the historical source of the still important village goddess (*gramadevata*) of South India.

The Greek, Roman and Indian pantheon in particular are replete with female deities who often play a central role in the respective mythologies. But it is not so much the deification of the female form which interests us as the participation of real women in religious life. Here again we find in both primitive and ancient religions the widespread presence of women magicians, shamans, healers, visionaries and seers, prophetesses, and priestesses. Female visionaries played an important role in Germanic religion, and the women oracles of Greece were equally well-known, especially the famous oracle at Delphi (the marble base of whose tripod, by the way, ended up in a stately Yorkshire home, Castle Howard). Of great renown, too, are the sibyls, the prophetesses and fortune-tellers of old, considered to be the mouthpiece of a particular god. They were pictorially represented in Christian churches from the eleventh century

---

2. Cf. the section 'Die Frau' in F. Heiler, *Ersheinungsformen und Wesen der Religion* (Stuttgart, 1961), pp. 411-426.

onwards, the most famous example being Michelangelo's paintings in the Sistine Chapel in Rome. Female temple priests and attendants were known in many religions, for example, in Egypt, Sumeria, Babylonia, Greece and ancient Japan. Roman religions knew the vestals, the consecrated virgins charged with the perpetual care of sacred fire in the temple of the goddess Vesta. At the other end of the spectrum, we find the phenomenon of temple prostitution in several religions.[3]

Regressive trend

In earlier times, when religious practices were less formally organised and religious roles less institutionalised, it was easier for individual women to hold positions of religious authority. With the gradual development of the higher religions, a more definite institutionalisation of religious roles occurred. Sacred authority, like secular authority, rested with men and the exercise of religious functions, be it sacrifice, teaching, preaching, blessing or initiation, became a male prerogative. We can observe such developments as much in ancient Mithraism and Brahmanism as in Christianity and Islam. Thus we are faced with a certain regression in the participation of women in religious life. This is not to say that in the area of religion women once held a position above men. It only means that in an earlier, more undifferentiated age of development, certain areas of religious activity were open to women which later became closed.

This regressive trend can be found in many religious traditions, and it seems to express itself in two ways. First, there is the general decline of the oracular, prophetic and even priestly activity of women if one compares the situation in ancient cultures with that of more recent times. Then there is the specific regression of religious activities of women in particular religions if one compares the creative time of the founder with

3. Many ancient pagan practices continued in Christianity in medieval Europe. It has been said that sometimes a kind of secret priesthood was exercised by women; this custom is thought to be one of the reasons why the witch hunt was so vigorously pursued by the Church.

later practices. At the time of a religious beginning, when a charismatic personality, an enlightened being, shapes a new way of life, much is questioned and little taken for granted. In such a period of flux, women, in their support of a new movement, were often allowed greater freedom than was customary in their environment. Only later, after the newly emerged religion had become codified, were women's roles once again consigned to what they had previously been in that particular social milieu.

It is in itself a remarkable phenomenon that we do now know of any woman who was a great religious founder. Moses, Mahavira, Buddha, Jesus, Mohammed, are all men. However, this is not as extraordinary as it at first appears; the great statesmen, philosophers, writers and scientists of the past have almost invariably been men, too. Public life was, by and large, notwithstanding a few exceptions of remarkable women in history, the sphere of men. Women's sphere was not public but private life: home and family, the preparation of food and clothes, the birth and nurture of children. If one considers for a moment how much time and energy these activities required in traditional societies and keeps in mind the much shorter average span of life, it is not at all surprising that there was neither surplus leisure nor surplus energy available to women to achieve more. Only the changing patterns of life in very recent time have opened up an entirely new arena of freedom and possibilities for women.

If one looks at the women associated with the person of a particular religious founder, or with a particularly creative period in the history of a religious tradition, one can see that women were always present and often more actively involved in religious activities than was possible later. One has only to think of some of the outstanding women in the Old Testament, their active and sometimes crucial role in the early history of the Israelites. This contrasts sharply with, for example, the passive role of women in later Jewish synagogues. Even today, only the reformed synagogues allow women active participation in their service. A similar regression can be observed is Islam: Mohammed's spouse played a decisive role in early Islam; the prophet's daughter, Fatima, occupies an eminent position for Shia Muslims. Yet, women's activities in Islam are generally restricted to the private sphere. The use of the mosque on Friday is denied to them. Women may read the *Koran* but not preach it. Perhaps among the Sufis alone the distinction between the male and female tends to disappear. Thus a woman may reach the highest ranks in the hierarchy of Muslim saints. This greater equality of status may well be due to the fact that the mystic path, perhaps more than any other religious orientation, strives to realise the lofty teaching about the divine in all human beings on a practical level.

In early Christianity too, we find women making an important contribution. Their activities are associated with preaching, teaching, social work and even liturgical service. Yet, later, many of these activities became impossible through a retrograde development, often linked to a strong emphasis on male asceticism. Such a pattern of retrogression can also be shown in the development of Hinduism, and it is to the closer examination of the Indian religious traditions that we now turn.

Women and Indian religions

In the well known book, *The Position of Women in Hindu Civilisation*, A.S. Altekar[4] argues that Indian women in the distant past had a higher status than in more recent times. Women once enjoyed considerable freedom and privileges in the spheres of family, religion and public life; yet, over the centuries, their situation changed adversely. This better position applies more specifically to the Vedic age when women played a more active economic role and participated more in ritual. For example, for a long time girls in higher society were allowed to undergo the *upanayana* rite. During that time asceticism was far less prominent than subsequently. As far as we have any evidence, there was also no seclusion of women.

Later, when the ascetic *sannyasa* ideal became very dominant,

---

4. A.S. Altekar, *The Position of Women in Hindu Civilisation: From Prehistoric Times to the Present Day* (Delhi: Motilal Banarsidas, reprinted 1973).

the status of women deteriorated. Furthermore, just as the introduction of slavery revolutionised the position of women in the classical period of Greece, the emergence of the semi-servile Sudra Caste within Hindu society deprived women of many of the economically productive functions. Altekar sees the period of 500 A.D. to 1800 A.D. as one of progressive deterioration in the position of women in society; only the recognition of certain proprietary rights developed for the better. The *upanayana* rite for girls was completely abandoned; marriage was seen to be its main substitute. At the same time, the marriage age was increasingly lowered; child marriage became a common practice, precluding any formal education for girls, whilst the remarriage of widows was taboo. Through the influence of the Islamic custom of *purdah*, more strictly enforced in India than elsewhere, North Indian women in particular lived in great seclusion. Theologically speaking, women were classed in the same category of Sudras. They were not allowed to recite the *Vedas* nor to perform the Vedic sacrificial ritual. This right was extended to women only by the Arya Samaj, a Hindu reformist movement founded by Swami Dayanand Saraswati in the nineteenth century, which attempted to free Hinduism from later accretions by going back to the original customs of Vedic times. Traditionally, women had only a subsidiary role in worship, being associated with it at home and through their husband.

The great traditional ways to salvation were normally not open to women. However, the *bhakti* and *puranic* schools, which came to prominence by 500 A.D. and stressed devotion and faith, amply provided for women's emotional and religious needs. Thus women became the followers, custodians and patrons of devotional worship in Hinduism. Altekar stresses that women in the past were largely educated through the stories of *puranic* literature which inculcate blind faith rather than rational behaviour; with more time on their hands, women could visit temples, perform vows and submit to fasts with greater regularity than their menfolk who were preoccupied with other work. 'Thus the very women whom religion had once considered as outcastes . . . were the most faithful custodians of its spirit and traditions'.[5]

Orthodox Hinduism, as we know it today, associates woman mainly with the family but everything here is defined in relation to the husband. A modern Hindu writer[6] has stated this in the following words:

> A man's religious life is considered to be essentially deficient without his wife's active participation in it . . . Without a wife . . . the psychological and moral personality of man remains imperfect. She is his constant companion in his religious life, preparing for him the sacred articles used in worship, accompanying him on pilgrimages, present at all ceremonies . . . And finally, in her role as the mother, woman is regarded as divine, respected many times more than the father and the teacher.

Yet, at the same time, some of the special sacraments of Hinduism do not apply to women, especially not the important rite of initiation:

> The most important sacrament for a woman is marriage. After marriage a woman is generally considered to have no existence apart from her husband, especially so far as religious practices are concerned. Her husband is her proper spiritual preceptor, or guru, and in all spiritual matters she is dependent on him. The conscientious performance of household duties constitutes her proper ritual.[7]

This is the traditional Brahmanical position. The author concedes, however, that in popular Hinduism women are allowed greater freedom in worship and other religious practices. But granted the different levels at which Hinduism operates in

5. Ibid.
6. R.N. Dandekar, 'The Role of Man in Hinduism', in K.W. Morgan (ed.), *The Religion of the Hindus Interpreted by Hindus* (New York: The Ronald Press Company, 1953), pp. 140-141.
7. Ibid.

practice, it nevertheless seems paradoxical that women are given such a low, dependent status in all practical religious matters when the mythological and theological formulations of Hinduism express the motherhood of God and the female aspects of the divine, the *Shakti*, with greater force and beauty than those of any other world religion.

Path of renunciation

Hinduism also declared women ineligible for the path of renunciation (*sannyasa*). Not renunciation but the discharge of her family responsibilities is woman's specific *dharma*, her most sacred duty. This general injunction notwithstanding, we know of famous Hindu women saints—Lalla, Mirabai, Sarada Devi, to name only a few, and in our own age, Anandamayi. As in Christianity, asceticism appears to have had important repercussions on the status of women in Hinduism; and the fact that women were normally altogether excluded from the path of renunciation, must have had graver consequences still. The early *Dharmasutra* writers still regarded renunciation as an anti-Vedic custom. A hero of the *Mahabharata* epic has even been quoted as saying that renunciation appeals only to those who are unsuccessful in life. However this may be, it would be far too simplistic to merely accept that in the distant past, before the advent of renouncers in large numbers, all was well with women in Indian society. They may have had greater freedom of movement and a greater share in important economic, social and religious functions; yet, antifeminist views may have been more widely spread than one likes to admit in an egalitarian age.

Both Buddhism and Jainism, dating from the sixth century B.C. or earlier, do express such views in their writings. Buddha was initially opposed to the admission of women into the *Sangha* but the eventually gave way. Thus we find Buddhist nuns from the beginning, and the Jains have nuns too. However, the stricter *Digambara* Jains hold that women can never gain salvation unless they are reborn as men. Yet in spite of certain discriminatory practices, Buddhism and Jainism have both produced some distinguished women preachers. For Buddhism, the service of the *upasika*, the laywoman, is also very important; many such women lay followers are well known and have exercised influential patronage in the past history of Buddhism.

It would be quite inadmissible to explain the status of women in a particular society as being exclusively due to the dominant religious views held by that society. The image of women in a religious tradition is an important variable affecting the status of women, especially in a religiously oriented culture, yet it is not the only variable. A well-known Indian anthropologist[8] is of the opinion that

> the status of woman in India can be more understood in the context of Indian ethnology than in that of religion or Brahmanism. ...Brahmanic influence appears to have been overestimated, and the rigid mores of woman's conduct have been read in the context of the doctrines of *Karma* and *Dharma*, but if Brahmanism had such a great influence, how is it that the majority of social groups, castes and tribes escaped it or did not conform to such a ... system?

This brings us back to a point made earlier; religious teachings and attitudes to women are closely related to specific groups and the mores of a given society. Often enough, religious teaching underwrites the *status quo* but in certain instances, it may also contain the anticipatory capacity for a change of state. In a secular society, such a change of state is already occurring in the position of women; in the last fifty years or so, it has changed almost beyond recognition. Yet traditional attitudes die hard and, sad though it may be, these traditional attitudes towards women are sometimes both sanctioned and further reinforced by Christian tradition.

8. D.N. Majumdar, *Race and Culture of India* (New Delhi: Asia Publishing House, 1961), p. 206.

Women and Christianity

The historical and theological background of the Christian image of woman has been most comprehensively studied in the recent book, *Women in Christian Tradition*.[9] As this topic is of great relevance to our present discussion, it seems best to examine some of its main arguments. The book provides a much-needed balance to contemporary studies on women which are often too exclusively focused on present problems and questions without seeing how these are rooted in a past tradition. The image of woman in one particular religion, in this case Christianity, is far from being uniform; it always includes several aspects, possibly exclusive of each other. At certain times, some traits may become more prominent than others due to extraneous reasons. As the earlier views on women seem to be more differentiated than later ones when positions have become more fixed and rigid, we tend to react strongly against the image of the most immediate past, the image of women closest to us.

Two quite different images of the nature and status of woman can already be inferred from the two accounts of creation in the Old Testament (Genesis, chapter two, being the earlier version and chapter one, the later). The two divergent traditions can be followed right through Biblical literature. Social conditions assigned an inferior position to women but

> Jesus's behaviour, as recorded in the Gospels, does not follow traditional Jewish reserve. To his companions' surprise, he speaks with the Samaritan woman at the well. He heals women as well as men, entertains relations of friendship with Martha and Mary. The group of his followers includes both married and unmarried women. His teaching on marriage implies the equality of man and woman. This will be of great importance for the concept

---

9. G.H. Tavard, *Women in Christian Tradition* (Indiana: University of Notre Dame Press, 1973).

of womanhood in the early Church; it was at variance with the mainstream of the rabbinic tradition.[10]

However, the ambiguity of the status of women comes out strongest in the writings of St. Paul. There are those texts which clearly express the subordination of women. For centuries, Pauline teaching that women is the glory of man[11] and that women are not allowed to speak in Church[12] was taken as the scriptural justification of woman's subjugation to man and the exclusion of women from liturgical activity in Christian Churches. 'The married woman stands at the bottom of a hierarchy at the top of which is God. Christ and husband mediate in between, so that the woman seems further removed from Christ and from God than her husband'.[13]

Then, there are other texts which express the principles of equality or identity operating through Christian baptism: all Christians, whether male or female, slave or free, enjoy the same freedom based on their identity in Christ.[14] In Him Christian men and women are raised beyond the distinction of the sexes. A new spiritual freedom was experienced which led to much heavenly daring and experiment in the early Church and to a flouting of conventions.

This striving for an acting out of spiritual freedom found in baptism, and for a realisation of the kingdom of God on earth in tension with the given social environment, characterises much of the history of early Christianity.[15] In principle, there was the equality of women with men found through baptism; in practice, however, the living out of this spiritual freedom could only be realised through strong asceticism and lived by an ascetic elite. Logically, the spiritual freedom given to woman in baptism should have been followed by her complete emancipation in the world. This consequence, however, is only coming into force today.

10. Ibid., p. 20.
11. First letter to the Corinthians, 11, 7.
12. Ibid., 14, 34.
13. Tavard, op. cit., p. 28.
14. Letter to the Galatians, 3, 23-28.
15. Tavard, op. cit., p. 32.

Ideals of asceticism

Historically, the freedom of venture and new experiment was soon curtailed when the immediacy of the coming of the kingdom of God receded into the background as only a remote possibility. Christians became settled; the Church had to accommodate itself to the world at large. Injunctions for the behaviour and status of women were modelled on the example of the Hellenistic and Roman environment; women were assigned to their customary, subordinate position. Liberation, found in the New Testament through the experience of baptism, was now only possible through the strictest asceticism, a path theoretically open to both men and women. However, many ascetic writings also reflect a strong anti-feminist character. The view of woman as an embodiment of evil and, at the root of all sexual evil, gained strong support. Woman was seen as a creature of imperfection and congenital weakness.

It is not necessary to mention here the many Christian writers who through the ages, gave vent to their anti-feminist feelings. One reason for this is that the ideals of asceticism, contemplation and monastic life became closely associated with virginity. This is by no means always the case in other religious traditions; suffice it to mention the married Sufis in Islam and the married monks in certain forms of Buddhism. In Christianity, virginity was ranked higher than married life. There is no doubt that, apart from the Biblical sources, neo-Platonic thought with its contempt for the body, had a strong influence on these developments.

It is equally important to remember that only relatively late in the early history of Christian thought did marriage come to be considered a sacrament. In the first centuries, marriage was mainly a family and civic affair. The ordinary Christian woman had the status assigned to her by society. Only the consecrated virgin could claim equality with men as a member of an ascetic elite; as Tavard notes, 'the life of virginity was a prophetic anticipation of restored incorruptibility, a manifestation of the fullness of deification, of the final integrity of the image of God in man and in woman'.[16] Both Western and Eastern Christianity promoted the life of consecrated virginity but the Western Church tended to separate, much more than was ever the case in the East, the liturgical service of the Lord from contact with women. In the West, the marriage of priests was abolished by the decision of a Council in the twelfth century; instead of the custom dying out, however, we find much clerical concubinage in the fourteenth and fifteenth centuries when the desire of priests to marry reappeared. The Protestant Churches of the reformation all allowed their ministers to marry whilst the Council of Trent reiterated the prohibition of clerical marriage in the Catholic Church, this time with a great deal of success.[17] New questioning of this decision is only recurring in our own day.

No adequate model of woman

The double typology of womanhood—subordination or equality—is reflected in contemporary writings, both Catholic and Protestant. Referring to various Catholic models of womanhood, Tavard perceives as their central problem the open schizophrenia they imply.[18] There is the presence of

16. Ibid., p. 87.
17. Ibid., p. 119. Tavard points out the important relationship which obtains between women and those who build theological systems. In the West, theology has always been the speciality of a section of the clergy; thus, the history of both asceticism and celibacy has its bearing on the image and status of woman. He states emphatically that 'the separation between priests and women is bound to entail a one sided theology of womanhood, to which woman remains alien and from which she is likely to find herself alienated'.
18. Ibid., p. 149. But how do we discover the adequate categories of thought within which to envisage the role of woman? The author examines different orthodox models (the Greek Church Fathers; Soloview; Bulgakov; Evdokomov) and Protestant examples (Luther, Calvin, Barth, Brunner) yet all of them fall short of an acceptable anthropology for today. There are, however, some recent attempts to develop new theological perspectives that recognise the distinctive role of women in religion. See, for example, Letty M. Russell, *Human Liberation in a Feminist Perspective: A Theology*

Contradictory streams of thought to see woman as weak and as a symbol of temptation, and to idealise her as a symbol of transcendent goodness .... Thus it happens that Catholics who wish to promote the rights of women today confront us with the humanistic tradition of Simone de Beauvoir, with Freudian reconstructions or, at a lower level of sophistication, with statistical data on women in and out of wedlock.

The conclusion to be drawn from a survey of the Christian tradition is that there exists no fully adequate Christian model of woman which would meet modern women's requirements—and this can be said of the traditional image of woman in all religious traditions. Nor is there any model which would adequately express the spiritual freedom of the central Christian message. The Christian theological stance concerning woman, her function in society, and her place in the Church, was originally dominated by Jewish, Greek, and Roman patterns of thought and behaviour into which the Christian revelation 'wedged an element of newness, of fermentation, perhaps we may even say of revolution. Yet this element could only take shape in the context of the prevailing cultural forms which to a great extent contradicted it'.[19]

To achieve this disentanglement, to develop a comprehensive theological anthropology for both women and men, one also has to recognise the need of competent women theologians who can participate in this task. Who else can adequately express the self-understanding of women and create a richer, more balanced image of woman if not women themselves? Under different social and economic conditions, women today have come to claim a new position in society; they have acquired a new status of equality. Any outdated image which may still regard them, due to the one-sided idealisation or denigration, as either semi-divine or sub-human, cannot answer the needs of a new situation where women claim and fight to be persons in their own right.

(Philadelphia: The Westminister Press, 1974); Rosemary Ruether, *New Woman: New Earth* (New York: Seabury, 1975).

19. Ibid., p. 188.

Women and the modern world

Let us briefly examine the reasons why the status of women is changing in modern society.

The largest single factor affecting the status of women today is the changing family pattern coupled with the increased access to formal education, even though the percentage of women in higher education is still considerably lower than that of men. In all countries where data are available, there is evidence of a strong correlation between educational level and the employment rate of women. The more highly educated married women are the more they are motivated to continue in or return to their careers, irrespective of their husbands' social status or income group. Earlier it was feared that a girl's prolonged education might diminish her marital prospects; now we have a development whereby education provides additional prestige and represents an important asset for marriage. This can be witnessed in contemporary India; it also accounts for the rapid increase of women students in countries as different as Argentina, Italy and Japan.

It is erroneous to believe that the employment of women, especially married women, is a new phenomenon. Women have at all times and in all types of economy made a substantial contribution to the production and distribution of their communities' resources. But whilst the economic unit in pre-industrial society was the family itself, industrialised society introduced a strict separation of the home from the place of work. What is new, therefore, is the fact that women are employed outside the home, as independent individuals, receiving monetary rewards. Thus the emphasis is more on *going out* to work than simply on work.

The changed position of women in society together with an increasing emphasis on the nuclear rather than the joint family pattern and other social changes affecting the contemporary family, make the husband-wife relationship of crucial importance. Marriage nowadays is increasingly seen as a partnership where family life becomes a cooperative venture. Thus, the compatibility of marriage partners is of the utmost importance; the leading role in a family may depend more on temperament than on accepted conventions. In the process of mutual adjustment towards a situation of equal status, women are increasingly stretching their interests beyond the home whilst men, in turn, are becoming more home-centred than in the past. This new situation also affects the relationship between parents and children which, due to the smaller number of children and the nuclear family structure, allows for a more intensive but less authoritarian pattern. The most revolutionary factor affecting women's lives today is certainly the availability of birth control and family planning.

These changes deserve closer scrutiny than is possible here since many of them may have an inherently ambivalent character. This brief survey is only intended to bring out the deep changes which have revolutionised the status of women in industrialised societies. Of great additional importance is the increased expectation of life together with a drastic reduction in the years a woman devotes to the bearing and rearing of children. All these changes will increasingly affect the entire female population of the globe, whatever their religious traditions may teach about the status of women.

At present, no religion can offer an adequate model for contemporary women's self-understanding. The newness of the situation has to be matched by a corresponding new creative effort on the part of religious leaders and thinkers male and female alike. Otherwise, women, the most faithful devotees and upholders of religious traditions through the centuries, may well have to abandon religion itself as being an instrument of their subjection.

Women and religion today

Whilst women have reached a critical stage of self-reflection and a new status in the contemporary world, religion itself is undergoing a crisis at present. None of the religious traditions has so far been able to offer an adequate spirituality for the needs of men and women today although many religions contain excellent counsels and models of holiness. But what was adequate for the past may not be so for today. Even when the position of women at the earliest period in religion can be seen as a relatively better one, it is far from being comparable to the contemporary situation. It was usually in her social role as wife and mother that woman's position was assessed. In the past, woman's status has always been closely dependent on her child-bearing role. This can be seen especially from the stigma traditionally attached to barrenness, and the tremendous importance placed on male offspring.

The new social and economic conditions which, at last, have given women the freedom to be persons in their own right (whilst not precluding their roles as wife and mother), require a corresponding theological elaboration of the image of woman. Perhaps the time has come, during a period of religious crisis and renewal, to work out in practical terms the basic religious teaching about the essential equality of human nature. Wherever the ascetic ideal has been too prominent in religion women were denigrated. The counsels of ascetic spirituality have in the past been largely addressed too men only, to the exclusion and detriment of women. What about women's own spirituality? Women's views have rarely been heard or asked for in religion, and women's 'nature', so well projected by men, needed little on its own account. All too often the faults of men have been blamed on women. The ascetic ideal which has often had a nefarious influence on the status of women, needs to be replaced by a richer and more balanced spiritual ideal which both men and women can share. Women who still care for religion and see the importance of religious values today, can only plead with religion to give them a fuller share in all religious activities.[20]

In India, too, the traditional ideal of womanhood is often strongly modified in practice. Many outstanding women leaders were deeply involved with the struggle for national independence. The successful contribution of women to the independence movement accounts for the fact that in India

20. This is now increasingly happening. The World Council of Churches has promoted the collaboration of men and women for many years. Certain Christian denominations have had women ministers for quite some time. Today, there are strong movements for the ordination of women in both the Anglican and Roman Catholic Churches.

there are, relatively speaking, more women active in politics than in Western countries. Theoretically, however, the supreme ideal of Indian womanhood is still modelled on the Brahmanical tradition and linked to a strongly patriarchal structure of society.[21] In religion, too, women still occupy the traditional place.

It is most interesting to note that recently a woman of the Lingayat sect in Mysore has begun to propagate the religious equality of woman by fighting for women's right to become a *guru* and to initiate disciples. This is just one example which shows that if women want to improve their status in the sphere of religious belief and practice, it is up to women themselves to assert their right and presence. Today, in a time of much religious transformation and renewal, women themselves have to make sure that their voice will be heard and listened to. The religions of the past have not been able to offer an adequate model for the image of woman, but all religions in the future will be under greater pressure to be more just in representing, and responding to, the aspirations of *all* members of the human community. The challenge presented by the modern world and the status of women in it has to be taken up in a creative way. Women alone cannot achieve this task; the status of women in religion may be worked out more satisfactorily if both women and men have an equal share in influencing the development of religious thought and practice.

---

21. This paradoxical situation between Indian theory and practice is well brought out in the detailed sociological study on Indian women by Maria Mies, *Indische Frauen zwischen Patriarchat und Chacengleichheit: Rollenkonflikte studierender und berufstaetiger Frauen* (Meisenheim am Glan: Verlag Anton Hain, 1973).

8 Muslim Women in Uttar Pradesh: Social Mobility and Directions of Change

Zarina Bhatty

Muslims in India are a heterogeneous community. While there is conformity in ideals and beliefs, derived from the Quran and the *Hadis* (sayings of Prophet Mohammad), the general pattern of living, the system of social stratification, customs and attitudes regarding women have been greatly influenced by the dominant Hindu culture of India. Early conversions to Islam usually meant the acceptance of a different faith while the mode of living remained more or less unchanged. What Ibbetson says of the Muslim convert of Punjab is also true of Uttar Pradesh: '...His customs are unaltered, his rules of marriage and inheritance are unchanged, and almost the only difference is that he shaves his scalp lock and the upper part of his moustache, repeats the Mohammadan creed in the mosque and adds Mussalman to the Hindu wedding ceremonies'.[1]

An important reason for the retention of Hindu customs was that very often instead of a few individuals in a village community, a caste group as a whole accepted Islam. Such a group escaped the brunt of social pressures to abandon its cultural heritage. In Kasauli[2]—a village in the former Oudh

---

1. D.C.J. Ibbetson, *Punjab Castes* (Lahore: Government Printing Press, 1916), p. 14.
2. Kasauli is a pseudonym for a village which is 25 miles east of Lucknow and 8 miles from the town of Bara Banki. The majority of the

region of Uttar Pradesh which I studied and shall frequently refer to for empirical support of my comments and conclusions—the Sakas (the caste of water carriers) still have the symbolic fire as a part of their wedding ceremony, the bride and her groom do the ritual rounds along with the Muslim *nikah*. The position of women in Indian Muslim society is thus influenced both by Islamic injunctions and Hindu traditions. And, as has often happened in the compounding of two sets of influences, the conservative and the restrictive elements of one have tended to dominate or neutralise the liberal elements of the other. This has become glaringly apparent since the enactment of the Hindu Code Bill which has given equal rights, at least in law, to Hindu women while the tenacious adherence to the outmoded Muslim Personal Law continues to keep the lot of Muslim women unaltered.

Islam, at its inception, also represented a reformist movement.[3] In Arabia, at that time, women were no more than chattels and even female infanticide was practised. Islam brought about significant improvements in the attitude towards women and their rights so that Muslims were usually considered to have a higher social status than their Hindu sisters before the passage of the Hindu Code Bill. However, the reforms of centuries ago are completely outmoded and obsolete in the realities of the twentieth century. It is this fact that Muslim society in India has persisted in not recognising.

Social stratification

Muslim society in India is sharply divided into two distinct sections—the Ashrafs and the non-Ashrafs. The Ashrafs represent the upper social strata and comprise the equivalent of a hierarchy of four castes: the Sayyads, the Sheikhs, the Mughals and the Pathans, in that order. It is believed that these upper castes are of foreign origin and thereby superior, while the

population is Muslim. This paper is based on data collected during field work in 1962, 1964 and again in 1973.

3. Zarina Bhatty, 'Social Status of Muslim Women in India', *Roundtable* (March, 1975).

non-Ashrafs are mostly converts and inferior. In the Oudh region of Uttar Pradesh, Ashrafs form the bulk of the Muslim landlord class. One reason for this may be that the Nawabs continued to rule in Oudh till as late as 1856. This might also explain why a distinctly feudal culture is associated with the Muslims of Uttar Pradesh and, particularly, with those who hail from the region of Oudh.

The division between the Ashraf and the non-Ashraf strata of Muslims is clearly reflected in their attitudes towards women. The Ashraf concept of a woman is derived entirely from her role as a wife and a mother and is garnished with the traditional feminine virtues of pre-marital virginity, beauty, tenderness, modesty, self-denial, graciousness, sensitivity and devotion to the family. These virtues, however, are not superfluous trimmings but prerequisites for the role assigned to her in which she upholds the honour of the family, ensures the continuity of the lineage and passes on to the new generation the 'noble' tradition. A girl, right from birth, is moulded for marriage and motherhood. Romance, an inevitable adjunct of her assigned role, is sung about but in practice tabooed. The daughter, in fact, is regarded as a potential alien in her father's house, for she belongs to the patrilineal lineage of her future husband. She is referred to as *amaanat* or *paraya dhan* (another's property). Mrs. Hassan Ali, an English lady married to an Indian Muslim, who lived with her husband in Lucknow in the early years of this century, writing about Ashraf Muslim families in Uttar Pradesh says:[4] 'It is generally to be observed in Mussalman families even in this day that the birth of a baby girl produces a temporary gloom, while the birth of a boy gives rise to a festival in the Zenanah. Some are wicked enough to say that it is more honourable to have sons'. Today, three quarters of a century later, the gloom at the birth of a girl baby persists.

The reason for this gloom among Muslims is the same as that advanced in Hindu society, namely, that the girl is a liability, her birth commits the family to exorbitant outlays for her

---

4. M. Hassan Ali, *Observations on the Mussulmans of India*, (ed.), William Crooke (London: Oxford University Press, 1917), p. 186.

dowry or marriage gifts and expenses, and though she does not really belong to her parents, she must be cared for, guarded and preserved until she is claimed by those who expect her to be thus guarded and preserved for them. It is not surprising therefore, that Muslims, while expressing their displeasure as begetting a daughter, use the phrase 'a guest of four days' to describe her.

Patterns of marriage and work

Islam does not envisage a woman having the liberty to choose her own man to marry, but it does give her the privilege to approve the man she is married to. The Quran is quite explicit on this issue: 'A woman ripe in years should have her consent taken (in marriage). While she remains silent her silence is her consent, but if she refuses she will not be married by force'.[5] But in Uttar Pradesh, particularly among Ashraf Muslims, not only is a girl's consent not taken but it is regarded as scandalous if she expresses her preference for a man. The custom of *purdah* which is enjoined upon a Muslim woman, whereby she has to cover herself with a superfluous garment specially designed to conceal her feminine appearance, drastically curtails her freedom and ability to move about. This custom springs from the attitude that women must not be seen by men lest they be attracted towards them. The implicit presumption is that once being attracted the men are not expected to exhibit any self-restraint. The onus of protecting themselves lies with the women. Thus if a man misbehaves with a woman, the fault most likely is hers and hence no sanctions in this respect need be invoked against the man. And there are none.

Clearly a life so hemmed in by constraints, so laden with impositions, could not possibly come naturally to women. Indeed, the desired attitude of complete submission to male authority, whether it is the father, brother, husband or father in-law is assiduously taught to girls. A song that is sung when a bride

---

5. T.P. Hughes, *Dictionary of Islam* (London: W.H. Allen, 1835), p. 314.

departs from her natal to her conjugal home depicts this attitude very aptly:

> Babul ham tore khoonte ki gayyan,
> jhidhar baandho bandh jayen
> (We are your cows, O Father;
> whichever stake you tie us to,
> There we shall remain bound.)

Non-Ashraf women by comparison are freer. To begin with, they do not as a rule observe *purdah*.[6] And since *purdah* is one of the insignia of respectability, these women are not considered as respectable as Ashraf women. While they play the role of wives and mothers, they are also partners in the daily struggle for earning a livelihood and, the harder this struggle, the greater is the importance of woman as a partner in work. The dominance of this struggle, often pursued grimly in the midst of poverty, leaves little room for the leisurely feminine virtues though they may be admired and even aspired to. Non-Ashraf women too are subordinate to male authority, though they need not be as submissive as their Ashraf sisters. Their movements are less restricted and, being equal partners in earning the daily bread, they have more opportunities for asserting themselves. Virtue is valued and expected of a woman more than it is of man, but it is not so rigidly conceived nor are deviations so severely frowned upon. Non-Ashraf women, therefore, find room for their emotional fulfilment; romances are not uncommon and even elopements occur. Divorce permitted by Islam still carries a strong stigma among the Ashrafs, but to a much less degree among the non-Ashrafs. In Kasauli I found that divorce, remarriage after divorce and marriage of widows were

---

6. The differential observance of *purdah*, which has been well documented, is influenced by socio-economic factors and has consequences for both the independence and social status of Muslim women. See, for example, A.R. Saiyed, '*Purdah*, Family Structure and the Status of Woman: A Note on a Deviant Case', in Imtiaz Ahmad (ed.), *Family, Kinship and Marriage Among Muslims in India* (New Delhi: Manohar, 1976); Shadbano Ahmad, 'Education and Purdah Nuances: A Note on Muslim Women in Aligarh', *Social Action*, 27 (January-March 1977), pp. 45-52.

more frequent among the non-Ashrafs than among the Ashrafs.

Legally, a Muslim man can take up to four wives. He can also divorce his wife at will, without assigning any reason, and simply by saying 'I divorce you'. He is not required by law or custom to pay any maintenance to the wife thus divorced, though he is obliged to pay a compensation of *mehr*[7] fixed in the marriage contract provided the divorced wife or her family insists on it. On the other hand, it is very difficult for a woman to secure a divorce. Not only does she have to go to court but the conditions under which she can seek divorce are also very stringent. Even if she succeeds in getting a divorce, she forfeits the *mehr*. Incidentally polygamy is not recognised as a reason for seeking a divorce. Fortunately, however, polygamy is almost negligible. Nevertheless, the absence of any safeguard for the woman clearly demonstrates the inequality in the status of man and woman in Muslim society.

In matters of inheritance too a woman is discriminated against in law as well as by custom. Islam stipulates that a daughter is entitled to one-third of her father's property, that is, to half of what her brother gets. This rule seldom applies to landed property which is almost never inherited by daughters. I found in Kasauli that, to camouflage this denial, the custom of cousin marriage with a preference for parallel cousins has been well established. In fact, this custom is common throughout Uttar Pradesh and particularly among those who have landed property. Non-Ashraf families generally do not own land or any other property worth considering and therefore the occasion for any discrimination in inheritance does not arise. There is

---

7. *Mehr* can be literally translated as dower. This is the amount fixed at the time of *nikah* which a husband is required to pay to the bride before consumating the marriage but in actual practice it is not paid unless or until the husband wants to divorce the wife. But if wife initiates the divorce proceedings then he is not obliged to pay the dower. But since a Muslim man can have up to four wives without divorcing the previous wives, it is seldom that a man starts the divorce, he can always discard his wife unofficially and marry another. In Pakistan, as Korson notes, '*Mehr* is not only a tradition, but is required by law, and can be enforced by law'. See J. Henry Korson, 'Modernisation and Social Change: The Family in Pakistan', in Man Singh Das and Panos D. Bardis (eds.), *The Family in Asia* (New Delhi: Vikas, 1978), pp. 169-207.

a sense of common ownership of whatever little is possessed because it is acquired through the joint effort of both husband and wife.

The fact of joint effort at making a living is perhaps the most important differentiating feature of the non-Ashraf families. I found non-Ashraf women in Kasauli moving about freely with their men and working alongside with their husbands in the fields or at crafts in which the family specialises. A division of labour based on sex is commonly practised. For example, among Manihars (the caste of bangle sellers) men manufacture the bangles or journey to the nearby city to buy their stock of bangles, while both men and women sell them in the village streets or at at their shop. Women have an edge over men in selling because they can reach Ashraf women in their home which the men, on account of *purdah*, cannot. The division of labour between men and women is more clearly defined in the caste of Nais (barbers). Men cut hair and shave, carry messages regarding births, deaths or marriages and cook at ceremonial occasions for Ashraf as well as non-Ashraf families. Nai women carry and deliver sweets that are customarily distributed among relatives and neighbours at festivals or ceremonial occasions, help Ashraf women in their toilette and at childbirth (it is usually a woman of the Nai caste who delivers the baby) and also massage new mothers and the new born babies. These women are paid a wage for their services or, as in Ashraf homes, they receive a traditionally fixed payment at harvest time and other customary gifts.

Education and employment

A change in the attitude towards women is clearly observable both in Ashraf and non-Ashraf sections of Muslim society, but the change is in different directions. It was discouraging to find that, while upper class Ashraf Muslims in Kasauli were moving towards a more liberal attitude, the non-Ashrafs were becoming more conservative and were trying to emulate those very traditional customs of Ashraf society which the Ashrafs themselves were giving up.

The greatest change in Ashraf attitudes towards women has come about in the matter of their education. The worth of education has come to be established so well in their own minds that they not only find it impossible to deny it to women but also actively encourage it. The partition of India, in this respect, had an advantageous effect on those Muslim families which decided to remain in India. Immediately after partition many families allowed their sons to go to Pakistan either out of fear of discrimination or to exploit the job opportunities in the new country, while the girls remained with their parents. Older people from families which owned land tended not to migrate for reasons which included the prospect of losing their property.

This happened in Kasauli too. While hardly any from the older generation migrated, quite a few young men opted to do so. Many joint families broke up on this account and, in some families, the burden of earning a living fell on the women. Necessity forced many families to yield to the pressures of time and to allow their daughters to take up jobs. Further, a side-effect of the Hindu-Muslim riots immediately after partition was that many Muslim women gave up *purdah* because in the *burqa* they were immediately identified as Muslim. Once a woman gave up *purdah*, though for a short-term practical reason, she seldom returned to it. Meanwhile, the doors of education were opening to girls and both these changes made more and more women to come out of their seclusion to seek jobs and take their place in spheres which had hitherto been closed to them.

In Kasauli today several girls, married and unmarried, are not only holding jobs, one of them is a Minister in the State cabinet. However, I found that while higher education for women is now desired and even facilitated by male members of the family, when it comes to taking up a job, some resistance is still encountered. Here, traditional attitudes towards women and values regarding status and prestige both play a role. At the time I was doing my study in Kasauli, an unmarried daughter of the leading Muslim family was working as a teacher in the village school. Another woman of the same family, now a Minister, was a member of the U.P. Legislative

Assembly. While the family showed no resistance to the candidature of the latter for the Assembly seat—in fact, was proud of it—it debated for long whether the other girl should be allowed to take up school teaching in the village. This, notwithstanding the fact that the Assembly candidate was forced to mingle with all sorts of people on terms not consistent with the traditional values of her class. Such exposure was tolerated because to be a member of the State Assembly carries high prestige, but similar exposure in the midst of the village folk at the relatively low prestige level of a school teacher was clearly undesirable. This lingering resistance in fully accepting the break is evident in many other ways as well.

It should be noted that though the worth of education is being accepted, at least among families that can afford it for their daughters, in matters of marriage and the granting of other personal choices, women are still treated differently from men. The alternatives available to them are still very limited and traditional attitudes continue to regulate their lives. In Kasauli girls are not encouraged to make their own choice of husbands or even to express their preference. They marry whoever is chosen for them by their parents and the majority of marriages take place within close relatives. Some deviations have taken place in the last decade or so, but these were resisted and strongly disapproved. In the matter of accepting jobs too the resistance has not worn off. Two years ago when a girl from the leading landlord family took up a university lectureship, the echoes of disapproval from the older members of the family were clearly audible.

Judged in the context of the present day urge for equality, the status of Muslim women in Uttar Pradesh surely falls short of the desired. Let me add immediately that I do not hold with equality in the sense of similarity of roles for men and women in society. But an individual's status in society does depend on the totality of rights—political, legal, economic and social—enjoyed by him or her. In other words, the status of an individual within any social system varies inversely with the impediments imposed by society deliberately or otherwise to restrict self-realisation. On this criterion Muslim society has been and still is discriminating against women. A Muslim woman has the assigned role of mother and wife, but this role is looked upon as inferior and serious constraints are placed on her if she wishes to supplement it with out-of-home interests. The encouraging sign, on the other hand, is that some rethinking is taking place and a few deviant women are emerging even in the Muslim society of Uttar Pradesh.

Social mobility and emulation

The situation among the non-Ashrafs is almost the reverse. Women in this segment of Muslim society are losing the freedom they had in an effort to emulate the Ashrafs.[8] In Kasauli I found that the Ashrafs were acting as a reference group for the non-Ashrafs. On the one hand, urban influences were percolating both directly and through the upper classes and on the other, rising incomes and a greater social and political awareness were giving them a more palpable stake in the village community and its traditions. The net result of these two strands of influences was rather curious. The lower class women were trying to imitate the upper class women, who are now more urbanised, in matters of dress styles, manners and language. This imitation extended further to attitudes towards education, religion and family structure.

But the desire was to become more like the upper class families in the traditional village structure rather than in their present day context. For example, the urge for education has expressed itself in the opening of Madarasas in the village, where the Quran along with some Urdu is taught. The practice of religion has become more ostentatious. There is a marked tendency among those non-Ashraf families who have done relatively well to put their women in *purdah* and to withdraw them from the family work force. It is now said in praise of a husband that he is able to give his wife the leisure to 'stay in

---

8. For a fine discussion of reference group behaviour and 'emulation' in a caste structured society, see Owen M. Lynch, *The Politics of Untouchability* (New York: Columbia University Press, 1969).

bed,' instead of forcing her to work in the field.[9] In Kasauli, a family of Telis (caste of oil pressers) made good and built a partly *pucca* (brick) house. Previously the women in the household used to help in working the *ghani* (oil press) and also in

Diagram: Social Mobility and Directions of Change

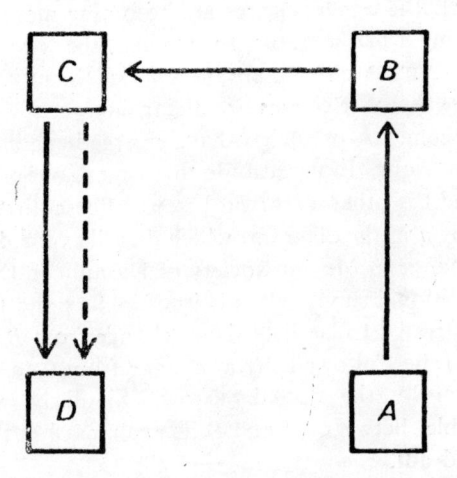

A poor class families; *B* lower class families who become relatively well off; *C* traditional upper classes; *D* liberal upper class families.

---

9. Zarina Bhatt, 'Status and Power in a Muslim Dominated Village in U.P.', in Imtiaz Ahmed (ed.), *Caste and Social Stratification Among the Muslims* (New Delhi: Manohar, 1973); Zarina Bhatty, 'The Problem' in *Seminar*, 165 (May, 1973), pp. 10-12.

vending mustard oil in the village streets. Now the young daughter-in-law does not work and has taken to *purdah* while the mother-in-law continues to work and does not observe *purdah*. Consequently, the authority of the husband has also increased and the woman has been pushed back into the limited roles of wife and mother.

The same regressive process with respect to the status of women in the lower classes has been observed by Srinivas who describes it as the process of 'Sanskritisation' among the lower caste Hindus.[10] Thus in Hindu society too it has been found that while the upper classes are becoming more modern and are according a better status to women, the lower classes, in an attempt to emulate them, are accepting the attitudes and values which these upper classes are discarding.

Two new segments of society have emerged exhibiting new patterns of behaviour. In its attitude to women, one represents a backward and the other a forward step. These directions of change are shown in the diagram which describes the dominant character of change in Muslim society of Kasauli. In the future, since the traditional upper class is itself in flux and the lower classes are motivated to emulate them, change from B to C can be expected to be followed by a change from C to D shown in the diagram by the dotted arrow. Similarly, while no change is visible between A and D its emergence in the future cannot be ruled out.

Directions of change

The major influence for change operating on the upper classes are education and urbanisation. On the lower classes, the major influence is economic progress, or more specifically, a rise in per capita income. It is the latter influence that needs to be examined further because it concerns the bulk of the Muslim society. The starting point here is poverty or near poverty—a condition in which work is hard (made harder by

---

10. M.N. Srinivas, *Caste in Modern India* (Bombay: Asia Publishing House, 1970).

poverty, a physical incapacity for hard work) and the rewards meagre. Women work because they have to, and not because they find in it a means for greater freedom, economic independence or self-expression. In a measure they already have these. When income rises and it becomes possible to substitute the labour of the woman in the family by a hired hand or the addition to the income contributed by the woman does not seem worthwhile, the attraction of withdrawing from work appears too strong. While the modulation of women's working hours or character of work or both with the possibility of giving the increase in family income a greater impetus might appear a more rational solution, it is rejected due to the psychological satisfaction of appearing closer to the behaviour pattern of the upper classes.

This analysis shows that while there are similarities in the status of women in the liberalised sections of the upper classes and the poorer lower classes (no *purdah*, freedom of movement, participation in economic activity) and the distance between them may appear relatively small, at least in one respect the similarity is entirely superficial, namely, the approach to work. Since this is fundamental, a direct movement from *A* to *D* in the diagram must be viewed as highly improbable at least in the forseeable future. The process of change as far as the lower classes is concerned, therefore, would continue to be circuitous, though its time span will be less the faster the rate of growth of family income.

Despite the dynamics of change, whose alternate directions appear to be towards a more liberal and a more egalitarian status for women, there is an island of stagnant rigidity—the Muslim Personal Law. Unless this can be submerged and replaced by legislation similar to the Hindu Code Bill, it will stand solidly in the way of Muslim women attaining what their sisters in this country or abroad are now likely to achieve.

9 Purdah and Public Space

Ursula M. Sharma

In this paper I shall consider some of the conventions which control the use of social space by women in North India, in particular the restrictions upon their free and uninhibited use of public areas. Generally, these conventions have been discussed in the context of *purdah*. *Purdah*, I would agree, is a complex of norms having three main dimensions: (*a*) those rules which govern the behaviour of married women towards male affines and neighbours. I have suggested elsewhere[1] that practices such as *ghungat*, avoidance of certain male members of the husband's family and village, etc., have the total effect of cutting women off from communication with those who are likely to hold power in the village; (*b*) those norms which define the separation of the sexes. The imperative that women should have minimal contact with unrelated men operates in favour of men in the sense that it is considered the responsibility of women to avoid men rather than that of men to avoid women. This means that it is difficult for a woman to engage in public, political or economic processes which involve contact with unrelated men since it is her business to withdraw from such situations Effectively, these norms re-inforce all other norms which define women's

---

1. U.M. Sharma, 'Women and their Affines: The Veil as a Symbol of Separation,' *Man*, N.S., 13(1978).

role as essentially domestic;[2] (c) those norms which govern women's mobility, and even visibility, outside the home. It is these which I shall concentrate on here.[3]

Village men and women, when they refer to *purdah*, usually use the term to include all these aspects, or whichever of them operate in there own community. I do not distinguish these aspects myself simply for an academic exercise in typology. Having separated the different dimensions of purdah practices, it is easier to discuss the local variations in *purdah*, and especially between Hindu and Muslim *purdah*. In these terms, Muslim *purdah* differs from the Hindu version of the institution in that it places relatively little insistence on norms of category (*a*), i.e. those regulating married women's interaction with affinal males, but a great deal on norms of category (*c*), those controlling women's mobility in public places. Hindu practice, on the other hand, accents (*a*) at the expense of (*b*) and (*c*). Hindu and Muslim *purdah* can be seen as variant combinations of a set of culturally available norms and concepts, which have very similar function so far as the structuring of women's relationships in the local community is concerned. There are further variants within the Hindu and Muslim groups, related to local conditions, social class, caste practices, etc.

If we wish to take a comparative approach, we can see all these practices as particular instances of a broad category of institutions found in peasant societies (and indeed in other kinds of society as well) which have the effect of excluding women from the public sphere, i.e., the sphere of publicly acknowledged political and economic processes and interactions. *Purdah*, seen in these terms, no longer appears as a cultural

---

2. See U.M. Sharma, 'Segregation and its Consequences in India,' in J. Bujra and P. Caplan (eds.), *Women United, Women Divided* (London: Tavistock, 1978).

3. To some writers, segregation is the most important aspect of *purdah* and the norms governing women's mobility outside the home are treated simply as the logical consequences of norms regarding the segregation of the sexes. See for instance, C. Vreede-de Stuers, *Parda* (Assen: Van Gorcum, 1978). This approach may be appropriate for Muslim communities in South Asia, but I think that among Hindus, the norms of category (*c*) are as well organised and conspicuous.

peculiarity of Islamic societies or of Hindus in South Asia. It is one way, among others, of controlling women and restricting them to the domestic sphere, ensuring that they step outside it only with difficulty, i.e., in the face of imputations of dishonour or in spite of practical difficulties. Some, such as Rogers,[4] would hold that these restrictions are not necessarily a disability if the domestic sphere is 'where the action is' and if the kinds of public power which a peasant male can expect to exert are very weak. Roger's argument is certainly constructive in so far as it draws our attention to some of the informal political processes which occur, as it were, 'off stage' and from which women are not excluded by the rules which constrain their appearances and behaviour in public. On the other hand, I would hold that in South Asia, these rules are much more than simply a means of maintaining the 'illusion' of male dominance. They really do contribute to the dominance of men in certain specific spheres, although their effect is not totally negative.

But I do not wish to pursue this comparative theme further here. I will limit myself to demonstrating that *purdah* does have a function in structuring relations in the local community, a *political* function in the broad sense of the word. With this emphasis, I hope that this contribution will complement the excellent analyses of *purdah* already available. Papanek, for example, has dealt with the way in which *purdah* is experienced by women and has demonstrated its relationship to the division of labour by sex and social class.[5] Jacobson has described *purdah* practices largely in terms of the way in which female sex roles are organised and only tangentially tackles the way in which *purdah* affects women's roles in production and public life. However, her account has the positive value of demonstrating the subjective satisfactions which their roles offer to women in spite of the

---

4. S. Rogers, 'Female Forms of Power and the Myth of Male Dominance: A Model of Male/Female Interaction in Peasant Society', *American Ethnologist*, 12 (n. 4, 1975).

5. H. Papanek, 'Purdah: Separate World and Symbolic Shelter', *Comparative Studies in Society and History*, 50 (n. 3, 1973).

apparent circumstances which they must accept.[6] Rama Mehta's study of Oswal women is probably the best study of *purdah* as practised by a parcticular caste community, showing how the institution responded to political and economic pressures to change.[7]

What I would like to add to these discussions is some consideration of the role of *purdah* in structuring social relations at the level of the local community. *Purdah* norms contribute to the restriction of the range of activities and opportunities open to a woman in the village where she lives. In so far as *purdah* contributes to the ordering of the political and economic life of the village it needs to be discussed alongside such institutions as caste and factions, not only in the context of sex roles and domestic organisation.

The following account is based largely on fieldwork carried out in Punjab during the winter of 1977-78 in Harbassi, a large village in District Hoshiarpur. But I have also utilised material gathered in two Himachal Pradesh villages, Ghanyari and Chaili, during periods of fieldwork conducted in 1967 and 1978 respectively.

Harbassi has a population of about 6,000 which includes agriculturists of all kinds from large capitalist farmers to farm labourers, and a commercial sector, comprising shopkeepers, traders and hawkers. There are also those who service the agriculturists—mechanics, government employed advisers, irrigation engineers, etc. There are artisans of all kinds (potters, cobblers, smiths, etc.), and a small service sector including sweepers, porters, domestic servants, etc. Ghanyari and Chaili situated in the lower foothills, have a far less complex occupational structure and are much smaller settlements, having populations of roughly 350 and 700 respectively. They are dominantly agricultural communities, but the farmers of this part of Himachal are not of the capitalist type, being exclusively peasant cultivators and their tenants. Both the villages have a few artisans, car-

---

6. D. Jacobson, 'The Women of North and Central India: Goddesses and Wives,' in D. Jacobson and S. Wadley, *Women in India: Two Perspectives* (Columbia: Asia Books, 1977).

7. R. Mehta, 'From Purdah to Modernity,' in B.R. Nanda (ed.), *Indian Women* (New Delhi: Vikas, 1976).

penters, smiths and the like, but Chaili also has a modest bazaar with a few shops and public offices. In both Chaili and Ghanyari there is a far narrower range of socio-economic differentiation, but in spite of Harbassi's larger and more complex population, its inhabitants had a strong sense of collective identity and perhaps a greater sense of 'civic pride' than either of the Himachali villages I studied.

When I first arrived in Harbassi something that made a very strong impression upon me was the fact that the women of well-to-do families (the wives of large capitalist farmers, professional people and shopkeepers or traders) moved outside the confines of their homes very little. Santosh K., a Brahmin woman whom I came to know very well, told me that she 'hardly stirred outside these four walls'. Her house, like many others in the village, did not face onto the street but onto a private courtyard surrounded by high windowless walls. A couple of small shuttered grilles enabled her to look out into the neighbour's courtyards; but access to the street was only gained through a pair of high wooden doors, firmly bolted at night. Santosh could view what was going on in the streets and fields around the house by climbing the stairway which led to the roof. From the roof one had a good view of any comings and goings in the street below, as well as of other women sitting on their roofs in the winter sunshine, sewing, knitting, cleaning grain. One could watch the public life of the street, but distanced from it, as a spectator rether than as a participant.

I had taken Santosh's remark about 'not stirring outside these four walls' as a complaint, since she had been recently widowed and lived alone, her two sons being employed in other parts of the country. But afterwards I realised that it had been made in a spirit of pride; to be able to conduct one's daily life without the need to stir outdoors was a privilege only the prosperous could afford. Poor women, such as the farmer's widow who came to wash Santosh's dishes daily, the washerwomen who collected her laundry, and the sweeper who cleaned her latrine could not afford such a secluded life.

On the other hand, differences due to social class should not be exaggerated since all these women were subject to certain general conventions which governed their appearance in public places. Women of the lower classes might be obliged to move abroad to cultivate their fields, fetch provisions from the bazaar or sell their services in the village, but they might not linger unnecessarily in the public streets. They might not, for instance, stop to take tea or chat at the eating houses in the bazaar unless accompanied by a male relative. Nor might they raise their voices in laughter or anger as they might in their own courtyards or alleyways or attract attention to themselves in any way.[8] When I say that women 'might not' do these things, I do not mean that they were meted out some kind of instant punishment if they did. Women in all the three villages studied experienced a sense of unease in public places which was sufficient to inhibit their behaviour. Women accounted for this feeling in various ways. The daughter of one large landlord, for instance, told me that she never went to the bazaar because 'men take wine there and get drunk so it would not be a good thing to go there'. Others accounted for this avoidance less in terms of the hostility of the space itself than in terms of their own lack of confidence. Thus a farmer's wife in Chaili told me that she did not go to get her shopping herself, but would always send her son or husband because 'I am uneducated and I am always afraid that I would be cheated and made to look foolish'. Another farmer's wife, Vidya, used to visit her neighbours often, but always taking a very circuitous route to reach their homes via several footpaths at the back of the main street. When I asked her why she did this, she said that she did not like to go through the main bazaar 'because there were men there, and they might look at us'. The sense of being 'out of place' in the main street or bazaar is enough to ensure that women go about their business discreetly and then return home briskly when it is done. Women are not actually debarred from using public space and in cities there may be segregated facilities which make it easier for them to do so without loss of reputation. But their appearance in public is conditional—conditional upon discreet behaviour and having some specific business. They cannot use

---

8. One of Jacobson's informants stated that 'at a religious drama, a man can laugh loudly but a woman has to laugh quietly. She shouldn't raise her voice, and she should obey her husband'. Jacobson, op.cit., p. 67.

public space in the casual manner permitted to men. Respectable women do not without good reason, expose themselves to contact with strange men—and as we have seen from Vidya's remark, simply to be looked at by a strange man counts as contact.

Unlike men, women should not gossip out of doors or chat casually in public places unless they wish to incur the criticism of others. Kanta, an agricultural labourer's daughter in Harbassi, told me 'I have to go out in order to do my work in the fields, but you will not see me hanging about the village or sitting in other people's houses. I do my work and then come home'. Women do, in fact, gather to gossip in each other's houses or in the alleyways that run between them, but what Kanta's remark shows us is that it is difficult for women to *admit* to purposeless activity outside the home. Poor women are not in a position to observe the norms which regulate women's use of public space as strictly as women of the wealthier classes, but these norms do, nonetheless, affect the way they present themselves outside the home and the way in which they evaluate their own and other women's behaviour. In spite of differences in actual practice there was general consensus as to the kinds of place which are considered as dangerous or unsuitable for women.

The basic fear which motivates the sense of unease in public places is the fear of breaking the norm that forbids women to receive attention from unrelated men, and the idea that in inviting such attention (however unconsciously) a woman jeopardises not only her own good name but that of her family. It is assumed without question that in public places men will look at women. They will certainly stare at them, possibly tease them by passing crude comments on their appearances or by jostling them. This, it is felt, is a fact of social life which one cannot alter. This being so, it is women's responsibility to avoid places where this might happen. For Muslim women, as Papanek has suggested, the *burqa* offers a form of shelter for the woman, a screen from such attentions which still allows her to be mobile.[9] For Hindu women, the veil with which a few

---

9. Papanek, op. cit., p. 295.

married women in Harbassi still cover their faces when venturing into public places, provides a less satisfactory alternative. But however wrapped and swathed, a woman is still distinguishable as a woman when she goes outside her home and the most cursory male glance at her bundled form logically constitutes a violation of the monopoly which her own menfolk should enjoy. The best protection of all for women is not to enter public areas more than they need.

The evaluation of social space: public and private

In rural India, the areas of a village are graded according to how public they are, and are subject to a moral evaluation in terms of the degree of danger they hold for women. But what kinds of space are defined as public? In Harbassi, the areas which women avoided when they could included the bazaar, which consisted of a low winding street, running roughly parallel to the main road; the grain depot and wholesale vegetable market; the main road which runs right through the village, and is lined with public buildings such as schools, offices, a library etc. The bus stand, which is situated at the junction of the main road with country lane also tended to be avoided. These public areas were acknowledged to be male preserves; women often had to venture into them, but would not linger there longer than their business obliged them to. The network of back alleys between the bazaar and the main road was felt to be less public and women did not mind being seen there. Most could reach the houses of friends of kin via these back streets without needing to cross the more public areas. Similarly, the footpaths and by-lanes which linked the village with its surrounding hamlets were also felt to be less dangerously public for women.

A group of wealthy ladies who lived near to each other and who observed the maximum seclusion known in this part of India used to take a stroll together in the evenings down the lane which leads from their houses to a watercourse in the fields. None of them cared to go alone, and they always returned by dusk, but they did not feel that their reputation could be damaged by being seen in this part of the village. The footpaths through the fields near the village were evidently felt to be in quite a different category from the bazaar and the main road, even though they were quite public (in the sense that anyone could use them) and women would use them freely to reach their own fields or to visit the houses of friends or kin in adjacent hamlets.

Agricultural land is social space of yet another type. Many women are obliged to work in the fields, being employed seasonally by local farmers to reap or weed. This is considered a disagreeable necessity, but more because it involves entering into economic relations with non-kin and because it involves unpleasant manual work, than on account of the actual location of the work. One's own land is really an extension of one's own home and women can move about their own fields and estates with confidence that they will not be censured. The preference for farmers' wives to withdraw from agricultural labour if they can afford to seems to be quite as much due to the degrading nature of manual work as to the effects of being seen outside the home. The wives of rich farmers would sometimes visit their estates either for relaxation—a kind of picnic outing—or to help their husbands to supervise operations. Santosh, for instance, would travel with her eldest son by bus to the hamlets where their land was situated. She would have a cot drawn up under a tree beside the road so that she could watch the boring of a tube well in shade and comfort, not at all concerned by the fact that she was visible from the road. Her sister-in-law, Kaushalya, enjoyed accompanying her husband to their fields, especially on sunny winter mornings. These outings were not undertaken very often, but there was a feeling that one's own land was so much a projection of one's own domestic space that one had as much right to be seen there as one had in one's own courtyard. One was only publicly 'visible' in the sense that one was 'visible' to someone peeping through a grille in the private courtyard. On one's own territory one need fear no censure.

I remember that on evening I had accompanied Santosh and Kaushalya to their fields and we missed the bus which should have taken us back to Harbassi. We set out on foot, but we had not gone far when it started to get dark,[10] so we decided to go back to the hamlet where Santosh's tenants lived. Her son was still there talking to some of the tenants and we would travel back perched on the mudguards of the tractor—not a very dignified way to travel, but in the dark who would see us? Both my companions had become rather nervous as dusk fell, but as soon as we set foot on Santosh's land again, she remarked with an expression of relief, 'Well, at least we are in our own fields now. No one can do anything to us.' In point of fact we were on a lonely path and had anyone wished to rob or rape us there would have been no one in earshot to came to our help. But the idea that she was back on her own ground gave Santosh a sense of security and confidence again.

Those women who are obliged to labour in their family's fields grumble far more about the tedious nature on the work, the back-breaking toil in the hot sun at threshing time and the monotony of weeding, than the fact that this work takes place outdoors. In the Himachal villages I studied, there were hardly any woman who could afford to observe any kind of seclusion, but the view that agricultural work was *dishonourable* for women was a point of view put forward more often by men than by women. The latter usually saw it simply as disagreeable. One's own fields are an extension of private space beyond the actual walls of the home. Some wealthy farmers in Harbassi would build a small hut over a tubewell pump which would not only protect the pump but also accommodate such homely articles as cots, rugs and tea making equipment, which the farmer and his family could use to make themselves comfortable when they visited their fields. One farmer even had a small library of books kept in his hut, and another woman had a spacious room built at the head of her tube-well. She termed this her *dera* (encampment) and she would spend a good deal of time there each day under the pretext of taking her husband and their labourers the food which she had prepared. She could do this without fear of censure, since though she was publicly visible,

10 Times is subject to social evaluation as well as space A respectable woman gets up early to do her work and is not seen out of doors after dark unless accompanied by some kind of chaperone.

she could not be said to be loitering in public space.

Another category of social space which is evaluated in quite a different way is the jungle. The term 'jungle,' of course, refers to any uncultivated ground; it need not be actual forest. In Punjab there is little land of this category left. Population expansion and the increase in the value of land and its products have ensured the utilisation of every last acre of cultivable ground. All that remains near Harbassi is a few narrow strips of coarse scrub and grass along the borders of the *cho* (seasonal watercourse). As one approaches the Himalayan foothills these areas of waste ground become more extensive, and in the vicinities of both Chaili and Ghanyari one village is separated from the next by tracts of deciduous scrub or pine forest. In both Punjab and Himachal the land categorised as jungle is used for a number of purposes, the most important of which is grazing and the collection of fodder for cattle. In Himachal it is also used for the collection of firewood and dead leaves used to provide bedding for domestic animals. In both areas people go to waste land near the village in order to defecate.

Women of most social groups, therefore, will sometimes be obliged to cross space categorised as 'jungle' in going about ordinary activities (indeed in both areas cutting grass for fodder is a predominantly *female* activity). But there is also a feeling that the jungle is not a good place to linger in and that it is potentially dangerous. The feeling is not only experienced by women; in Punjab there is the fear (on the whole, I think, a real one) that anyone who hangs about in lonely places at night is liable to be attacked and robbed. In Himachal the predominant fear is that of evil spirits or ghosts, who ambush unsuspecting travellers in the dark or in the hot still hours of noon. But for girls and women the jungle holds special dangers. Kishan Das, a high caste farmer who lived near Chaili, told me that he did not like to send his daughter to the high school in Chaili since she had to walk through the woods to get there. He and some of his relatives were pressing that a high school for girls be established in the village where they live so that their daughters did not have to make this journey (they were not so worried about their sons). Many girls in the hamlets around Harbassi stated that their education had been discontinued after they had completed the fifth grade, for then they would have had to attend the high school at Harbassi. Their parents had been unhappy about the fact that they would have to cross several *cho* to get there and they did not like their daughters to have to go through such jungly places. This could have just been a rationalisation of their inability or unwillingness to bear the expense of the girls' further education, but certainly more girls attend high school in Harbassi now that a good bus service links it with the outlying hamlets.

There can be hardly any doubt that the fear underlying this avoidance of waste land and forest was the fear that the woman who ventured into such places might be molested by strange men, or even raped. Indeed, several villagers expressed this fear quite explicitly. As in the case of the bazaar, the sexual attentions of men are the danger which women must avoid. But in the bazaar (the public space *inside* the village) such attentions are unlikely to go beyond teasing and rude remarks, whereas in the jungle (the public space *outside* the village) there would not be spectators present to deter really violent behaviour. I did not hear of any women who had actually suffered such an attack from a stranger but there were several women in Ghanyari who claimed that kinsmen of their husbands had tried to force their attentions upon them when they had been cutting grass in the jungle. Both the jungle and the bazaar constitute areas of public space where a woman ventures at her own risk. No one else can be held responsible for anything that befalls her if she traverses such areas unchaperoned. But she herself is responsible to her family for any loss of reputation which they may suffer as a result of her behaviour (or the behaviour of others to her) in public places. So long as a woman stays in her own home or her own field she can claim that any violation of her honour has taken place in spite of the protection of her menfolk and her own due care. She ventures outside this private space at her own risk.

This definition of public space as essentially male territory is not, of course, peculiar to Indian society. Even in many European towns there are streets which are effectively 'no-go' areas for women; that it, women who enter such streets at night do so at their own risk. If, having done so, they suffer molestation or loss of reputation it is considered that they have somehow brought it upon themselves. (Soho is one such area which is well known, not to say notorious, in London.) As a student, I once had lodgings in an area of London which was respectable enough in itself, but to reach my house from the railway station I had to walk down a street known to be frequented by prostitutes. That is, I supposed that it must be frequented by prostitutes although I seldom saw any, for men in cars would feel free to approach any woman walking down this particular street whether or not she looked or behaved like a prostitute. There was no point in complaining about such behaviour since people in the locality assumed that as everyone knew the character of this street, it was a woman's business to avoid having to go there at night. It is only very recently that public houses (where alcoholic drinks are served) have ceased to be such no-go areas for unaccompanied women, and even now there are not many public houses where a woman would feel at ease in going alone to order a drink for herself. Feminists in the West are now questioning the assumption that it is women's business to avoid such areas rather than men's business to refrain from molesting them there. In the past year 'Reclaim the Night' marches and demonstrations have been held in several cities, asserting women's right to 'walk down any street, night or day without fear of sexual attack or harrassment from men'.[11]

Villagers in Harbassi often stated that in the past the restrictions on women's mobility outside the home had been even tighter, at least so far as women of the landowning classes were concerned. I was told that women of 'good family' did not venture out at all before 1947 without swathing themselves in heavy shawls over their saris and completely covering their faces. One old woman stated that her mother had never been to school

---

11. Claude Enjeu and J. Save have described the effective exclusion of women from certain parts of the city in an article 'The City: Off-Limits to Women,' *Liberation* (July-August 1974); 'Because women are apparently mingled with the urban crowd, there is an illusion of equal mobility and access. Yet it wouldn't be far fetched for a cartoonist to sketch out a "street guide for the ladies". Throughout the city their paths are studded with keep-out signs and danger signals'.

because it had not been considered proper for girls of respectable families to go out unchaperoned (nowadays girls have a good deal of freedom to run about the streets until they are eleven or twelve years old). She herself had been the first girl in her family to get an education, and that only because by that time the family could afford a maidservant to escort her to and from the school, which was only a few streets away. Villagers explained this greater rigidity in terms of the presence of Muslims in the village, and the fear that girls would be kidnapped by them. (There was a substantial Muslim minority in Harbassi until 1947 when they emigrated *en masse* to Pakistan.) Whether or not Hindu girls were in greater danger of abduction than Muslim girls I cannot say; the point is that Hindus believed that they were. Hindus considered that they were not so much emulating Muslims in enjoining their women to observe *purdah* as protecting them from Muslims. Certainly the period leading up to 1947 was experienced as one of declining law and order and public safety. Many girls of both communities were raped or abducted. This makes it difficult to judge whether the modern relaxation of *purdah* restrictions represents part of a long term trend or simply a recovery from the tense pre-Partition period.

Domestic space

The antithesis of public space is domestic space, where women feel secure from the various kinds of physical or moral danger which might assail them outside. In the home they can, within the limits of their roles in the family, behave in a more uninhibited way. The epitome of domestic space is the kitchen. This area is presided over not by men but by the women of the household; it is the women who both prepare and serve food and who control access to the cooking area, which must be kept ritually pure. Khare notes that 'a central axis ... must always develop between the women of the house and the domestic hearth'.[12] So even if modern cooking methods or labour saving

12. R.S. Khare, *The Hindu Hearth and Home* (New Delhi: Vikas Publishing House, 1976).

devices are used which cut down the amount of time and work involved in cooking, and even if a servant is employed to prepare meals, the women of the family have the fundamental duty to supervise the cooking and serving of food. The cooking area, the moral centre of the household, is the area where a woman is most 'at home' even if she spends much of her day at work outside the house.

But space inside the house is also zoned and evaluated in terms of its degree of 'privateness', although just how strongly marked the separation will be depends on the size of the house and the status of its inhabitants. Santosh K.'s house had two courtyards. One opened on to the street itself through a high doorway. A sitting room had been built facing on to this courtyard, and this room along with the outer courtyard had been used a generation ago, by the menfolk for eating, sleeping and entertaining male guests. The inner courtyard, onto which faced a couple of living rooms and the kitchen had been the domain of the women of the family. A servant had been employed to take food from the kitchen to where the men would be sitting in the outer courtyard, but male visitors would not penetrate beyond the door that separated the two courtyards, leaving the inner part of the house as a purely private zone.

This pattern of household zoning has fallen out of use in Harbassi, although it is true that in all but the poorest dwellings there is some crude division into 'inner' and 'outer' domestic space. Some room or part of the courtyard will be distinguished for the reception of guests, especially male guests, and screened off somehow from the cooking area which is the preserve of the woman.

Women, therefore, experience social space as divided into zones of differential danger or risk. At the centre of her social world is a woman's own kitchen and the cooking hearth around which she busies herself with the greatest sense of moral and physical security. Beyond that are the outer parts of the house, then the alleys, footpaths or fields around the house where she need move about with only a little more constraint and circumspection. Beyond these again are various kinds of public space which she may not be able to avoid entering, but which are negatively evaluated for women. Most remote and dangerous of all is the jungle—that space which is outside society altogether, or rather which is least under the control of men. The further she moves from her own hearth, the more she is held to run the risk of moral danger—symbolic violation through the impudent gaze of strange men (even, at worst, real violation) and the loss of reputation which she risks through her vulnerability to this kind of danger.

Married and unmarried women

How far are these restrictions applied differently to married and unmarried women? Certain female practices (veiling, avoidance of affines) are only enjoined upon women after marriage, and there is some suggestion in the literature that unmarried women have more freedom of movement than married women.

Marriage for a woman initiates a period of movement between her parents and her in-laws' home. She now becomes aware of the distinction between *peke* (her natal kin and village) and her *saure* (her in-laws' home). During the first year or two of marriage she will travel a good deal between *peke* and *saure* until her residence with the latter is stabilised and she is fully incorporated into her husband's household. However, she does not undertake such journeying alone. It would reflect ill on the family that sent her if they let her go unescorted. Men tend to rationalise this in terms of women's lack of confidence in travelling alone, the inability of a young inexperienced girl to find her way without difficulty. Women are less likely to see it in terms of their own incapacity. One Himachali woman told me that women might perhaps be afraid to travel alone, but immediately qualified what she had said with 'Well, they might not really be frightened, but they would be worried about what people would say about them.' Travel involves the use of public space and the use of buses and railway trains (except where segregation facilities are provided) evokes the same feelings of unease and being out of place for many women. Santosh K. told me that she felt nervous in buses and did not even like going to Hoshiarpur to visit her relatives (this involved a bus ride of not more than half an hour). On the other hand, many women are experienced travellers and have journeyed through many parts of India with their husbands and fathers; for them, a male escort is a matter of form and family honour.

I feel that it is age rather than marital status that governs the strictness with which a woman must observe the norms governing women's movement in public. Since the fear underlying such restrictions is the fear of the sexual attentions of men, it is women who are both old enough and young enough to receive such attentions who need be most scrupulous. Little girls of good family may run from street to street and will be sent on errands to the bazaar, and elderly women have somewhat more licence to move about as they wish. It is possible that young married women are expected to behave more circumspectly than unmarried women, but I do not think the difference is great. This expectation would be consistent with the pattern of etiquette by which a married woman avoids the senior male kinsmen and neighbours of her husband and does not allow her to face them, and with the convention that a daughter in her own village is in some sense the daughter of the *whole* village and thus should be immune from the danger of unwelcome attentions from men. Yet in some respects an unmarried girl is under more rigid surveillance than a young bride, since any false move may jeopardise her reputation and hence her chances of making a good match. I think that the difference between the rules which apply to unmarried women and those which apply to married women lies not in the kind of areas they may or may not visit, but in the notions of authority and good form which they feel they must respect. A daughter-in-law may be less free to go out in any case as she is likely to have more domestic duties than an unmarried girl, but several young wives mentioned that they did not feel they could ask their mother-in-law's permission to go out more often if the senior woman herself was not fond of going out. It would not be good form to claim a greater freedom than the senior lady of the household. (An unmarried girl, on the other hand, could ask her brothers to escort her without violating ideas of seniority and precedence.)

One's 'Own Place'

Many women, (especially upper class women) have spent a good part of their lives in a place where they are known as neither daughters nor daughters-in-law. Santosh, for instance spent more than twenty years in a city in Haryana where her husband was employed as a college professor, and she only returned to Harbassi on his death. Kaushalya spent many years living in the village and towns of Himachal Pradesh while her husband was employed as a Forestry Officer, and returned to Harbassi on his retirement. Manjit Kaur was neither born nor married in Harbassi but lives there because her husband was employed in the Electricity Board there, and they expect to move to his natal village when he retires. Santosh noted that while she was living in the city she had not observed *purdah* in the sense that she observed it in Harbassi; she had moved about the city fairly freely without thought that her behaviour might be censured. But, she said, the city was not 'one's own place' (*apni jegeh*) and so no one had expected such scrupulous observance of seclusion. The concept of *apni jegeh* refers to a place where your family are not strangers or outsiders and where it has an established reputation to maintain. In 'one's own place' your family already has a reputation, a niche in the local hierarchy carved out by former generations, which it is your responsibility to (at least) maintain, and (if possible) enhance. This does not mean that behaviour outside one's own village is a matter of indifference. Obviously Santosh did not mean that she travelled about in the city with total disregard for the local norms that defined proper behaviour for women in public places. She meant that she structured her social life without reference to a particular status which her husband's family had already established there. A married woman in Harbassi, on the other hand, would be constrained by what her parents-in-law regarded as proper behaviour and as suitable friends. It would be her duty to maintain contacts with families with whom her parents-in-law had cordial relations. In a town where her family had no such established niche, a woman is more free to associate with those whom she herself chooses as friends.

Precisely the same applies to men in many respects, i.e., men

Purdah and Public Space   231

in their own village have to consider the wishes of their elders with respect to their associates and are expected to maintain the relationship that their parents have established. They too must conform more closely to local conventions of etiquette, caste custom etc. But for men this code does not include restrictions on their movements and therefore the contrast between 'one's own place' and a place of temporary employment is not experienced in quite the same way.

For women who have spent much of their lives outside the village, or who have been brought up in a different kind of community, returning to Harbassi where the code is much stricter may be anticipated with some gloom and despondency. Lata, Santosh's daughter-in-law, had been brought up in a Punjabi city and since her marriage had spent much of her time in the U.P. city where her husband worked. When she came to Harbassi to visit her mother-in-law she was, she said, bored to tears since there was 'nowhere to go and nothing to do'. She and her husband had led a fairly full social life, frequently dining out or going to the cinema with other employees of her husband's firm, visiting local parks with friends for picnics and outings. In Harbassi, not only were there no such public venues where women could go with their families for pleasure and relaxation, but even her interaction with the neighbours had to be regulated by the wishes of her mother-in-law. She did not mean that her mother-in-law actually forbade her to go out, but that it would have been bad form for her to initiate visits or to go out if her mother-in-law were not so disposed. Kaushalya's daughter Veena also complained that her life was very boring now that she had come to live in Harbassi after her father's retirement. She had completed her education outside the village and therefore did not even know many of the other girls of her own age. There was no acceptable meeting places for young people and so, now that she had finished her M.A., she had nothing to do but stay at home and help her mother with housework.

Santosh, on the other hand, had not found the return to Harbassi so frustrating, for as she pointed out, 'One is never respected in another town as one is in one's own place. Here everyone knows who I am, even if I have not lived here much myself, because they all knew my husband and his father. They respected them, so they respect me'.

In 'one's own place,' one is committed to membership of the community and the community is committed to allowing you to participate in the reputation acquired by previous generations of your family. Outside 'one's own place' there is not much mutual commitment—you only have the reputation which you earn personally. But the mutual commitment in 'one's own place' means that you must follow the norms of etiquette and public decency already established in the community with greater circumspection than you might outside. This leads to the apparent relativity of norms regarding women's behaviour in public which has been noted by Jacobson, and others.

If Muslim women throw off their *burqas* when they travel outside their home towns, to don them again when they approach their own back alley, it is not because they are hypocritical and jettison cherished values when they think they can get away with it. It is rather that a good name among strangers is of little social value. It is one's reputation in one's own place, or in a place where one intends to spend a good deal of time, that constitutes real social capital.

Women's relations with each other

To what extent do restrictions on their movements outside the home affect women's patterns of interaction with other women? Jacobson suggests that they have the effect of limiting a woman's capacity to form relationships with women outside her own family and thus of isolating her. One farmer's wife in Harbassi told me that as she seldom stepped outside her home, she 'did not have any friends'. She presented herself as isolated, and yet most women in her situation did in fact lead a fairly full social life. For one thing, women living in actual seclusion may, and indeed will, receive visits from other women who are not. Santosh K. for instance was visited daily by the following: a sweeper woman who cleaned her latrine; a poor farmer's widow who cleaned her dishes twice a day; a washerwoman who collected her clothes for pressing; an elderly teacher, her friend and neighbour, who called on her every morning before going to work. Periodically she was visited by the barber's wife, who would massage her head and dress her hair. In former times she would have received twice daily visits from the women of water carrier caste who would bring water from the public well, but now that virtually every household has its own pump installed this is no longer necessary. Santosh also had a daily call from the farm servant who did most of the farm work while her sons were away, as he would take instructions from her before going about his day's work. As well as those visitors, who would usually see her sister-in-law Kaushalya or others of Kaushalya's family, as the two houses were adjacent, separated only by a private alleyway which was closed off from the street by a wooden gate. Thus, a woman who was observing the strictest form of seclusion practised in this community would meet a large number of people in the course of her day, perhaps more than a British housewife, isolated in an impersonal block of flats. She and other women in a similar situation could be aware of each other's activities through the numerous functionaries who provide services to a number of adjacent households.

The self-consciousness which women feel about using public space does not, in any case, prevent them from visiting each other via the maze of back alleys, which they use freely and which do not have the same inferior moral connotations as the bazaar itself. Idle visiting, roaming the streets in search of gossip, going from home with no better business than to pass the time of day, would not be approved. But a certain amount of mutual visiting is allowed and indeed enjoined. There are occasions when a visit is positively demanded by neighbourly duty. One such occasion is when there is a death in a neighbour's household. Some representative of the household must visit the bereaved family at least once, preferably during the period of initial mourning, or as soon after as is convenient. This is known as *afsos kerna* (to express sorrow) and it is a duty which is taken very seriously. Even a woman who was not particularly closely acquainted with the deceased will go to mourn and weep with his or her female kin. Men do undertake such mourning visits, but are less likely to visit families who are not closely related or very well known to them. Pure 'duty' visits are left to the women folk. Another occasion when a visit is demanded is after a wedding when the bride is brought home. The women of the household then dress in their best and then troop off to see the new bride and present her with *shaggan*, a ritual gift which usually consists of a sum of between Re 1 and Rs 11, according to the status of the family and the intimacy they enjoy with the bride's in-laws. The women will sit together to discuss the wedding and exchange news and will be offered sweets before they go. A similar pattern of visiting takes place when a baby is born. *Shaggan* is presented to the infant and visitors will be offered sweetmeats. Indeed even before a visit is made, a birth or wedding will be announced through gifts of sweets made to neighbours. Any crisis or unusual event in a family, whether auspicious or unfortunate, may be the occasion of such visiting, e.g., a sickness in the family, a son or daughter returns home after graduation, a buffalo calves, a married daughter returns home for a visit, etc.

So women are, strictly speaking, true to their own assertions that they 'do not sit about in other people's houses' in the sense that they do not indulge in purposeless visiting. But there are so many legitimate purposes for visiting that women do in fact, lead a very active social life, in spite of the norms that restrict their appearance and movement in public. In fact it is worth noting that it is a specifically female duty to maintain good relations with neighbours, kin and old family friends through such visiting, and to represent the family at weddings, religious ceremonies and the like. In a community like Harbassi, then, it is far from being the case that women are cut off from the social life of the village, though they may be debarred from direct participation in some aspects of it.

The negative effects of Purdah

Purdah, as we have seen, does not seriously inhibit the relationships which women are able to entertain with other women in the same village. But it will be obvious that there are certain activities which it must effectively rule out for women, some opportunities to which it must effectively close the door. Any participation in the formal political and judicial processes of the village is rendered extremely difficult in so far as these processes are public and open. I asked the *sarpanch* of a village near Chaili whether women brought many cases to the *panchayat*. Hardly ever, he replied with some pride. He claimed that either he or one of his colleagues would visit a woman who had a complaint against a kinsman or neighbour and would endeavour to persuade her to obtain some kind of settlement outside the *panchayat*, mediating themselves if this was necessary. It would be a source of shame to the community, he said, if women were obliged to come and settle their disputes in a public place, when they could be settled in private. The *sarpanch* of a village near Harbassi told me that in his village a woman member of the *panchayat* would be sent to interview any woman who wished to bring a case in the *panchayat*. She would try to obtain all the necessary information so that the woman herself would have to submit to only the minimum of public questioning. A problem in both areas I studied was finding women who were prepared to stand for election to the *panchayat*. Frequently the statutory woman member could only be obtained by co-opting a wife or kinswoman of one of the elected members. Now, women obviously do participate in politics in India, possibly more than their sisters in Europe or America. But for village women, whose reputation (and whose families' reputation) is invested in their not making themselves in any way conspicuous in public, active participation is rendered difficult by the norms I have discussed here.

More significant perhaps, is the effect on women's economic opportunities. Women, we have seen, do enter the bazaar, but not on the same terms as men. The marketing of farm produce is almost entirely in the hands of men save for petty quantities of milk or eggs which a peasant wife may sell to neighbours or friends in the vicinity of her home. Some women market small amounts of cotton to the Khadi Bhandar in Harbassi, where other women come to buy up similarly small quantities for spinning at home. But the publicness of major transactions makes it hard for women to participate in marketing at any higher level. Selling in the *mandi* is exclusively a male affair. It is also worth noting that the interpretation of the *purdah* ideal in this part of India debars women from a means of making a small income which is very important in other areas, namely petty trading and hawking. In pre-industrial England it was common for women who had no husband, or whose husband could not provide an income sufficient for the family's needs, to earn money through small scale street trading especially of foodstuffs. In many Third World countries today this is a common means for a woman to earn her livelihood as it requires little or no capital and can be combined with the care of a family. A woman can hope to achieve some kind of independent income in this way, however limited. In some parts of India one does see women hawking vegetables and other goods, but this is unusual in north west India, being totally at variance with the preference that women should not be seen conducting business in public.

The exclusion of women from public space affects their position in the labour market. There can scarcely be said to be a 'public' labour market for men in a rural area like Harbassi, but even less is there any for women. I will illustrate this by examining the case of tailoring, a trade practised by both men and women. In Harbassi there are several tailoring establishments in the bazaar. Here, customers can get shirts and pyjamas made up, and women can get their saree blouses and *salwar-kamiz* suits stitched (though many women have some sewing skills and can make up their own clothes at home). These entrepreneurs are all men, and employ other men to help them in their shops. It would be unacceptable for a woman of any social class to sit in an open shop in the bazaar at a sewing machine. There are, however, several seamstresses in Harbassi who make up clothes for customers. They operate entirely from their homes, and include several unmarried girls. They operate independently and do not employ others. They have no means of advertising their services and work entirely on the basis of personal recommendation. This does not mean necessarily that they are at a disadvantage compared with male tailors, as some of them achieve reputations for efficiency and style and can command good prices for their work. But they can do this only once they are established, and since they have no means for advertising their services, building a clientele is not always easy. In some small towns women may earn money as seamstresses by taking in work from some tailoring establishment in the bazaar. The tailor who runs the business takes orders and measurements from customers in his shop and puts some of the work out to women to make up in their homes. This work is usually paid at a very low rate indeed, far lower than a woman would earn if she set up her own private clientele, and lower than the male tailors who sit and stitch in the shop itself. The women literally pay for their public invisibility. They are permitted to sell their services, but since they cannot confront the public themselves, they require a male intermediary. This dependence lays them open to exploitation. Many Asian women in Britain have fallen victim to the same set of conditions. Many do work in garment factories and other places of work, but for those for whom this is impossible (due to small children) or unacceptable, selling their 'sweated' labour as home workers is the only opportunity for earning which is easily available.

Conclusion

What I have said here is not intended as an exhaustive discussion of the ways in which social space is categorised and evaluated, any more than it is an exhaustive account of *purdah* practices. The public/private dichotomy is only one dimension in the definition of social space. There is, for instance, the purity/pollution dimension, by which certain areas of the village are defined as impure. High caste people, of either sex in Harbassi would be unwilling to enter the sweepers' quarter and sweepers would be excluded from certain kinds of area defined as pure or sacred. The character of social space is such that men as well as women are excluded from certain kinds of area. Also the differential evaluation of the cardinal points, the left hand/right hand distinction affects both sexes in various departments of life, from religious ritual to domestic architecture. A full account of the social organisation of space would include these and many other characterisations of space.

It could also be contended against what I have said here, that I have argued from the most pronounced case of seclusion—that of high caste women of superior social class, living in an area of India heavily influenced by the former presence of Islam. Could it not be said that the forms of seclusion and exclusion which I have described are much more weakly felt elsewhere?

I think that it is certainly true that it is in communities like Harbassi that *purdah* takes its most conspicuous form. The exclusion of women from public space would certainly not be the first thing one would notice in a hamlet like Ghanyari, as it was for me in Harbassi. In neither the tiny hamlet nor the large city is one so aware of the norms of seclusion and avoidance of public space. A settlement like Ghanyari is too small to have very much space which can clearly be defined as public; there is, after all, no bazaar nor any main thoroughfare which is not used more or less exclusively by a small group of families, apart from the main road which links Ghanyari with the next village.[13] Women can conduct their routine activities without even taking thought about the considerations of reputation which I have discussed here. In large cities, on the other hand, there is little accessible space that is not public. Alleyways and back streets are less likely to be regarded as 'belonging' to the families that live in them. There is also more accommodation to that fact that women need to be able to use public space both in the sense that there is greater provision of segregated facilities (separate sections for women in eating houses, cinemas, etc.) and in the sense that there is greater liberality in regard to women being seen in public. It is more important to a woman's reputation to avoid being seen *alone* or at *night* than to totally avoid public areas as such. Harbassi is neither so small that it has no public space, nor so large that a looser set of norms operates. The principles that underly the ideal of

---

13. A dispute arose during the period of my fieldwork in Ghanyari which illustrates this. A *panchayat* member of carpenter caste had applied to the *panchayat* for a grant to pave the pathway outside his home. The Brahmans of the village protested that this was an illegitimate use of public money as the path 'really belonged to carpenter families'. It was really used by members of various castes, but it was not difficult to argue that it was not really a public path at all.

seclusion which the wealthy ladies of Harbassi observe are only a more pronounced form of norms that every farm labourer's daughter observes. Harbassi should not therefore be seen as some kind of bastion of archaism. Rather, it is a community where certain norms which are implicit in the behaviour of *all* rural women receive explicit expression in the practices of a limited but influential section of society. The Harbassi housewife who declares that she 'never goes out' is able to act out the principles which inform the behaviour of her sweeper and her tenant's wife who cannot afford to observe seclusion in its most structured form.

10 Etiquette among Women in Karnataka: Forms of Address in the Village and the Family

Helen E. Ullrich

Recent studies on linguistic etiquette have focused on a macro level of several languages[1] and of a language as a whole.[2] The emphasis has been on pronominal usage and on the use of 'plural' forms to show 'politeness'.[3] There is a dearth of material regarding etiquette for women and linguistic etiquette for the structure of a caste-stratified village. The purpose of this paper is to show how forms of address are related to the social structure of a village in Karnataka State[4] and how these forms reveal women's place in the social structure on the village level and the family level.

Politeness as a term has frequently been used to refer to the

---

1. R. Brown and A. Gilman, 'The Pronouns of Power and Solidarity', in T.A. Sebeok (ed.), *Style in Language* (New York: John Wiley and Sons, 1960).
2. S.S. Bean, 'Meanings of Grammatical Number in Kannada', *Anthropological Linguistics*, XVIII: 1 (Jan. 1975); H.S Biligiri, 'How to be Polite in Kannada and Other Important Matters', unpublished paper, Symposium on Politeness Exchange in Indian Languages (Mysore: Central Institute of Indian Languages, April 23-25, 1975); Clifford Geertz, 'Linguistic Etiquette', *The Religion of Java* (Glencoe, Ill: The Free Press, 1960).
3. S.S. Bean, op. cit.; S.S. Bean, 'Two's Company, Three's a Crowd', *American Anthropologist*, 72 (1970), p. 72.
4. Data for this study were collected during a year's residence in a Karnataka village. Field work was made possible by a Senior Research Fellowship, American Institute of Indian Studies.

use of plural forms of address for those in a position requiring deference. In a number of languages the plural form of address is used to people in a position of relative power, higher status, and unfamiliarity; whereas the singular form of address may be a manifestation of lack of power, low status, intimacy. To recognise the use of plural pronouns as indicating 'politeness' seems to be confusing the issue. The implication is that one is more 'polite' with those of greater power. I argue rather that etiquette is a preferable term and that the etiquette appropriate to those in various social positions differs. Hence the occasions for the use of singular address and the occasions for the use of plural address, as well as the people to whom these various forms should be used all belong under the rubric etiquette. In examining etiquette appropriate to women in a Karnataka village, the family and village will be examined. The perspective, as revealed by means of address, will include ideal usage and actual usage including attempts at change in the social system. Unless otherwise indicated, the data were collected from women.

Materials for this paper are drawn primarily from the women of six castes in Totagadde,[5] a village in the Western Ghats of Karnataka State. The methodology used in gathering material was both participant-observer and direct questioning of the manner of address used. Women of the different castes were asked how they would address members of other castes whose names they knew and whose names they did not know. Another very important aspect of village intra-communication was observation of women who went to various hamlets and for what reasons.

The first portion of this paper will focus on the village setting so that there will be background for the following sections which deal with the manner in which forms of address reflect the power structure and caste hierarchy. The limited communication among women of different caste groups is significant in preserving and reinforcing social distance. Forms of address within the caste and the family reflect that nature of family and

---

5. Totagadde is a pseudonym referring to the two major crops—*tota* (areca nut plantation) and *gadde* (rice paddy)—grown in the village.

caste relationships, as well as direction of change. The sections on intracaste and intrafamilial communication focus on one caste, the Havik Brahmins.

Setting

The village, Totagadde, has a population of approximately seven hundred. The three major caste areas may be ranked as high(Brahmin), middle (Sudra), and low (former tribal and Harijan). The lower castes reside in the southern part of the village; the Havik Brahmins, in the centre; and the Sudras, in the northern part of the village. Members of the two lowest castes, Harijans and Girijans,[6] reside in separate hamlets and have little social interaction with members of other castes. They work primarily for Havik Brahmins who occupy two hamlets and are the dominant caste economically, ritually, and politically. Haviks are the second most populous caste in the vilage—the most populous caste is the Divaru (Halepaika), a Sudra group which also occupies two hamlets. The difference in numbers between the two castes, however, is less than fifty. The four castes located in the northern part of the village are the Lingayat, Potter, Divaru (Halepaika), and Vokkaliga castes. The Potters, Lingayat family, and Vokkaligas reside on one side of the rice paddy (see Diagram). There is much visiting back and forth among the members of the Sudra group. When Sudras pass the Girijan hamlet, they usually stop to visit, but the visiting is non-reciprocal. The higher ranking Sudra women initiate all conversation with Girijans. The six castes from which data have been drawn are the Brahmins, Lingayats, Vokkaligas, Divarus, and Harijans.

Totagadde is a structural entity in itself. An outsider asking a villager his *uuru*[7] (village) would receive the answer Totagadde.

---

6. Girijans, literally 'mountain people', are reputed to be former tribals. The terms Girijan and Harijan are used only by the Brahmins. Members of other caste groups are not familiar with the terms and refer to Harijans and Girijans by caste names.

7. The retroflex form is indicated by a capital letter, e.g., *huDugu*. The long vowel is indicated by a double letter, e.g., *uuru*.

It not only has its own post office and a store, but more importantly the people residing here are linked to each other ritually. There are village gods who mark Totagadde boundaries and whom members of all castes worship. At festivals there is a more specific ritual linkage. For example, at Dipavali Brahmins give all who ask areca flowers, areca nuts, and betel leaves needed for worship and non-Brahmins reciprocate by providing ropes to tie the cow for cow worship. *uuru* has other usage showing the various levels of social identity for the village: When the temple god is taken on his annual tour of the village, he visits all of the hamlets except the Harijan hamlet. Indeed, no god visiting the village goes to the Harijan hamlet. When a *panchayat* is held for the *uuru*, this usually means a particular caste *panchayat*. When the *uuru* is summoned to weddings, *uuru* refers to the caste group for the Brahmins, Girijans, and Harijans; but to both Sudra hamlets for the Sudra castes and Lingayats. *uuru* (village) then has four different points of reference in Totagadde—caste, the Sudra area of town, all hamlets except the Harijan hamlet, and the village itself.

Forms of address: village level

The three basic types of address in Totagadde intercaste usage are determined by relative caste rank—those of higher caste than speaker, approximately equivalent caste to speaker, and lower caste than speaker. For those women considered inherently high in rank, the term *amma* is used. *amma* among Brahmins and Lingayats designates the kinswoman mother; for all the other castes, it designates the kinswomen in the category, grandmother. This includes all female kinfolk of the second ascending generation. Among those castes relatively close in rank, i.e. the Vokkaligas, Divarus, Girijans, numerous kinship terms are used. Among castes where many kinship terms are used, there is a difference in ranking which is realised by not accepting food from the lower ranking castes and by the lower ranking castes having to wash their own drinking vessels. While relative purity and pollution are observed, those castes which use reciprocal terms have visiting and gossip patterns suggesting a considerable interaction. In the one multicaste hamlet this extends to intercaste borrowing of valuables such as gold ornaments. The third type of address is to those considered much lower in caste rank. Either the term *huDugi* (girl) or personal name without kinship term is used. Some only use personal name; others use *huDugi* exclusively.

One might view the three forms of address as metaphorically referring to a family. The Brahmins as the parents have charge of remedying any problems and of the religious well-being of the village. The Sudras comprise a liminal category in which they are neither dependent nor completely independent of the Brahmins. The Sudras own and manage their own lands and are not completely dependent upon the Brahmins for religious services. Some do depend upon the Brahmins for economic assistance in times of need and advice for dealing with officials in town such as doctors and police. Each Sudra household has a particular Brahmin whose advice is sought on these matters as well as on questions of ritual. Sudra women, especially Divaru women, are active in both the economic and ritual spheres. While Divaru women rarely come in contact with Brahmin women, when they do, forms of address serve to reinforce the relationship with the use of *amma* (mother) to Brahmin women and generally personal name to Sudra women.

The low castes, to a large extent, are dependants of the Brahmins. A Brahmin household generally hires members of one particular low caste family. In some cases the relationship began when the Brahmin family lent the low caste man marriage money. That man and his family theoretically will work for the Brahmin family their entire life receiving medical care, food, clothing, and daily wages in return. Forms of address serve to reinforce the relationship with the use of *amma* to Brahmin women and girls who use *huDugi* to address low caste women, even elderly ones.

Dimension of power

The ways women have of addressing each other may be viewed in terms of power. Roger Brown and Albert Gilman in their article 'The Pronouns of Power and Solidarity' define power in the following manner.[8]

> One person may be said to have power over another in the degree that he is able to control the behaviour of the other. Power is a relationship between at least two persons, and it is non-reciprocal. ...

Those exclusively addressed as *amma* (mother) have both ritual and economic power. The Lingayats and the Brahmins both provide priestly services for the entire village. The Brahmins are the only ones to hire people on a regular basis. The power ascribed to the men who are in charge of the religious wellbeing of the village, of most of the occupational opportunities, and a refuge in times of financial stress is also inherent in the women. Brahmin women, as well as men, frequently direct maidservants. These maidservants are the ones usually addressed by *huDugi* (girl).

The various caste groups may be divided into those which have power and those which do not. Intercaste relationships are regulated by the power differential. Power may be regarded as possessed by those whose advice is sought, those who are requested to perform worship, those who lend money, those who serve as links between the village and the town, those who own land, and those who are the employers. From the perspective of power, one may regard different groups in the village as marked by a distinctive feature with dyadic priorities—a plus sign indicates the presence of the feature; a minus, its absence; plus and minus signs together indicate the feature is sporadically applicable. The use of distinctive features along this classification may be seen in Chart I, where Brahmins are shown as powerful; Sudras, in the middle rank, and untouchable as powerless.

With the exceptions that Sudras employ people on a temporary basis, that they own land and are semiliterate, the

---

8. Roger Brown and Albert Gilman, op. cit., reprinted in Joshua A. Fishman (ed.), *Readings in the Sociology of Language* (The Hague: Mouton, 1968), p. 254.

Etiquette among Women in Karnataka

CHART 1: Dimensions of Power within Totagadde

Power Attributes	Brahmin Male	Brahmin Female	Sudra Male	Sudra Female	Low Caste Male	Low Caste Female
Employer (Permanent)	+	—	—	—	—	—
Employer (Temporary)	+	±	+	+	—	—
Advisor	+	—	—	—	—	—
Religious Authority	+	—	—	—	—	—
Money-lender (outside of caste group)	+	—	—	—	—	—
Arbitrator in disputes	+	—	—	—	—	—
Landowners	+	+	+	+	—	—
Literacy	+	+	±	—	—	—

Key + indicates presence of a characteristic
— indicates absence of a characteristic
— indicates sporadic occurrence of a characteristic

Sudras and the low castes belong to the same category. With the exceptions that Brahmin women belong to households which have permanent employees, hire employees on their own sporadically, and are literate, Sudra women belong to the same category as Brahmin women. Land ownership, literacy, and employment are the categories which provide a continuum of power differences. According to Chart I, Sudra women and Brahmin women are roughly equal in power. With regard to independent decision-making, the borrowing of money, participation in the daily life of their hamlet Sudra women, especially Divaru women, exert an influence similar to the men. For all non-Brahmins, the power differential between the sexes on an all village level is not significant. Among Brahmins it is. The respect and power Brahmin men have is ascribed to Brahmin women as indicated by terms of address.

Taking into consideration terms of address, the Sudras fall into a middle category (see Chart 2) in which the highest group calls them by the term *huDugi* (girl) whereas the lowest group, the Harijan, calls all higher ranking groups *amma* (mother).

Note that the Girijans, one of the low castes, receive the *amma* form of address from the Harijans. However, Girijans are subsumed under the low caste category because they are regarded as untouchable by some, are landless, and because previously they borrowed marriage money from the Brahmins which resulted in a permanent indentureship.

CHART 2: Linguistic Dimension of Power within Totagadde

Caste Grouping	Power	Form of Address
Brahmins	+	Called *amma* (mother) by all groups
Sudras	±	Called *huDugi* (girl) by Brahmins; *amma* by Harijans
Low Castes		
Girijans	±	Called *huDugi* by Brahmins; *amma* by Harijans.
Harijans	—	Called *huDugi* by all castes

The Harijans illustrate their position at the bottom of the ranking by calling all women except the Lingayat *amma* (mother). Harijans indicate a position of extreme distance from Brahmin women and girls by occasionally calling them *ammnooru* (*amma* plus an honorific *avaru* which is realised as *ooru*). A similar suffix is used in addressing Lingayat women, only the suffix is added to *akka* (elder sister), that is *akkanooru*. This serves to differentiate among Brahmins, Lingayats, and Sudras-Girijans in terms of address.

amma is widely used as a form of address to Brahmin and Lingayat women (see Chart 3). In addition, it is used by Harijans to every group except the Lingayats. The use of the term *amma* to express rank has dimensions of power which extend into the economic and political realms as well. Accompanying the use of *amma* is the use of grammatical plural in commands. The metaphorical distance which the use of *amma* and plural forms creates also correlates with a lack of knowledge of the groups about each other's practices. Brahmin women expressed surprise on learning that Divaru women have ritual practices surrounding childbirth and that Divaru marriages needed to be performed at a propitious time (*muhurta*). On the other hand, non-Brahmin women follow the example of Brahmin women or their idea of Brahmin women's behaviour, of their dress, and of their cooking. Brahmin ritual control is exemplified by the observance of menstrual taboos by every group in Totagadde. Even the Lingayats, a group which does not ordinarily follow menstrual taboos, does so in Totagadde. As non-Brahmins become more prosperous and their women are able to take time away from work, menstrual taboos are elaborated. Those groups which use kinship terms among themselves do not emphasise the ritual distance which separates the caste groups, but instead emphasise a common relationship of being from the same village. Those who are addressed only as *huDugi* (girl) are without economic or ritual power of any sort. It is obvious that the means of address serves to show the basic divisions within Totagadde, as well as the strong emphasis on hierarchy.

CHART 3: Receivers of Respectful Forms of Address

All non-Brahmins—————	*amma* (mother) to Brahmin women and occasionally to girls
Brahmins, all non-Brahmins with exception of Lingayat———	*akkamma* (elder sister-mother) *amma* to Lingayat women; Harijans also *akkanooru* (elder sister-respectful suffix)
Girijans—————————	*amma* to Brahmin women; Lingayat women, much older women *saNNamma* (little mother) to Brahmin girls Personal name plus *akka* to Brahmin girls
Harijans———————	*ammnooru* to Brahmin women and girls; *amma* to all women in village with exception of Lingayat

Limited communication

The use of *amma* in addressing Brahmin women serves to reinforce ritual and economic rank as well as to indicate a lack of familiarity with non-Brahmins. People from all non-Brahmin groups request Brahmin men to perform *puja* (worship) when disaster or illness occurs. Brahmin men are called upon to settle disputes and to provide one of the three types of financial help—marriage money to low castes, money for oxen to the Divaru, and money in times of need to members of any caste. Only the first type is not expected to be repaid but rather indicates the beginning of a lifelong indentureship for the low castes.[9] Plural forms of power, respect and etiquette are used to address Brahmin men. Brahmin women and children share in the etiquette which requires address by plural forms, of which *amma* may be regarded as an example.

Although Brahmin women are no longer restricted as they once were, they are rarely seen outside of their own hamlets. Rather Sudra women come to the Brahmin women to have clothing stitched or, in the case of Harijans, to clean the barns and to do outside work. Both patterns reflect the differences in the skills of the women concerned. The Harijans provide unskilled labour whereas the Brahmin seamstresses provide skilled labour. For Brahmin women to work outside of the home or to work for other castes is a new pattern. Ten years ago only one Brahmin woman knew how to sew; now at least a half a dozen women sew.

Those Sudra women who have clothing stitched in Brahmin households might be surprised to discover that they are more frequently identified in terms of their husbands' than by their own names. Indeed, Brahmin women do not know the names of many non-Brahmin women; however, the non-Brahmin reaction in many cases to the inquiry about how higher caste people were addressed when the personal name was not known was that it was inconceivable in such a small village not to know the names of all the people residing there. Indeed, not only does a Brahmin woman rarely know the names of non-Brahmin women, but the only view she usually has of non-Brahmin hamlets are those located on the road to relatives' houses. In 1975, when a Brahmin woman went to the Divaru hamlet on her husband's business, she created a sensation. That year she

---

9. This has changed and the lower castes no longer repay this debt. In reaction to this Brahmins are no longer lending marriage money.

was the only Brahmin woman to venture alone in a non-Brahmin hamlet. The social structure is such that Brahmin woman have little contact with non-Brahmin women and are not likely to have reason to develop more extended contact with them in the near future.

As the Lingayat family lives in a hamlet with Potters and Vokkaligas, the Lingayat women necessarily have a lot of contact with non-Lingayats. The Lingayat women rarely go outside of the two hamlets on the northern end of town. Indeed they only go over to the Divaru hamlet for *puja* (worship) or for other religious functions and even then rarely do they appear. In spite of the lack of mobility of Lingayat women, they are not physically isolated from women of other castes. Ritually and linguistically the Lingayat women retain strict segregation from women of other groups in the village. This separateness is demonstrated by the forms of address *amma* (mother) and *akkamma* (elder sister-mother) used to Lingayat women by all groups in the village. On the other hand, recognition of Lingayat subordinate ranking to Brahmins is illustrated by a Lingayat comment when asked how Lingayats address Brahmin women, 'one cannot call members of higher castes by name'.

Since Harijans and Girijans work in the Brahmin hamlet, there exists extended contact between women of these castes and Brahmin women. The relationships vary from friendly to completely neutral to antagonistic. Most of the relationships I observed were friendly or neutral. Low caste women spoke when addressed, but did not initiate conversations. In cases where there is a friendly relationship, gossip and stories are exchanged while the women are working. The neutral relationship is characterised by conversation being limited to instruction for work.

Inter-caste address

The use of inter-caste kinship terms includes at some level all the non-Brahmins of Totagadde (see Chart 4). There is considerable variation in usage among castes. The Divarus are the only ones to have provided terms for affines as well as for metaphorical consanguineal kin. The Divarus provide this extended terminology for all non-Brahmins, with the exception of the potters. This is curious, as the potters of all the groups in the village are the ones whose speech patterns most closely resemble those of the Divaru. The Divaru have the greatest number of extended kinship forms for the Vokkaliga who rank above the Divarus and emphatically do not reciprocate. Vokkaligas insisted that they did not use affinal forms with the Divaru. I have also not observed such usage. The Vokkaliga and Divarus are also similarly occupied with rice paddy and vegetable growing. This extended terminology might be an upwardly mobile gesture along with the recent donning of the sacred thread by several younger Divaru men, the emulation of Brahmin cooking at Divaru ritual gatherings, a remodelling of house design to parrallel Brahmin houses, and Sanskritisation in naming children.

The Vokkaligas and Girijans both reported that among Sudras and lower castes they use only the personal name for women younger than they. In observing Vokkaliga women talking with Girijans, however, it was clear that a Girijan would only call a Divaru child by her personal name. An older Girijan woman addresses an adult Vokkaliga woman by personal name plus *akka* (elder sister). There is an ideal of reciprocity which just does not exist.

Visiting patterns among all the non-Brahmins, except the Harijans, is extensive. The greatest degree of communication is Vokkaliga-Divaru, Vokkaliga-Potter, Vokkaliga-Girijan. The Vokkaligas are the ones the Divaru generally visit on their way to and from the fields; the Potters visit the Vokkaligas when they have spare time. Never have I seen a Vokkaliga in a Potter house, in spite of the two castes residing in the same hamlet. The only times I have seen Vokkaligas in the Divaru hamlet has been for religious events. Girijans do not frequent the Vokkaliga hamlet, but whenever Vokkaliga women pass the Girijan hamlet, they sit and chat. Despite the considerable amount of interaction between the Vokkaliga and other non-Brahmin groups, Vokkaliga speech is different from that of other groups. Vokkaliga women are quick to point out a form which they label Divaru and to deny using such forms. Vokkaliga

Etiquette among Women in Karnataka 253

CHART 4: Use of Kinship Terminology for Inter-caste Address

Lingayat girls	Non-Brahmins
akka (elder sister)——————————all non-Brahmins	

Vokkaligas — **Divarus**
atte (father's sister)————————personal name
attige (father's sister's
　daughter) if married——————personal name
　to village
doDDawwa (mother's sister)————personal name
　if native to village
personal name+*akka*——————*akka* (elder sister)
　if same age or younger
personal name+*akka*——————personal name if younger
　if elder
personal name+*akka*——————*amma* (mother) if much older

Potters
personal name+*akka*——————personal name

Girijans, Harijans
personal name+*akka*——————personal name+*akka*
personal name————————————personal name+*akka*[10]
　if younger

Divarus — **Vokkaligas**
atte (father's sister)——————personal name+*akka* (elder
　to old woman[11]　　　　　　　sister)

Vokkaligas, Potters
tangi (younger sister)——————personal name+*akka*
　if younger

Potters
akka, if elder————————————personal name+*akka*

Girijans
akka, if elder————————————personal name

Harijans, Girijans
tangi, if small——————————*amma* (mother) if old woman
　　　　　　——————————personal name+*awwa* (mother)
　　　　　　　　　　　　　　　if old woman
　　　　　　——————————personal name+*akka*, if elder

10. Contrary to the elicited data, Vokkaliga women were observed being addressed by personal name *akka* by considerably older Girijans.
11. As reported by Divaru, but not practised. In practice, the Vokkaligas use *amma*.

attige (husband's elder————————attige, if somewhat equal in age[12]
sister[13])

Girijans	Harijans
personal name————————personal name	
	Divarus, Vokkaligas, Potters
personal name————————personal name+*akka*, if elder	

children can be heard to use Divaru-Potter forms. Although Vokkaliga children sometimes use Divaru-Vokkaliga forms in play, they also enjoy ridiculing the forms specific to those groups. The rapidity with which Vokkaliga women point out forms belonging to other castes seems to be significant in retaining separate forms, forms which resemble colloquial Kannada. While terms of address show a close relationship among non-Brahmins, dialectal forms as maintained by women give each group its separate identity.

Unlike kinship terms which stress an actual or fictional relationship the use of *huDugi* (girl) as a means of address points to a clearly hierarchical structure. Its use is considered entirely appropriate by those so addressed. Basically the structure is for the highest ranking group to address lower ranking groups in this manner when the name is not known. In cases of considerable hierarchical difference, the name although known is simply not used. However, there is some change occurring in the use of *huDugi*. Some families use personal names; others substitute *tangi* (younger sister). Still others use *huDugi* regularly for relatively high caste help if the woman works quasi-permanently in a particular household (see Chart 5 for the use of *huDugi*).

Address in the Havik Brahmin caste and family

Within the Havik Brahmin caste relative age is the primary determinant for terms of address in the village. (See Chart 6).

12. The glosses provided are that of the basic kinship term.
13. In effect this is not reciprocal as reported by the Divaru. In practice the Divaru are not called *attige* but by personal name.

CHART 5: Use of *huDugi* (girl) in Inter-caste Address

Brahmins —————————*huDugi* (girl) to all castes except Lingayat
——————————*muduki* (old lady) to older Vokkaliga women
——————————personal name if know personal name; otherwise *huDugi* to Vokkaligas, Divarus
——————————*huDugi* even if know personal name to Girijans, Harijans
Vokkaligas——————————personal name; if do not know personal name use *huDugi* to Harijans
Girijans——————————*huDugi* to Harijans

With the exception of young girls, the form of address is invariably proper name or proper name and a suffix. If the woman is younger or approximately the same age, she will be addressed by her proper name alone; if older and in the same generation, by proper name and *akka* (elder sister); if of an older generation, by proper name and *amma* (mother). Those

CHART 6: Havik Brahmin Forms of Address

Old woman——————————Personal name + *amma*, e.g., *LakSmamma*
Older than speaker but same generation——————————Personal name + *akka*, e.g., *Padmakka*
Younger than speaker——————————Personal name
Young girl——————————*kuusu* (girl), *ammi* (girl). Personal name, diminutives of personal name[14]

characterised by a very close friendship evolve several variant forms of address. This, however, is limited to those approximately equal in age.

In contrast to forms of address among caste members, there is a rich proliferation of terms within the family. The terminology can be regarded as falling into categories of relatives belonging to the patriline and those potentially related by marriage. (See Chart 7.)

---

14. Divarus use *tangi* (younger sister), personal name + *amma*, and *amma* (jf not know child's name).

CHART 7: Havik Kinship Terms of Address

ammamma	grandmother
amma	mother
hiriamma	mother's elder sister, father's elder brother's wife
cikamma	mother's younger sister, father's younger brother's wife
cikki	mother's younger sister, father's younger brother's wife, only used if very close relationship
atte	father's sister, mother's brother's wife
attema	mother's brother's wife, elder brother's wife's mother
attegaLu	mother-in-law
akkayya	elder sister
akka	elder sister, husband's elder brother's wife
tangi	daughter, husband's younger brother's wife
personal name+akka	elder sister
attige	mother's brother's daughters, if older, son's wife's mother, daughter's husband's mother, husband's sister, brother's wife
proper name	daughter-in-law, grand-daughter, younger sister, daughter
ammi, kuusu, tangi	daughter

Changing relationships: the family

Although family structure among the various castes of Totagadde has undergone considerable change, the greatest change has been among the Haviks. Women in the other castes have enjoyed relatively greater freedom, perhaps related to their being essential to the agricultural cycle. Havik women have in the past remained primarily at home, with the exception of going to other Brahmins' houses to husk areca nuts. In this section I will first discuss the relative positions of women in two castes, the Havik Brahmin caste and the Divaru caste, and then relate this to ways of addressing children and husband and wife.

In a model fitting the Havik family the eldest man in the family is the *ejmaanru*, head of household. He has complete power to make all the decisions with regard to all matters in the running of the household and the areca plantation. He manages all the money. The *ejmaanru* even dictates the dishes to be cooked. When daughters arrive at a marriageable age, he has the task of arranging the marriage. In the past he had total power even in this. However, now the daughter has a veto power and has been known to break engagements to which she had previously agreed. The *ejmaanti*, the wife of the *ejmaanru*, regards her husband as a personal god and does his bidding. Younger brothers and sons are in a similar position. Metaphorically speaking, the ship has one captain and all work together for a common cause, the good of the family. This system may have been more functional at a time when women were married before puberty and trained in the ways of a household from a young age. The raising of the marriage age from pre-puberty a generation ago to between eighteen and twenty-five and the education of girls have been factors in changing this structure. Two case studies follow. Case A provides an example of a crisis and settlement of the crisis. Case B is an example of a new type generally approved of by both men and women.

CASE A. Gange spent many years happily married. Her husband's gambling did not overly concern her until she discovered he planned to sell land to settle gambling debts. She let it be known that there would be trouble if anybody bought the land. With advice from her brothers she took over the management of the land. At the time that this land quarrel was occurring between husband and wife, her husband was pitied by the other women of the village. After she obtained control of her and her children's share of the land, her husband simply left. Gange has proven a competent land manager and has gained access to groups such as the Havik *panchayat* which previously were all-male. She goes to town alone, something not done by any other Havik woman. Because all this is in the line of work and because of her success, she has been able to combine both management and motherly duties. Although her sons have reached an age when they could be managing land, she continues to do so. The label, 'Indira Gandhi' written on her door by a prankster aptly sums up her role in her family.

CASE B. Lalita and her husband are considered the happiest couple in town from the viewpoint of other women. She, as president of the village women's club, frequently goes to conferences. When the daily paper arrives, she and her husband divide the paper so both can read at the same time. Lalita does not stay in the background, but participates in conversations. The ease with which she enters conversations with men has brought her some criticism, as the old pattern was that a woman should only participate in conversations with relatives. However, now people think that a woman should be able to deal with visitors; so Lalita's behaviour is regarded as preferable to the older pattern where a woman stayed in the background or retired to the kitchen. Like Gange, Lalita can take over if her husband is not present. The ease with which Lalita talks with others—both men and women—and her ability to handle affairs when her husband is away provide a model of new type of woman.

While the old model where the woman is helpless and incapable of managing on her own is true for many older women, younger women have become much more independent. As Case *A* illustrates, a woman may go to rather extreme measures to protect property and the means of livelihood for her family. At the moment such extremes are tolerated; indeed Gange (Case *A*) is not even criticised for her independence. Rather, her independence is accepted as necessary for the job she has undertaken, namely the management of family lands. Lalita (Case *B*) better fits the ideal, a complement and not a subordinate of her husband, one who can help and take over when the occasion demands.

Havik women in the past tended to view their identity in terms of their husbands. To a large extent this is still true. However, with a high school degree now considered the minimum acceptable education for marriage, a woman is more inclined to be independent. The change from wide age differences between husband and wife to that of approximately the same age is recent.

Yet this new pattern is accepted by all to the extent that an engagement which in the past would never have been broken was when a younger man appeared. Engagements are theoretically not broken among the Haviks; however, in this case a young girl was engaged to a much older man. Younger Haviks in Totagadde thought the engagement was best broken; older people also think that there should not be a wide disparity in the ages between husband and wife. However, older people think that under no circumstances should an engagement be broken.

In contrast to Brahmin women who in the past had no responsibilities outside of the household, Divaru women are important contributors to agricultural work. Some of the work is specialised. Only men do the ploughing; only women, the sowing and transplanting of rice. Although both transplant other crops such as chillies the women are more likely to be involved in the transplanting of rice; the men, in the irrigation of newly transplanted plants. Both work side by side. Both men and women prepare the fertiliser. Only women do the cooking unless a woman is observing menstrual taboos. Women control the food that is served and the money. Upon a girl's marriage, she is given a chest with a lock which has only one key which she keeps around her neck. This is the chest where the girl keep her money; should she become the *ejmaanti* (female head of household), this is the chest where the household money will be kept. Women are as likely as men to go to town for shopping. In contrast to Brahmin women who never argue openly or criticise their husbands in public, Divarus have no such inhibitions. Consequently, it is somewhat surprising that women do not tell folktales if a man is present. The man is given precedence in this realm.

In a model fitting the Divaru family the eldest man in the family is the *ejmaanru* (head of household). He is in charge of the farming and making decisions affecting the household. Unlike the Brahmins, however, the Divaru *ejmaanru* does not have total power. This is shared with the *ejmaanti* who has no inhibitions in expressing her opinions. As Divaru women work alongside their husbands in the fields, they have first hand knowledge about farming. The Divaru widow rises to a position of even greater power in the household; the Brahmin widow loses her position to her son's wife. Divaru women are basically in charge of the home and child care; however, this is in addition to their other work. The women have the authority to run the household as they see fit. In effect, this means that the *ejmaanti* has the authority and is responsible for supervising the work of her daughter-in-law.

Divaru marriages are arranged by the girl's and boy's male relatives. The girl does not see her husband until the wedding day. She has no veto power, but there is the possibility of divorce and remarriage.

The importance of the distinction between male and female children is clear from the forms of address. There is no merging of the terms for the Brahmins; there is for the Divarus. Brahmin boys are called either *maani* or *appi*; girls, *kuusu* or *ammi*. Among Divarus, on the other hand, there is a common term *eppi* for addressing either boys or girls. Although sons are preferred a number of Divaru households have only one daughter. Divaru girls, as well as boys, have a ritual first hair-cutting. Unlike the Brahmins, the Divarus have the same number of life ceremonies for boys as for girls—the first haircutting, marriage, crisis childbirth ritual pollution, and death. This suggests that Divarus value girls more than the Brahmins value girls.

Both Divarus and Brahmins have a taboo against saying the spouse's name. This taboo which still applies equally to husbands and wives among the Divarus, does not apply to Brahmin men. Brahmin women in their thirties do not hesitate in saying the husband's name if the husband is not present. Older women will not say the husband's name at all. Younger women will say the husband's name in front of the husband if the situation requires that she say her husband's name. Among both groups there is the use of the plural-respectful form when speaking about or to the husband and the singular form when the husband speaks to the wife. When angry at their husbands the Divaru will use the singular, but not Brahmin who try to swallow their anger in silence.

Conclusion

Forms of address have been discussed on three levels, the village, the caste, and the family. On the village level the basic three-way division in the village of Brahmin, non-Brahmin and low caste is portrayed both in terms of address, occupational patterns and ritual hierarchy. On the family level the change in the authority structure, while not indicated by terms of address, has led to an increase in the wife's use of her husband's name. Contrasted with the Divaru the relative equality of importance in terms for sons and daughters seems to be illustrated by a lack of differentiation is the most common term for addressing a child.

Etiquette in Totagadde consists of knowing the proper behaviour towards other people. Avoiding the uttering of a husband's name is as much a part of etiquette as calling a lower ranking woman by the term *huDugi* (girl). The use of only singular forms among Haviks is as appropriate as the use of grammatical plural is by non-Brahmins to Brahmins.

Change in the relationships may be seen on the village level by the incipient usage of *tangi* (younger sister) or personal name to those on a lower ritual level. Claims for greater status by members of non-Brahmin castes are seen in the adoption of what were Brahmin names and the adding of the suffix *amma* (mother). That this claim is projected with some caution is obvious by the fact that when a Brahmin requests the names they are supplied without *amma*. On the family level a decrease in the gap between husband and wife among Brahmins may be illustrated with a decline in the taboo of saying one's husband's name. All of these changes suggest a reordering in the social organisation of the village, a reordering of etiquette from what was exclusively hierarchical to what is more egalitarian.

Schematic Diagram of Totagadde Hamlets

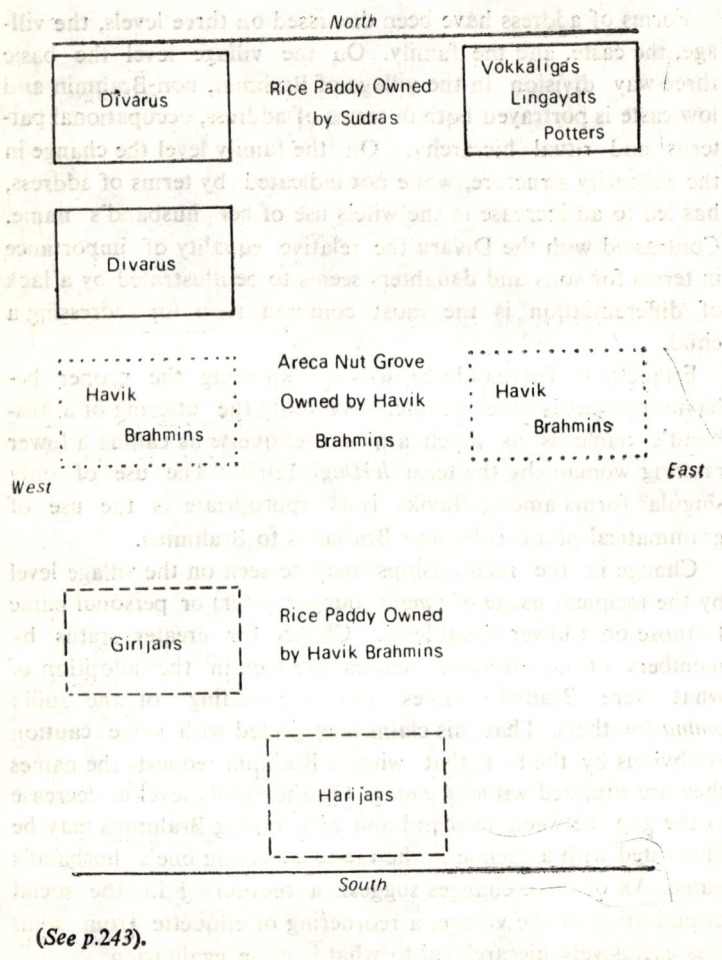

```
                     North

   ┌─────────┐   ┌──────────────┐   ┌──────────────┐
   │ Divarus │   │ Rice Paddy Owned │   │  Vokkaligas  │
   │         │   │    by Sudras     │   │  Lingayats   │
   └─────────┘   └──────────────┘   │   Potters    │
                                     └──────────────┘
   ┌─────────┐
   │ Divarus │
   │         │
   └─────────┘

   ┌─────────┐   Areca Nut Grove    ┌──────────┐
   │  Havik  │   Owned by Havik     │  Havik   │
   │Brahmins │     Brahmins         │ Brahmins │
   └─────────┘                      └──────────┘
West                                                East

   ┌─────────┐   ┌──────────────┐
   │Girijans │   │ Rice Paddy Owned │
   │         │   │ by Havik Brahmins│
   └─────────┘   └──────────────┘

                 ┌──────────────┐
                 │   Harijans   │
                 │              │
                 └──────────────┘

                     South
```

(See p.243).

11 Asian Women in Britain: Strategies of Adjustment of Indian and Pakistani Migrants

Verity Saifullah Khan

South Asian migrant women in Britain are as diverse in life-styles and attitudes as indigenous British women and manifest a far wider variety of cultures and languages.[1] Any discussion or statement about their situation in Britain involves making broad generalisations, but there are, however, certain justifications for treating South Asian women as a general category. Firstly, the majority of South Asian women do manifest significant similarities in their life-style and values *in comparison* with the white indigenous population of Britain. These include some of the distinctive characteristics of South Asian culture as compared to Western culture and the factor of skin colour with its acquired social significance (which South Asians share with certain other ethnic minorities).[2] Secondly, South Asian women, like British women, are subject to different conditions and different problems, compared to their men and these are particularly evident in the migrant situation. And thirdly, South Asian women are a

---

1. In this article the terms Asia and South Asian refer to the Indian Sub-Continent and its peoples, most notably Indians, Pakistanis and Bangladeshis.

2. In Britain there is a large minority of people from the Islands of the West Indies and a far smaller group of Africans. In general parlance the terms 'coloured' and 'black' are used to refer to these two minorities and the Asian population.

relevant category because the white indigenous population perceives them as such. Whether through indifference, ignorance or prejudice the indigenous population remains basically unaware of the internal diversity among South Asians. Consciously or unconsciously the differences between 'we' and 'they' are stressed by utilising generalisation and stereotypes which maintain and justify the lack of, or limited, social interaction. A further justification is that concentrating on any particular South Asian population (e.g., Gujarati, Sikh, or Bangladeshi), or section of a population, will not be typical of the whole.[3]

This paper restricts itself to the 'first' generation migrant women and points to some of the specific and fundamental factors relating to the position of South Asian migrant women in Britain. The immense variation of background and degree of adjustment found among the South Asian population will be hinted at by incidental reference to particular groups, and only passing reference is made to the 'second' generation of British born South Asians.[4]

It is easy to discuss the position of South Asian women in Britain in the context of the clash or meeting of two cultures and this has been the main perspective of the very limited amount of

---

3. There is a wide diversity not only between the various South Asian populations, but also within them. This is based on ethnic/religious/class differentiation (see V. Saifullah Khan, 'Perceptions of a Population: Pakistanis in Britain', *New Community* 5 (n. 3, Autumn, 1976) and the different demographic and environmental factors (see V. Saifullah Khan, 'Ethnic Identity Among South Asians in the U.K.', in M. Gaborieau and A. Thorner, *Asie du Sud: Traditions et Changements* (Paris: CNRS, 1978).

4. Suggestions for further reading about these specific populations include for Sikhs works by R. Ballard and C. Ballard, 'The Sikhs: The Development of South Asian Settlements in Britain', in J.L. Watson (ed.), *Between Two Cultures: Migrants and Minorities in Britain* (Oxford: Blackwell, 1977) and A.F. James, *Sikh Children in Britain* (London: Oxford University Press, 1974), and for Pakistanis B. Dahya, 'Pakistanis in Britain: Transients or Settlers', *Race* 14 and 'The Nature of Pakistani Ethnicity in Industrial Cities in Britain', in A. Cohen (ed.), *Urban Ethnicity* (London: Tavistock, 1974) and P. Jeffery, *Migrants and Refugees: Muslim and Christian Pakistani Families in Bristol* (Cambridge: Cambridge University Press, 1976).

material on the subject.[5] It is argued here, however, that it is important to start an analysis of the position of South Asian women in Britain within a far wider perspective. The nature and quality of the South Asian woman's life in Britain is dependent on a multitude of interrelated factors beyond the control of the individual woman. The structure of British society and the economic and political conditions in Britain and the Indian Sub-Continent are the fundamental relevance as well as the more specific factors such as the life she had led back home, the number of years she has been in Britain, the place in which she is living and her personal family circumstances, particularly the attitude and prospects of her husband.

After a brief outline of the typical daily routine and conditions of life for South Asians in Britain, past and present socio-economic and political conditions in Britain and the Indian Sub-Continent will be outlined. Some of the major determinants of the nature and quality of the life of South Asian women in Britain will be underestimated without this perspective and the related process of migration.

In 1971 there were 652,800 persons of South Asian origin in Britain and of these 268,200 were born in Britain. There were 483,100 persons of Indian origin and 169,700 persons of Pakistani origin (including at that time Bangladeshis), those born in Britain numbering 226,800 and 41,400 respectively. There were 254,300 males and 228,800 females of Indian origin and 114,300 males and 55,400 females of Pakistani and Bangladeshi origin. Thus in 1971 there were approximately 284,200 females of South Asian origin in Britain of which 137,500 were

---

5. The dearth of material on Asian women in Britain and of the woman's world in other societies, particularly those with a marked segregation of the sexes is due to the predominance of men in the field of social science research and the tremendous difficulties associated with fieldwork. In such a society a male researcher cannot hope to gain entry and acceptance into the woman's world. A female researcher does so by adopting the life expected of a woman and thus restricting her movement in the man's world, and even in certain other sections of the community. As an outsider she may assume a certain role flexibility which can be manipulated to her advantage, but this involves a careful management of impression to maintain a consistent picture of herself.

born in Britain in comparison to 363,600 men of Asian origin of which 130,700 were born in Britain. The number of Asian women born in India, Pakistan or Bangladesh and now living in Britain has increased considerably and this has been faster than the numbers of their male counterparts because immigration since 1965 and particularly 1971, has been restricted almost wholly to dependants (i.e woman and children). Therefore, the sex ratio, especially uneven among Pakistanis, is now more balanced than it was in 1971 (124 Indian males to 100 females and 295 Pakistani and Bangladeshi males to 100 females).[6]

The daily routine and conditions of life

The majority of South Asian women in Britain are from rural areas of India, Pakistan and Bangladesh and have limited, or no, command of the English language. Like the poorer socio-economic strata of British society they live in terraced or semi-detached houses[7] which are concentrated in the 'inner-city' area of the towns and cities (particularly the large industrial cities of the Midlands and the North). These areas consist of a zone between the central shopping and commercial centre and the public housing estates and the smarter new suburbs on the edge of the city where the more prosperous inhabitants of the inner-city areas have moved with the advent of slum clearance, the influx of immigrants and the availability of higher standard housing. Their housing is usually the oldest in the city, often subject to short-term leases but in some areas undergoing re-development schemes if not eventually marked for slum clearance. South Asian settlers in Britain have shown a marked preference for ownership of their houses[8] and it was in this area of the city that the cheapest

6. All figures are from the 1971 Population Census of Great Britain. For details see G.B. Gillian Lomas, *Census 1971: The Coloured Population of Great Britain* (London: The Runnymede Trust, 1973).

7. Terraced houses have common side walls, i.e., you cannot walk down the side of the house. Semi-detached houses have one wall attached to another house and one open, i.e. they are built in pairs.

8. David J. Smith, *Racial Disadvantage in Britain: Summary of Political and Economic Planning Reports* (Harmondsworth: Penguin, 1977).

housing was available and there was the least organised resistance (from neighbours, estate agents and local authorities) to the influx perceived as undesirable by many local inhabitants. By the time the larger influxes of migrants arrived in Britain the original population of these areas was dispersing, leaving a high proportion of the old, the single and students or workers in rented accommodation; often the poorest and among the 'down-and-outs' of British society.

The houses in these and other parts of the cities of England frequently consist of two living rooms on the ground floor and a kitchen on the same floor or in the basement. The front door of the house leads into a small corridor or, in the smallest of Victorian houses, directly into the 'front' room and then the stairs lead up to the first floor. On the first floor there are two or three bedrooms and usually a bathroom and sometimes there are one or two bedrooms in the attic. At the back of the house there is often a small yard or garden. The variation in size, quality and comfort of these houses differs considerably from area to area, city to city and according to the priorities, preferences and finances of the owners. The utilisation of rooms is often similar to the British neighbours; the 'front' room is used and decorated as the 'best' room where visitors are received and children are under more careful surveillance. The 'back' room is the heart of the household where young children spend much of their day. This division is convenient for South Asian households who to some degree or another observe the system of *purdah*. Women and children remain in the family quarters when visitors arrive and the men occupy the front room.[9] Other distinctively Asian features are found in many houses including brightly coloured furnishings, a *tawa* and *koonda langree* in the kitchens and plastic buckets and jugs standing in the bath.[10]

Except for a few religious men, the majority of South Asian men wear Western dress. Many of the earliest Sikhs in Britain

9. See V. Saifullah Khan, 'Purdah in the British Situation', in D.L. Barker and S. Allen (eds.), *Dependence and Exploitation in Work and Marriage* (London: Longmans, 1976).

10. Most British bathrooms contain baths, not showers. Rather than adopt the Englishman's seemingly dirty habit, Asians stand in the bath and wash themselves in traditional style.

cut their hair in order to get work and a certain number of teenagers do so voluntarily but this trend seems to be on the decrease and it is now usual for Sikh children entering school to have uncut hair. South Asian women, however, have in most cases maintained their traditional clothes, either *sari* or *shalwar-kameez*. The increased popularity of the trouser suit is due to the influence of prevailing fashions in urban India and Pakistan, its practicality in the British climate and may also reflect more fundamental changes in attitude. The fact that the *burqa* has rarely been seen in Britain is not so much an indication of change but an acknowledgement that in Britain it defeats its purpose; it brings attention to, rather than hides, its wearer. Many South Asian girls are still wearing *shalwar* or trousers to school despite initial hostility from some educational departments, and there remains parental objections among certain sections of the South Asian population to daughters attending co-educational schools and, for example, girls wearing gym-shorts at school.

The majority of Asian men in Britain belong to the category of unskilled or semi-skilled workers and they are concentrated in certain fields of employment.[11] Many men work long hours to supplement their relatively low pay and/or maximise their savings. Asian women rise early in the morning to prepare a meal for their husbands before they leave for work, or on their return from a night shift. The children leave for school between eight and eight thirty and return between three and four o'clock in the afternoon. In the evening the husbands either return from work or get up from a day-time sleep to go on a night-shift. The majority of Asian women stay at home with their young children for most of the day except for visiting nearby shops or friends. Some women, who have no young children or arrange to leave them with friends or relatives, go out to work and some others do not venture beyond the house alone, leaving the shopping to husbands or sons and visiting only when chaperoned. Most family visiting takes place at the week-ends when families may travel long distances to visit close relatives

---

11. These include textile, transport and engineering industries, and transport and health services. See David J. Smith, *Racial Disadvantage in Britain: Summary of Political and Economic Planning Reports*, op. cit.

and friends.[12]

Many South Asian men and women live among their own people and have minimum contact with the British world around them. The majority of primary and most meaningful relationships are with relatives and friends from the same regional and socio-economic background in South Asia, whether they live near-at-hand or some distance away in another part of Britain. The majority of other relationships are with their own countrymen, either as workmates or neighbours. Most relationships with the white indigenous population or other ethnic minorities are restricted to formal, impersonal relationships with, for example, superiors at work and officials in offices, hospitals, clinics and schools.[13]

The wider perspective

The very presence of a large number of South Asians in Britain, rather than in any other European country is, of course, due to the historical fact of British Imperialism. In order to achieve her essentially economic motive for colonisation Britain established a political, administrative, judicial and educational system to support it, whose influences are still evident today in the structure and values of the society. Imperialism in India increased the ever widening gap between the rich and the poor nations of the world and thus provided prerequisite of subsequent mass, international migrations. It has carved the routes for such migrations by facilitating or forcing movement of labour and fostering rising expectations, and has influenced the structural development of British society and the formulation of prevailing values and stereotypes.

To the customary British distrust of strangers was added the traditional disparagement of colour. Sociologists investigating the character of prejudice against the new immigrants

12. V. Saifullah Khan, 'Pakistani Women in Britain', *New Community* 5(n. 1-2, Summer, 1976).
13. See V. Saifullah Khan, 'The Pakistanis: Mirpuri Villagers at Home and in the City of Bradford', in J.L. Watson (ed.), *Between Two Cultures: Migrants and Minorities in Britain* (Oxford: Blackwell, 1977).

discovered a sediment of racial conceit among whites of all classes, produced by relics of imperial myth in school textbook and story; the acquired arrogance of many who had served in the empire as soldiers, technicians or minor administrators. . . .[14]

Until recently the villager's conceptualisation of life in Britain was similarly influenced by past and present effects of the British Raj. Britain, or *vilayat,* was believed by villagers to be a rich, advanced and a desirable place to live where everyone was wealthy, well educated and happy. The remittances and inevitably one-sided feedback received in the villages from migrants tended to confirm this view. But villagers in India and Pakistan and migrants to Britain also hold another more critical conception of the West; the 'immorality' of its life-style and values in relation to the family, marriage, social interaction between the sexes, etc. This view was confirmed in the South Asian setting by the British and American films shown in urban areas and on television, and by those migrants who did not conform to the expectations of their family. For those migrants in Britain with limited contact with the English world around them these notions were also reinforced by media images and the behaviour they saw. But most migrants underwent a reappraisal of life in Britain when it did not meet their expectations of the 'golden land'. And now a more balanced appreciation of the difficulties and dilemmas of life in Britain has filtered back to the villages of the main emigration areas.[15]

The composition of the South Asian population in Britain is similarly explained by economic, political and historical factors. The main emigration areas in the Indian Sub-Continent are invariably areas that have had a tradition of migration due to over-population (e.g. the Punjab of India) and/or unfertile agricultural land (e.g. Mirpur, Azad Kashmir, Campbellpur in the Punjab of Pakistan, Sylhet in Bangladesh) and/or political disturbances (e.g. at Partition in the Punjab and Kashmir).

14. R. Segal, *The Race War* (Harmondsworth: Pelican Books, 1967), p. 307.

15. For more details of the migrant ideology see V. Saifullah Khan, (n. 13 on page 269).

Gujarat in India has a fifteen-centuries old trade route with East Africa and Sikhs have settled abroad prior to this century (e.g. in British Columbia, the Fiji Islands).[16] And there has always been the internal migrations in the sub-continent from the northern mountain areas to the plains, rural-urban migration and the settlement of newly irrigated tracts of land.

In the early decades of this century many Indian doctors and students came to Britain, few taking up permanent residence. But small numbers of unskilled South Asians came to Britain by way of the merchant navy of British army and small groups of Sikhs settled as craftsmen or peddlars. Subjects of British rule as citizens of the empire were entitled to free entry into Britain. Some stayed, others returned and some encouraged relatives to join them by the same means or by sending finances. Men from the areas mentioned above were often anxious to seek alternative sources of employment and when there was a demand for labour in post-war Britain, which coincided with political upheavals in the Indian Sub-Continent, networks or 'chains' developed between settlers in Britain and potential emigrants. The majority of the subsequent influx of migrants were not the poorest of villagers but small landowners joining kin or fellow villagers in Britain. The poorer landless tenant farmers and artisans depended on the 'migration chains' and gained financial, emotional and organisational support from their kin group.[17]

It is these factors which explain the amazing selectivity in the Asian migration to Britain; a large percentage of migrants coming from specific regions, and within the regions specific districts, *tehsils* and villages. And this selectivity, and its influence on settlement patterns in Britain, has contributed to the degree of separatism manifest in the different populations, and the perpetuation of existing prejudices and stereotypes. This is no doubt exacerbated by the tendency of the British population to categorise all South Asians as one, or presume

---

16. See H. Tinker, *The New System of Slavery* (London: Oxford University Press, 1974); *The Banyan Tree: Overseas Emigrants from India, Pakistan and Bangladesh* (London: Oxford University Press, 1977).

17. See V. Saifullah Khan, 'Pakistani Migrants and Social Stress', in V. Saifullah Khan (ed.), *Minority Families in Britain: Support and Stress* (London: Macmillan, 1979).

there is a coherent and organised Pakistani, Indian, Bangladeshi 'community'.[18] Concentrated areas of emigration and settlement facilitated the maximum feed-back to encourage further emigration and, in the long-run, has proved a major impetus to socio-economic change in the emigration area, but a major deterrant to social change in the settlement areas in Britain. The mechanics of such selective migrations also facilitate the establishment of 'institutions' of migration facilitating movement between the sending and receiving areas (e g. travel agents, banks, new air routes) and providing facilities to soften the initial difficulties of life in an alien situation (e.g. estate agents, doctors, shops, restaurants, *hallal* butchers' etc. run by Asians). An establishment of these large South Asian settlements with their own facilities and institutions in the short-run helps, in the long-run hinders and in the meantime restrains individuals branching out and facing the new conditions in which they are to live and gain their livelihood.

The small but noticeable percentage of South Asians from an urban-educated background were less dependent on the migration chains which so greatly facilitated the movement of villagers. They were less restricted by the imposition of successive immigration controls[19] and more able and willing to communicate with the indigenous population and other middle-class Asians of different ethnic and linguistic backgrounds. They are, however, more exposed to and often conscious of the (subtleties) of discrimination.[20]

The migration of women

It is only within this background of the processes of migration and the present economic and political situation in both countries that the position of South Asians in Britain can be clearly

18. See V. Saifullah Khan (n. 12 on page 269).
19. Successive immigration controls in 1962, 1965, 1968 and 1971 have changed the pattern of immigration from one of mainly unskilled workers to one of professional and skilled workers.
20. David J. Smith, see n. 8 on page 266.

appreciated. It is often wrongly assumed, for example, that migrants are atypical, in character and/or background, of the majority of their home population. This is frequently true of the earlier migrants who established footholds for subsequent migrants and who have often adopted relatively quickly a new life-style and values. These men are likely to have been of adventurous spirit, social outcastes or driven by economic necessity. But once the migration 'chain' develops this no longer holds true; the element of individual choice is considerably reduced. The new alternative becomes a natural, less drastic choice as time passes. A Punjabi or Pathan family thinking of sending their son to find lucrative employment with the help of a cousin in Karachi now consider the alternative of sending him (six times the distance but for greater financial reward) to a brother or uncle in Britain.

In the late 1950s and 1960s the preponderance of men in the migration indicated the essentially economic motive for migration and the migrant's belief in its temporary nature. The gradual increase in women migrants reflected an acknowledgement of the need, or desire for an extended stay, partly due to economic pressure (the increasing cost of living in Britain but the relatively higher wages and lower employment), and partly reflecting a change in attitude and orientation.

The migration of women is significant in several, often unrecognised ways. Firstly, if the close family and kin ties among South Asians are acknowledged the migration of women can be seen as a force strengthening, not severing ties with home, although altering patterns of remittances and expenditure and custom. A migrant now has to consider his expected role in relation to his affines and in the case of Muslims a further bond with his kin group. Secondly, the different South Asian populations have reflected different trends and priorities in the migration pattern. Indians, on the whole, settled in larger numbers earlier than Pakistanis but they also indicated a greater swiftness in calling their wives.[21] This reflected recognition of

---

21. Thirty-four per cent of the total female immigrants from India arrived before the end of 1961 (compared with 41 per cent of males), and 35 per cent came after the beginning of 1961 (23 per cent for males). Only

their wives' earning power, less concern for the restrictions of *purdah*, and a greater acceptance of their intention to stay for an extended period. Pakistanis tended to observe a stricter form of *purdah* and many villagers from Pakistan and Bangladesh felt particularly threatened by the impact of Western values. This perceived undermining of valued, cultural and religious principles and the lack of confidence due to limited social and linguistic skills contributed to an insecurity which has, in recent years, been enhanced for all South Asians due to the political climate in Britain.[22]

Thirdly, the marriage preferences of the various populations have reinforced, to varying degrees, the other constraints against change. Among all South Asians in Britain there has been a preference for sons to have an arranged marriage with a girl from home. This preference for a less independently-minded, domestically orientated and submissive girl is, however, altering as boys brought up in Britain demand different qualities of their brides (notably those of companionship and comparable education) and seek different life-styles, e.g. a nuclear household, a working wife. Thus, the restricted marriage market for British-educated South Asian girls may expand correspondingly.[23] But where more specific marriage preferences (relating to family, kin or caste) are retained, the number of eligible individuals in Britain may be small. In the case of marriage with kin, especially cousins, pressures to maintain the tradition will be strong because it will guarantee another member of the kin group

7 per cent of the Pakistani females (including Bangladeshi) arrived before the end of 1961 and nearly 70 per cent came after the beginning of 1967.

22. This has involved an increased politicisation of the 'race' and 'immigration' debate which is typified by 'the numbers game' focusing on 'problems', 'restrictions', and 'evasions' of the more easily identifiable West Indian and South Asian populations. There has also been a notable increase in the number of right-wing and fascist groups and violent incidents in the last few years.

23. This also expanded when the legal position altered to allow British women to bring their male fiancees to Britain. The policy causes a peculiarly difficult reversal of the normal expectation of the bride adjusting to her husband in the arranged marriage situation. Men brought up in a South Asian village find their wives not only more confident, but more educated, and knowledgeable about the English world around them.

entering Britain. But parents are increasingly aware of the inherent problems of, for example, sending a daughter 'home' to marry in India or bringing a boy from the Sub-Continent, as more 'disaster' cases emerge and are publicised.

Finally, it is important to remember that all the first generation South Asian women migrants have come to Britain as (actual and legal) dependants. In certain populations and in subsequent generations an increasing number of South Asian women will be legally and economically independent and will not feel such strong ties with the homeland, nor the same pressures to conformity in Britain. Loyalty to the family and the maintenance of other Asian values must not be underestimated, but at the same time the existence of an alternative, whether utilised or not, is bound to affect the Asian woman's appreciation of her own situation. The pressures to conform from family and kin ties, the reflection of the honour or shame of an individual into the group and, at times, the ferocious gossip networks still tend to restrain deviants. And many apparent alternatives are not real options for someone initially socialised into a South Asian system.[24]

It is the South Asian woman's status as a dependant which makes her movement a reliable indicator of the future intentions of her husband or group. When the Pakistan Act was passed in 1973, the rush to call wives to Britain or to get British nationality for wives already resident in Britain reflected the suspicion of a complete halt in immigration, even of dependants. The problems such wives and children face before they eventually reach Britain are yet another indication of their dependent

24. This is particularly evident in the case of an Asian girl who wants to marry an English boy or an Asian boy of the 'wrong' religious affiliation. Usually rejected by her own and her partner's family she not only faces a sudden separation from them but a new existence in which only one relationship (that with her husband) monopolises her time and emotions, and where she is more exposed to prejudice and may not be accepted. See also C. Ballard, 'Conflict, Continuity and Change: Second Generation South Asians', in V. Saifullah Khan (ed.), *Minority Families in Britain: Support and Stress* (London: Macmillan, 1979); National Association of Asian Youth, *Which Half Decides? A Contribution to the Debate on Sex Discrimination, British Nationality and Immigration Laws* (Southall, Middlesex: National Association of Asian Youth, 1979).

status and the vulnerability of migrants in general.[25] But it also indicated that many husbands who spoke of returning soon to Pakistan would not do so or had hopes of returning in the distant future. While the more isolated and relatively recently arrived woman acted as a strongly traditional and home-orientated force (through her lack of understanding of her situation, linguistic difficulty, sense of insecurity and uncertainty), there is every indication that this more 'conservative' woman has become, in many instances more Britain-orientated than her husband. For both husband and wife visits to the homeland force the migrant to assess the relative advantages and disadvantages of both countries, and to appreciate their changed expectations and values. Many women admit that they would find it hard to return to life in the Sub-Continent. It is often the attainment of a greater social and linguistic confidence and/or capacity to earn and/or an appreciation of the future available to their children, which have a decisive influence on the woman's assessment of her situation.[26]

Problems of adjustment

Many of the initial problems of adjustment for South Asian women in Britain are common to all South Asians and many other migrant groups. These are the immediate physical problems of adapting to new living conditions and a new climate which may also compound other social and psychological problems of adjustment. The new climate demands thicker, and more layers of clothing; and nappies for children. Particular reticence

---

25. The immigration laws, their interpretation and the interview procedures have been under considerable criticism in Britain. For details see M. Akram, *Where do you keep your string beds* (London: The Runnymede Trust, 1974); and *Appeal Dismissed: The Final Report of the Investigation into Immigration Control Procedures in the Indian Sub-Continent* (London: The Runnymede Trust, 1977).

26. The dynamics of the South Asian family in Britain and the particular ways in which Asian women perceive and define themselves is the subject of a forthcoming book: V. Saifullah Khan, *The Worlds of Migrant Women*.

to change is evident in relation to footwear; the practical tights or socks and closed shoes are still not worn by some South Asian women of village origin even in the coldest of weather. The new climate, its lack of sunshine and restricted outdoor activity can be detrimental to health, particularly for women restricted by custom or necessity to the house.[27] The climate and type of housing in Britain combine to impose an in-door life-style restricted in space and frequency of social interactions which markedly contrasts with the out-door sociability of the family courtyard and village or *mohallah*. Rain and cold weather forces children to play in restricted space in-doors. Mothers have no help from other female family members to supervise the children, give them company and relieve the monotony and help with the larger amounts of washing and housework.[28]

Coupled with the natural homesickness for family and friends the impersonality and large scale of city life is striking, particularly for men and women who have never lived in a city in their own country. An in-door orientated life-style and the traditional reserve of privacy-conscious British limits the opportunities for communicating with neighbours and other contacts made in the daily routine. Frequently the lack of facility in English, and the mutual belief or prejudice that language and culture are a serious barrier to communication, perpetuate the tendency to ethnic exclusiveness. Formal, impersonal interactions, dealings with a complex bureaucracy, demand for punctuality and the faster pace of life in the industrial urban West bring added pressures.

Such external factors often exacerbate the natural human

27. For details of dietary problems see S. Hunt, 'The Food Habits of Asian Immigrants', in *Getting the Most Out of Food* (Burgess Hill: Van-den Bergh and Jurgens, No. 11, 1976) and 'Adaptation and Nutritional Implications of Food Habits among Uganda Asians Settling in Britain', unpublished Ph.D. thesis (London: London University, 1977) and for details of psychological stress, see P. Rack, 'Diagnosing Mental Illness: Asians and the Psychiatric Services', in V. Saifullah Khan (ed.), *Minority Families in Britain: Support and Stress* (London, Macmillan 1979).

28. Overcrowding of several families in one house, and the residential concentration of South Asians, in 'ghettos' are therefore an actual advantage for Asian women at least in the short term.

emotions and reactions of uncertainty and anxiety arising from adaptation to a new social world and the increased self-awareness and reappraisal it demands. For many South Asians in Britain it has been their first move from their 'ancestral' home and for the majority (of women in particular) it has been their first experience of urban life and of another culture. Thus, it is the first marked comparison with the known and valued. The degree of adjustments demanded in lifes-style and values has been gradually reduced at least in the short-term perspective. Newly arrived migrants could depend on the experience and expertise of their already settled countrymen and utilise the institutions of migration and ethnic institutions providing many of the facilities once only available through contact with the indigenous population.

Some of the more fundamental adjustments to life in Britain are noticeably greater for South Asian women than men. At home in India or Pakistan men were used, in differing degrees, to a physical mobility beyond the home and its immediate neighbourhood. For women journeys beyond the home locality were restricted to occasional visits to a local bazaar or visiting relatives. In Britain many men of village background have to adjust to the new demands of industrial wage-labour and often working on night-shifts. This work is separated from the family unit but they frequently work and travel with fellow villagers or countrymen. In certain industries and certain fields of employment ethnic work gangs or complete shifts are the norm,[29] but in many instances South Asian men do interact with work-mates or superiors from the indigenous population. This movement beyond the home and contact with others, while initially problematic, provides opportunities to learn and practice English and facilitates a longer-term adjustment to, and understanding of the wider community.

29. Many Asians explain this as a preference to work with their countrymen and/or an acknowledgement of the pressures of a multi-ethnic workforce. More fundamentally it is due to the lack of promotion possibilities (due to discrimination) and potential (due to limited facility of expected linguistic and cultural attributes), and the advantages of instant recruitment (through kin and village networks) and greater control for the management.

The South Asian woman is, however, more restricted by her new situation. It is often assumed by British community workers and professionals in contact with South Asian women that they are restricted in mobility by religion and/or custom as they were presumed to have been in India or Pakistan. But the Asian family systems and the social life of the city *mohallah* or village society mean that Indian and Pakistani women invariably spend their day in the company of other women. It is this 'women's world' and the encumbent emotional and physical support which is abruptly ended when South Asian women move to Britain.[30] The strength of village-kin ties in the alien situation enables a substitute system to develop, the most meaningful relationship being with other women of the same family, kin and/or home village and other relationships newly formed in Britain which are usually with women from the same region and socio-economic background. Distant relatives may establish a more binding relationship and newly acquired friends may assume features of a kin relationship, so filling a vacuum in the traditional scheme of relationships.[31] The majority of Asian women who work are Indians, Sikh or Hindu, because custom and/or religion restricts all but the urban-educated Pakistani and Bangladeshi from taking employment beyond the home (i.e. where contact with unrelated men is inevitable). The character of the labour market, with the inbuilt bias against women and minorities, and the women's limited social and linguistic skills, place a large percentage of working women in the poorer paid declining sectors of industry or in small workshops, both frequently employing a large percentage of minority and/or women workers. But also cultural constraints relating to the *purdah* system tend to reinforce this trend. For some women (e.g. the older, the more traditional Muslims) working outside the home is unacceptable. These women and others at a particular stage in the life-cycle (with

30. For a discussion of women's segregation and solidarity in an Indian village, see U. Sharma, 'Segregation and its Consequences in India', in P. Caplan and J. Bujra, *Women United, Women Divided* (London: Tavistock, 1978).

31. See V. Saifullah Khan, 'Work and Network: South Asian Women in South London', in S. Wallman (ed.), *Ethnicity at Work* (London: Macmillan, 1979).

young children) can only consider homework. For other women work in an all-South Asian female setting is preferable but working with other women is often accepted. If the only available work involves working with men, working with English men is more acceptable than working with Asian men.[32]

South Asian women who go out to work do have some opportunity to befriend others, learn a little English and something of the British world about them. They are likely to be more aware, and understanding, of the pressures and influences experienced by their children and some variety and stimulation in an otherwise claustrophobic domestic routine may compensate for the inevitable physical exhaustion. It is possible that, over time, South Asian husbands will assume a greater responsibility in domestic affairs and caring for children to relieve their wives at present coping with the two full-time jobs of home and outside work. South Asian women, like other women in Britain, suffer from limited child care facilities. Some women who live close to relatives or fellow villagers, leave their children with them and others utilise paid child-minders.

It is evident that many of these problems of adjustment are not specifically due to migration to the West. A Punjabi villager moving to Karachi or Delhi would experience similar problems due to the nature of urban living, the physical separation of the family unit and the transition to a wage-based economy. The wife can no longer work on the land or beyond the home with those known to her and, if her husband finds work, the necessity to work is reduced and, the family's status is raised accordingly. This move for a village woman, whether in Britain or the Indian Sub-Continent, may be a step up the status hierarchy but it is also a step away from the relatively greater physical and economic freedom of the village woman. In a subsistence economy the women's contribution to the family's economic situation is valued and she has a greater control over the products of their labour. In an economy such as that in Britain, the woman who does not work for cash is economically dependent on her husband. While no longer an economic

---

32. See V. Saifullah Khan (n. *31* on page 229).

advantage to the household she is valued more in terms of a marker of status for the family.

It is important to add, however, that some of the new features of life experienced by South Asian women in Britain are seen by some women as positive, rather than problematic features. The smaller family unit contributes to a woman's loneliness, loss of physical and emotional support and the acquisition of new responsibilities. While bewailing these factors many women admit the advantages. If a newly arrived woman finds help and support in the initial period and then establishes a circle of friends she may overcome the anxieties of, and begin to enjoy her new freedom and responsibilities. The absence of elders is bemoaned in a country where baby-sitters are so valued and yet may be outweighed by the absence of a particularly unpleasant mother-in-law, the greater influence over the socialisation of one's own children and the great privacy available to a husband and wife. The early years of separation due to the migration process, and the husbands working at a long distance from home may produce tensions between husband and wife resulting from their different aspirations and experiences and yet the couple's earlier acquisition of household and parental responsibilities, their relative freedom of elders and particularly the loss of alternative support (in the 'woman's world and man's world') encourages a closer relationship between husband and wife.

Some conclusions, predictions and questions

Many of the problems faced by South Asian women and often South Asian men in Britain are those experienced by any migrant group or ethnic minority, particularly if they are moving from a rural to an urban area.[33]

South Asian migrants in Britain clearly highlight the fact that migrants are usually a highly exploited group, vulnerable pawns in an international exchange of labour. Such migrations

---

33. See J.L. Watson (ed.), *Between Two Cultures: Minorities in Britain*, op. cit.

have benefited the receiving country (through the influx of foreign labour in time of labour shortage and to support declining industries and jobs no longer acceptable to the indigenous population) and the country of emigration (by the influx of foreign capital to the emigration areas and foreign exchange for the country as a whole). And yet there is rarely any recognition or acceptance of this contribution by alleviating or facilitating the human conditions and dilemmas it invariably causes. The migrant finds his status is dependent on both worlds. In one he achieves economic advancement and in the other he is accorded recognition of his success. But he is restricted physically to one world at any one time and thus he lives totally in neither. Life in Britain, and the migration itself, is meaningful only in terms of life back home. Having left the village and become associated with *vilayat* a return to village life as he originally knew it is a rejection of opportunities not only beneficial to him personally but also to his family and kin. The changing aspirations and awareness which the migration process involves makes such a return far more difficult than the migrant could have foreseen. The migrants' service to both societies and the absence of its recognition has tended to strengthen the *status quo* within and between both societies which was the fundamental cause of their migration in the first place and will continue to constrain their opportunities for economic and social advancement.

The instability and insecurity of such a transitional category is also, in the case of South Asians in Britain, related to their lack of representation in the wider society. Like women in general, South Asians in Britain are not found in positions of power in accordance with their numerical spread. In both cases this results from individual and institutionalised discrimination and particular restrictions relating to their past and present skills and orientation. One reason for the under-representation of South Asians in Britain, and their lack of grass-roots organisation and representative leaders is the differentiation within the South Asian population based on ethnic, regional, religious and socio-economic and national background. Communication between each population (Sikh, Gujarati, Mirpuri, Chhachhi, etc.) is restricted by the internal organisation based on village and kin ties, by the diversity of languages and the maintenance of prejudices, and within each population there is the marked distinction between the urban-educated South Asian and the majority of less educated villagers. Most of the leaders or spokesmen of the South Asian populations come from the former category and have no mandate for representing the majority to the British world. Their desire for a wider social standing has led consciously or unconsciously to their disassociating themselves from the majority with whom they know they are classified by the indigenous population. Many of these 'leaders' have minimal influence over the community and are not directly interested in its cohesion or preservation except as the foundation of their power. The majority of South Asians value their existence only for their ability to communicate to the wider society on important issues relating to external threats to their nationality or religious affiliations.[34] Traditional leaders, often elders or long-established migrants, do wield authority over smaller sections of the communities. In the case of the Sikh community, official representatives of the Indian Workers' Association are democratically elected and their organisation has a wider support from, and great involvement in, the welfare of the whole community.

The South Asian population's lack of power and of any foundation on which organisation and cooperation between its different communities could be based is evident and severe in consequence for its women. Sikh and Hindu women may pray and eat together on Sundays at the local *Gurdawara* or temple respectively, but the majority of Muslim women have no meeting point or social life beyond that of the home. Some of the new mosques are now catering for separate provision for women and community involvement. The local and national Pakistani, Bangladeshi and Indian women's associations are usually small in number and influence and organised and supported by women from an urban-educated background. Few have tackled the fundamental problems experienced by village women, the majority concentrating on arranging cultural

---

34. See V. Saifullah Khan (n. 12 on page 269).

shows and *meena* bazaars to raise funds.[85] An increasing number of South Asian working women are now joining unions and there have been several notable cases of women striking in demand of better conditions.[36] Some of these strikes and recent national meetings and conferences organised by South Asian women have been run by the articulate and confident East African Asian women of the first generation, but other more radical and politicised groups are now being run predominantly by 'second' generation British Asians.

Although the children of today's adult South Asians are facing other problems, they are breaking down some of these barriers, based on ethnic and class origin, and have a greater access and ability to participate in the wider society. Their future depends on the degree of rejection or acceptance they feel from British society, the opportunities available in the alternative world back home and of course their parents' plans and attitudes and nature of socialisation. It is inevitably the young Asian girls who are going to experience the greater problems, and particularly those with strict Muslim parents (e.g. Pakistani, Indian, Gujarati, and Bangladeshi).[37]

It is clear from this general outline of the position of South Asian women in Britain that many women are facing the same fundamental dilemmas as their sisters in the Indian Sub-Continent. These involve questions arising from rapid social change, Westernisation and urbanisation, and the emancipation of women amongst many others. The problems revolving around working women, 'love' versus 'arranged' marriages, female education, the generation gap, etc., are dilemmas faced in urban settings in the Indian Sub-Continent. The majority of migrant women to Britain are, however, from rural uneducated

---

35. For a parallel in the Indian scene see P. Caplan 'Women's Organisations in Madras City, India', in P. Caplan and J. Bujra (eds.), *Women United, Women Divided*, op. cit.

36. See A. Wilson, *Finding a Voice* (London: Virago, 1978) and J. Rogaly, *Grunwick* (Harmondsworth: Penguin, 1978).

37. See V. Saifullah Khan 'Socialisation, Identity and Ethnicity: First and Second South Asians in Britain', paper presented to Xth International Congress of Anthropological and Ethnological Sciences, Delhi, to be incorporated into *The Worlds of Migrant Women*, forthcoming.

background with little knowledge of contemporary trends in the urban areas of their homeland. They have telescoped the two fundamental steps or rural-to-urban and east-to-west into one generation and tend to see their problem as peculiar to the British situation. In their position as dependants in a migrant situation, and as members of an ethnic minority, it is surprising that they have adjusted and coped with life in Britain as well as they have. The strength of the South Asian family system has done much to buffer the difficulties of adjustment in such an alien setting. It would, however, be helpful if there was mutual appreciation and cooperation between women in Britain and the Indian Sub-Continent of the common elements they are facing, and the alternative strategies employed to tackle them.

12 The Aging Woman in India: Self-Perceptions and Changing Rloes

Sylvia Vatuk

This is a preliminary report on one aspect of an on-going research project concerning the social and cultural framework of aging in Indian society. The project is an anthropological field study being carried out in the city of Delhi in one of the so-called 'urbanised villages', former agricultural settlements which have been caught in the path of the expansion of the city in recent years. Their fields have been acquired by the municipality for the building of roads, residential colonies, and commercial and public edifices, and their economic base removed, to be replaced by earnings from rents, salaried jobs or wage labour, or interest from bank accounts and investments, in the now-surrounding city. There are many such urbanised villages within metropolitan Delhi—the one in which the present research is being undertaken (and which I will call Rayāpur) has been gradually incorporated into the growing city over the past 40 years, the last remnants of land having been lost to agriculture about 12 years ago. The Rayā or Ravā Rājpūt caste was the dominant

---

I have based this report on partial data from field research carried out in the Delhi area in collaboration with my husband, Ved Prakash Vatuk. This project, entitled 'Social and Cultural Dimensions of Aging in India', has been supported by the National Institute of Mental Health and the American Institute of Indian Studies.

caste of this village.[1] Because all but an insignificant amount of the village land had formerly been under the ownership of members of this caste, they have profited greatly from the acquisition of its territory for urban construction. While at present the financial status of the Rayā families still resident in Rayāpur varies widely (depending upon the amount of land originally owned and their success in keeping or augmenting the money paid in compensation), all of the local inhabitants of the caste are at least relatively well-off; all own their own homes and most have other real estate which they give on rent; all have the basic necessities of life and certain luxuries as well, while some are wealthy even by Indian urban standards.

Scope

The focus of this research is the life-cycle and social roles of the aged within the local caste community of Rayā Rājpūts. In this paper I will discuss these issues as they concern the life of Rayā women. The indigenous definition of old age (*buṛhappa*) has been treated from the beginning as one of the empirical questions to be researched, and therefore it was decided not to establish any *a priori* chronological age as a cut-off point for delimiting the universe of study. Indeed, to do so would have been to come up against a serious difficulty in the widespread ignorance of precise chronological age, especially among the elderly. While various devices, such as the making of a time-events table, can be used to get at a fairly close approximation of chronological age in such situations, it was felt that for our purposes it was more appropriate to select for study those who consider themselves and are considered by others as 'old' in the context of their own society, regardless of actual age.

While the self-perception and the perception of others as old obviously differs from one individual to another, and tends to

---

1. This is a localised and relatively small agricultural caste found in Meerut, Muzaffarnagar and Bijnor Districts, as well as occupying six villages of substantial size in the Delhi urban area. Formerly known as Ravās or Rayās, they have since the 1930s preferred the designation of Rājpūt.

depend to an important degree on such variable external signs of aging as tooth-loss and greying hair, the general consensus seems to place primary stress on life-cycle criteria. Thus the marriage of one's children—particularly of one's sons—marks the beginning of old age in this society far more clearly than does the passing of a specified number of years. We have, therefore, included in our 'aging' sample all persons with effectively married sons or adopted sons.[2] In case of sonless or childless persons, we have included them on the basis of their contemporaneity with those already in the sample. There are so few of these, almost all of a clearly advanced age, that ambiguities about proper assignment to the sample have been negligible.

The women of the elderly sample[3] are all either married or widowed—a significant number have been remarried after the death of a first husband, usually to his younger or elder brother.[4] None of the women was born in Rayāpur: because of the practice of village exogamy, all local 'wives' come from other villages and those of this older group come for the most part from villages in Meerut and Muzzaffarnagar Districts in Uttar Pradesh. A few were born in Rayā Rājpūt villages located elsewhere in the Delhi area. While it sometimes happens in this region that a separated woman or a widow will return to live in her natal village, or that a man without sons will invite a daughter and her husband to remain with him in her natal village (as *ghar jamāi*), there are no such cases within this caste in Rayāpur

---

2. By 'effective marriage' I refer to the coming of a wife to live with her husband after their *gaunā* or consummation rite. In earlier time this rite took place some 3 to 7 years after the wedding ceremony, commonly performed for girls before puberty. Today, however, most Rayāpur girls (and the in-coming wives of Rayāpur boys) are at least 16 by the time of marriage, and no more than a few months normally intervene between marriage and its consummation.

3. Because this research is still in progress and the collection and analysis of the data has not been completed, I avoid presenting here any absolute figures, percentages which might have to be altered in subsequent publications.

4. Among Rayā Rājpūts and some other castes of this region it is customary to remarry widows of child-bearing age, preferably to a brother or other close agnatic kinsman of the deceased. Failing this, a widow is sometimes remarried to an outsider.

among the elderly group.

The background of almost all of the women is rural—before and after marriage—and in some cases, until fairly recently, they were actively engaged in agricultural pursuits as well as in housekeeping, cooking and child care, for in this caste it was (and still is in the rural areas) customary for women to work in the family fields, to cut fodder for cattle, to fetch water from the well for all the household needs, and so on. Because of the fortuitous location of Rayāpur, these women now rather suddenly find themselves in a position to enjoy almost total leisure (if they so wish) and an urban middle-class life-style, and some have such comforts in their homes as hot running water, gas stoves, refrigerators, air-coolers and Saturday night television. While they are almost universally illiterate, their younger daughters and their grand-daughters are graduating from college, and they are observing, and even fostering by their tolerance, new standards for the relationship of husbands and wives as they marry their sons and grandsons to educated girls of their caste from the other Delhi villages.[5]

While similar changes are affecting the lives of millions of other older Indian women who at some point in their lives have migrated from a rural to an urban environment (and even in a lesser degree the lives of millions who remain in the also changing rural milieu), the situation of these Rayāpur women, and of others in villages similarly "swallowed" by the relentless march of urbanism, is unique in many respects.

Residence patterns of the elderly

The old women of Rayāpur live, with negligible exceptions, in

[5] Because of their new prosperity and urban character, the Delhi area Rayās have begun to restrict marital unions as much as possible to among themselves, rather than continuing their previous pattern of alliances with the more distant and still-rural U.P. settlements of their caste. Rayāpur is in a peculiarly advantageous position in this respect, not only because of its wealth (it is known within the caste nowadays as *Amrika* ('America'), but because the two exogamous *gotras* present in the village are not found in the other major Rayā settlements of Delhi, while several of the latter are

'joint' households of three and sometimes four generations.[6] The most frequent type of household includes an older married couple, one or more married sons and their wives and children, and unmarried children of the older couple as well. Many such households also have additional members, a widowed or separated daughter, a daughter's child or other young relatives come to attend school in Delhi. A few also include the elderly father or mother of the older couple, making a four generation family group. There are very few widows in the older sample, no doubt partly because of the custom of widow remarriage. The bulk of the 'older' women are in the 55-65 age range (based on reported ages and other means of estimation) and there are very few over 70.

While the residential norm is thus for the aging woman to hold the position of mother-in-law and wife in a lineal extended household, there are some exceptions: those who have no sons or whose sons are young despite their own advancing age. A small number of married couples in this category live with adopted 'sons' (usually a husband's brother's son or a daughter's son) or with their own unmarried young children. One couple in their late fifties lives alone with only a young granddaughter (a SoDa), their only son having died and his wife remarried out of the family. A widow in her mid-seventies lives with her teenage granddaughter (DaDa), who has come to stay in Rayāpur from her village home in order to look after her grandmother and attend high school. This woman never had a son and is on bad terms with her closest relatives in the village, her former co-wife and the latter's son, with whom she might otherwise reasonably expect to be able to make her home.

Preparation for old age

As the extended family residence pattern is the universally

---

inhabited by members of a single *gotra*, preventing intermarriage between them.

6. This is not to say that the majority of all Rayā households in the village are 'joint' in structure, as they are not.

desired one by and for old people, it is not surprising that preparation for old age security begins early in terms of assuring that there will be such a family in which to live when the time comes. This preparation manifests itself first in the attempt to have at least one son. While in the literature on Indian society the need for a son is typically given a religious, other-worldly rationale, for these villagers it is pre-eminently and most practically a matter of providing for someone to take care of one's need in old age. Childless couples, and those who have managed to produce only female children, begin at some point to consider the alternatives: remarriage, adoption (formal or informal), or the taking of a *ghar jamāī*. While men sometimes take a second wife during the lifetime of the first in order to have a son, women may remarry only after the death of their husbands. Remarriage is almost routine in this caste if the woman is still in her child-bearing years and does not already have growing sons on whom she can begin to rely for support. Although the custom is justified in a number of ways, one important reason given by the Rayās themselves is to ensure that the woman will not be destitute in old age.

Adoption is always of a male relative, a daughter's son or the brother's son of either husband or wife. Occasionally, a sister's son may be adopted. The adoptee is usually a child, but there are instances of the adoption of boys in their late adolescence, done with the explicit understanding that the arrangement is being made to ensure that there will be someone to 'serve' the adopter (*sevā karnā*) when the need arises. In some cases land or money is signed over to the adoptee at this time. Widowed women rarely adopt, although widowed and unmarried men do so not infrequently. There are, however, some widowed women now living with adopted sons who were taken in during the lifetime of their late husbands.

Taking a *ghar jamāī* seems to be a less attractive solution to the problem of care in old age, even though many women may be heard to maintain that 'only a daughter can really serve her parents with all her heart'. There is a certain awkwardness in the living arrangements of a couple with the wife's parents, no least for the live in son-in-law himself, who tends to be looked down upon by others as a young man with little to offer, reduced to living off his wife's family. In other ways also the situation reverses or makes impossible of maintenance many of the accepted kinship role behaviour patterns. While there are at least two cases of village sons who are living as *ghar jamāīs* elsewhere, there are no such cases among Rayās in the village itself, although there are a few village 'daughters' living with their employed husbands in quarters separate from those of their parents.

Whether an old couple or a widow has a son of their own, or has made arrangements to adopt a substitute, it is expected (and almost always followed in practice), that this boy when married will live on in the family home with his new wife and subsequent children. No other alternative is even considered initially, except in the rare case of a family with several sons where one is asked to marry as *ghar jamāī*. However, this arrangement does not always last indefinitely. When a man has had two wives, it is unusual for married sons of the first to live for long in a joint household with the second. And even in the case of a woman's own son, it often happens that after a number of years he and his wife will set up separate cooking arrangements and even cease contributing to the joint family budget (although he usually continues in joint ownership with his father and brothers of any family property). When a couple's sons are beginning to think about arranging their own children's marriages, it is common, at least nowadays, for a formal division of even this joint property to be undertaken, although for the 'prestige' (*izzat*) of the family, it is still considered best to marry one's grandchildren while the family is still 'together' (*ikatte*).

However, in spite of the desire and need for some degree of partition of the joint family over the years, one thing that is considered quite out of the question is to separate off the old couple—or a widowed parent—leaving them to fend for themselves in the preparation of meals. If the elder son's wife wants to cook separately, she will begin to do so only after her husband's younger brother has married. And if full partition among the brothers takes place while one or both parents is still living, arrangements will be made to have them live and eat with one of them. More rarely, all the *bahūs* will feed them together or in turn.

Even in such circumstances, sons remain in the family home. It should be stressed that the number of sons in Rayāpur who have actually moved out of the parental residence in the course of a partial or complete partition of the joint family while either of their parents was still living is negligible. At most, some have moved by mutual agreement to another house owned by their family in the village. In fact, there has been very little movement out of the village by any men of this caste, with the exception of several families who have bought rural land elsewhere with the proceeds of their own land compensation and have left to farm it. More typically, even these families maintain one or more of a set of brothers on the farm, while the main part of the family remains in Rayāpur. Even leaving the parental home because of the demands of employment is extremely rare for young Rayāpur couples. Because Delhi as a large metropolitan city provides employment opportunities of all kinds and at all levels, and because a few Rayāpur boys have obtained the kind of high-level position or highly specialised advanced training that might make it difficult to insist on remaining in the city if the most favourable job opportunities are to be availed of, the kind of mobility that is becoming typical of much of the educated middle and upper classes in urban India has not yet affected Rayāpur household structures appreciably.

It is evident that this lack of mobility is not accidental: parents consciously want to keep their sons at home and consider it a defeat and a cause of much unhappiness if the joint household dissolves during their lifetime—so much greater their distress if a son actually moves away from the village. Up to the present the very few cases of the latter have been the result of severe family dissension (either between the young couple and a parent or parents or between brothers and/or brothers' wives). Because of the view that such a breakup is something for the family to be ashamed of, they are usually presented to outsiders as cases in which the couple had to move because the son's place of work was on the other side of Delhi and it took too long to commute, or because the young family was very large and the son's employer provided living quarters free of charge, and so on. It remains to be seen if this pattern of joint residence can be maintained in the next generation, for aside from the pressure of space which is already becoming severe in some homes, village young men are increasingly aiming higher than the B.A. or LL.B. that only five years ago was a rare attainment for Rayā boys, and a few are even making plans for postgraduate education abroad. But because of the persistence of the traditional residence pattern for the aged at present living in the urbanised village of Rayāpur, we must still look at the elderly woman's life and earlier life history within the framework of this type of household structure.

Stages of a woman's life

Rayā women tend to think about their own lives, and those of women in general, in terms of three main stages or periods, each having its own character and characteristics, its own appropriate set of activities, its own duties and rewards. The first of these is childhood (*bacpan*), a time that from the perspective of the end of life is viewed as having been generally pleasant, carefree, without much responsibility and few demands for hard work or restraint of freedom. During this period a woman is felt to have received the only unqualified love and nurturance she will ever have, and the warm and pleasant associations of childhood, of life 'in the mother's kingdom' (*mā ke rāj me*) colour a woman's perception of her natal home and village (*pīhar*) forever afterwards. Women in their sixties still look forward to frequent periodic visits 'home', even when parents have long since died and other familiar faces are rapidly dropping out of sight as well. One of the most often heard laments in this age group concerns the inevitable loss of touch with the *pīhar* as the years go on, and with few exceptions, these women do manage to make such a visit at least once every year or two. Similarly, Rayāpur households receive periodic visits from elderly village 'daughters' married 40 or more miles away.

For most of these women, childhood ended abruptly with the onset of puberty or shortly thereafter. Although there are a few examples of women of this age-group who married in their late teens, the majority were married before the age of 12 or 13 and went to take up married life in their husband's household and villages (*sasurāl*) within two or three years. Some women claim to have been so young at the time of the wedding that they were unaware of what was going on. These, who may have been as young as 7 or 8 years old, did not, of course, join their husband's households until they were physically mature, many years later.

The second major period of these women's lives (ironically referred to in contrast to the earlier period as 'mother-in-law's kingdom' (*sās kā rāj*) began for almost all in the position of junior member of a large joint farm family, where the contrast with the natal home in terms of workload and the ability to move about and speak freely with household members and others was sharp and often traumatic. There was little time and less privacy in the first months and even years to develop a close relationship with the new husband ('those were "simple" times', as one such woman put it), and frequent lengthy visits to their natal villages were a welcome respite from the physically and often emotionally trying atmosphere of the *sasurāl*. The first pregnancy was eagerly awaited, and those who had difficulty conceiving or who aborted easily or whose first children died in infancy report trying various measures, spiritual, magical and medical, to help them become pregnant or to ensure that their children would live beyond the perilous first year. Most did succeed in this, although some were never able to have a son, seen as so necessary for a worry-free old age. They spent the succeeding years rearing their children (although in many instances this task was mainly pre-empted by their mothers-in-law) and gradually, as in-laws died and brothers and cousins separated, succeeded to the position of senior woman of their own household, making the transition into old age with the marriage of sons and the coming of their wives and later of grandchildren—'the kingdom of the daughter-in-law' (*bahū kā rāj*).[7]

---

7. It is interesting to compare this feminine version of the woman's life-cycle with that of the well-known injunction of Manu which advises keeping a woman under the successive protection (and control) of father, husband, and son.

Self-perception of woman's life

Since the purpose of this research has been to look at old age in the context of the entire life cycle, considerable attention has been given, in eliciting life-histories and in interviews, as well as in observing interaction and listening to spontaneous conversation involving the elderly, to obtaining an overview of their perception of the total life experience (in the present case, of the female experience), both in specific, personal individual terms, and in the broad, generalised aspect. What emerges from the data is often contradictory—there seems to be a marked discrepancy between the largely pessimistic, discontented, and resigned verbal utterances about 'woman's lot' and the sad fate of the aged, and the observed high level of good-humoured and extraordinarily active participation and interest in social work and family activities. Women's life has been described to us time after time as being 'nothing but hard work, trouble, and pain from beginning to end'. Our queries often receive such responses. 'How can you ask about the best time of a woman's life? There is no good time'. A typical answer to the enquiry 'How are you?' (particularly if the greeter is another old lady) goes something like 'I can only wish that God would take me right now, but I suppose I will somehow have to get through the days that are allotted to me, although I would rather be dead'.

Detachment from worldly concerns is espoused as a necessary and desirable part of successful aging, while those who recommend it most vocally are on the go from dawn to late at night managing the affairs of their family, visiting sick relatives, helping to arrange the marriages of neighbours' children, attending weddings and funerals, buying clothes for festival presents for their married daughters, grinding two kilos of wheat by hand in the morning before breakfast, and similarly demonstrating considerable attachment to the practicalities of life on this earth. Even taking into account the fact of individual variability—which is considerable despite a high degree of cultural homogeneity and general similarity of life experiences among the women of this one caste in a single village—there remains a good deal to be sorted out from these apparently conflicting impressions.

We may try to do this by discussing these women's perception of the period of life in which they are presently living at three levels. First, there is the level of ideals: how a woman's old age ought to be spent, how she should occupy herself and how she should be treated by others. Second, there is the way that these women perceive their old age, and the old age of other women they know, to be in actuality. Usually, the issue here is the degree to which their life as they see it approaches or deviates from the ideal. And third is the 'objective' observer's view of their lives and her interpretation of it. This is made up partly from direct observation and questioning, and partly from clues provided by the women's own (or their family members' and relatives' and neighbours') verbal reports of incidents in which they have been involved.

Rest and service in old age

In ideal terms, old age is supposed to be a time of rest and leisure, a time when work responsibilities should cease, and one should be 'served' by the sons one has raised for the purpose and by their wives. Elderly women describe a fortunate one among their peers as one whose *bahū-beṭe* ('daughters-in-law and sons') give them much 'rest' (*arām*) and 'service' (*sevā*). The stereotyped manner of praising a daughter-in-law is to say that she is hard-working and serves one well. The concept of *sevā* is a broad one, and implied in it is not only the performance of all necessary tasks for the comfort of the older person, but love, consideration, thoughtfulness, and devotion as well. However, this latter aspect is implicit rather than verbalised; when asked to explain the meaning of *sevā* women almost always do so largely in terms of physical care: 'I have a very hard-working (*bahut Karnerī*) and serving (*sevā karnevāli*) *bahū*. She gives me my meals, washes my clothes, prepares my bed at night. In all things, she serves me well'.

Certain more personal services are also included in the concept of *sevā*, such as scrubbing the older woman's back when she bathes, combing and braiding her hair and, most importantly and symbolically, massaging her legs at night and when she is ill or tired. Young women often relate how their *sās* makes them press her legs (*pāo dabvāna*) for hours at a stretch each night, until they drop off to sleep from exhaustion, at which point the old woman is perversely brought back to wakefulness, demanding that the massaging continue. The older women, on the other hand, maintain that in *their* day they *really* served *their* mothers-in-law, not like the *bahūs* of today: 'In those days, when one of us massaged my *sās's* legs, the others would be massaging her hands. But now!' They claim that the custom is unfortunately dying, that the old are no longer in a position to demand this kind of service, and they shrug of questions about the practice in their own homes with a cynical laugh.

Sevā also means care in time of illness. It is a common complaint among the old that members of the younger generation are not sufficiently sympathetic when an old person is not feeling well. 'Here I have been coughing like this for so many days, I can't get my breath, yet no one has asked "mother, what is the matter?" I keep my sorrows and sufferings to myself.' Yet, although modern medicine is widely accepted and utilised by persons of all ages it is rare for an elderly person to agree to go for a stay in the hospital, even in the case of serious illness. In fact, one might say that they are especially reluctant to go in case of serious illness, because of the fear of dying away from home and family. Therefore, it is not unusual for an old and helpless person to be nursed for months or even years by a daughter-in-law. There is no thought given in this kind of situation to the possibility of hiring a nurse or other outsider to take over the less pleasant or physically exhausting tasks involved in caring for an invalid, even though for many of these families there are no financial constraints to their doing so. And I know of no instance in which an old person has been sent away to a hospital against his will, no matter how difficult the circumstances. Yet, despite the fact that no fear of being sent to die among strangers hangs over these women, they are unanimous in expressing the wish to die 'while my hands and feet are still able'. The worst thing that can happen to someone, they say, is to become helpless in old age and to live on a burden to others and to oneself. Indeed, whatever their private fears of death may be, they speak of it openly, cheerfully, and with matter-of-factness. Typical is the statement of a healthy woman in her late fifties, a widow and mother of three sons, of whom the eldest is married: 'I have sons, a daughter-in-law has come, there are son's children (*pote-poti*) and daughter's children (*dhevte-dhevti*). What more do I need? I am ready to go at any time'.

While the actual work involved in doing *seva* mainly falls upon a woman's daughter-in-law, the son himself tends to share the credit—and the blame—for the quality of its performance. Some women are of the opinion that it depends mainly upon the son whether his parents are well taken care of in old age, and there is a dominant tone of pessimism when they discuss this problem in general terms. It seems to be felt that hard as one may try to ensure that one has a son to provide for one in old age, and as much as one may do for him in bringing him up, nursing him through illnesses, educating him, and so on, it is in the end an unpredictable matter 'how he will turn out'. They explain that, 'if the son is good, then everything will be fine. But there are very few sons like that nowadays—at the most one in a hundred can be found who will really care for his parents in their old age'. Some maintain that a really 'good' son will make sure that his wife serves her in-laws well, but others feel that one's fate really lies in the hands of the stranger one has brought into the family: 'The son may be good, but if his wife is of that kind she will turn his head (*isko sikhaegi*) against his parents, and then he will also neglect them'. There is a definite feeling that social change is having an adverse effect on the position of old people, and as evidence of this they point to the increasing tendency of young married men to separate from their parents shortly after marriage. Although this has not yet become an important trend within the village or in the caste as a whole, they see it as a real threat for the future, and claim that it is being learned from the Punjabis (a very visible outgroup in the neighbourhood to whom all unwelcome social deviance is credited), among whom it has become (according to them) the expected norm.

Work activities of older women

It is the minimum duty of a *bahū* to relieve her mother-in law (*sās*) of such household jobs as cooking the meals and washing the utensils and clothes. It is said that 'it doesn't look nice' (*acchā nahī lag'ā*) to have an older woman cooking if there are one or more daughters-in-law in the house, and although some mothers-in law continue to share the cooking if they have only one married son (usually in this case one woman will cook the morning meal, the other the evening meal), it is the more common and expected practice for her to cease cooking shortly after her son's marriage, except in emergencies such as the sickness or absence of the *bahū*. The appropriate feminine division of labour as described by Rayāpur women has the mother-in-law doing the 'outside work' (*bāhār kā kām*), while the *bahū* takes care of the work inside the house (*ghar kā kām*). This coincides with the traditional rural expectation that a young married woman should stay within the house as much as possible, and although young wives in Rayāpur are by no means completely confined to the home (or when outside it to the chaperonage of their *sās* or other older women) to the degree that these elderly women were in their youth, the standard is still recognised as legitimate and desirable, although perhaps not very practical of execution under present day circumstances. There are many families in the village whose young married women leave the home only occasionally, and then only for such things as an excursion to the movies with their husbands (itself a serious departure from the kind of behaviour suitable for young married women in the youth and middle-age of the present-day elderly).

'Outside work' in this urbanised village includes shopping for staple provisions and vegetables and doing other errands involving contact with tradesmen and artisan specialists, such as the weavers to whom hand-spun cotton is entrusted each summer for weaving into blankets, or the cot makers who may be called from time to time to renew the string webbing on the family cots. In all households some of these 'outside jobs' may be taken care of by the men—either the old woman's husband or son—but a large part of this work, and particularly its organisation, is considered the province of the senior woman of the house. Although financial arrangements vary greatly from one household to another, it is also usual for the senior woman to keep the money for running the household, so that her daughters-in-law and grand-children must come to her for money when they want to make any routine purchase. This household budget may be apart from money which her earning sons keep back for their own and their wives' personal use (so that it does not mean total control over all purchases by family members), but it is nevertheless an important element in her day-to-day managerial authority.

Care of animals is also in most families the province of older women. More than half of the households in which old people are present own at least one buffalo for milk and *ghī* and some own more than one and occasionally a cow as well. The symbolic significance of having one's milk own (*ghar kā dūdh*) is probably as great as its contribution to the family diet. For the older generation, to have to purchase milk is one of the signs of changing times that is most to be deprecated. Although in the rural past of the this village, men took a large share in the care of milch animals, this task in most Rayāpur households is now relegated mainly to women, and among them mainly to the old, for the young wives increasingly come to marriage unfamiliar with the intricacies of milking and the care and feeding of buffaloes. This job takes a great deal of a woman's time, and necessitates her being available in the home at almost all times. A buffalo must be fed and watered three times a day, washed down at least once a day, milked twice a day (and the milk churned and *ghī* made), and her stall must be cleaned and the manure patted into dung-cakes which are dried in the sun and later stacked and used for fuel. The latter job is one to which the older village women are so accustomed from their earlier days—and the savings so substantial when compared to the cost of wood, coal, or kerosene, not to mention bottled gas—that many who do not own an animal buy manure from one of the local dairies and make their own dung-cakes.

Other household tasks that are typically taken care of by older women—although young women may also do them—are those which are fairly sedentary, such as spinning into thread the old cotton from the family quilts each spring, tacking new cotton into the quilts before winter sets in, and making such household staples in the appropriate seasons as pickles and hand-rolled noodles.

A major responsibility of the older women in most households is the care of young children, particularly toddlers. A grandmother will take charge of a young baby while its mother is busy with the cooking and washing, but when a baby is very small her contribution will usually be limited to holding it and perhaps feeding it sugared water while its mother is otherwise occupied. Later, however, and particularly after it is weaned or another baby is born, she may take over almost all of its care, having it sleep beside her at night, feeding it, and taking it along with her on errands or when she goes to visit neighbours or to any social or religious event. Grandmothers say 'the interest is dearer than the capital' (*mūl se pyārī byāj*) to explain their fondness for their grandchildren, and their exceptional leniency and patience with the antics and whining of children whom they have hopelessly spoiled and to whom they allow liberties that they never permitted their own children. It is not unusual for grandmothers in this way to attempt —and often succeed—in weaning a child's affection from his mother. But, young mothers, by and large, seem to accept the special relationship of grandmother and grandchild—perhaps partly because it relieves them of a significant burden of work—and are more apt to resent a mother-in-law who does not show special affection for their child or who shows favouritism to one of his cousins.

While the classical Indian four stages of life (*āshramas*) are not clearly articulated in reference to the female life-cycle, either in the traditional literature or in the folk conception, Rayā women do frequently use the classical terminology to refer to the second and major stage of life, that of the householder, *gṛhastha*. Ideally, they express the view that in old age a woman should leave *grahastha*, should detach herself from concern with the day-to-day running of the household. To leave *gṛhastha* involves two aspects: first, a readiness on the part of the *bahū* to take over the onerous household tasks formerly performed by the *sas* (with the indifferent assistance of her daughters), and second, a readiness on the part of the older woman to give up her managerial role and her feeling that she alone is responsible for and capable of managing household affairs. These two rarely coincide. While the former is generally more or less accomplished within a week or two of the new daughter-in-law's arrival, the latter is typically a very gradual process of withdrawal that may take many years and may never be completed before the senior woman's death. The symbolic act of 'handing over the keys' to the daughter-in-law is often resisted up to the end. In fact, although elderly women are often chided—and chide one another—for being 'too much bound up in *gṛhastha*', it is actually rare in this community for any woman to voluntarily cease taking some responsibility for the work of the household and its organisation until she is either mentally or physically quite incapable of doing so.

Religious participation of the aging woman

It has long been a tradition in Indian society—and in other societies as well—to regard religious activities as particularly appropriate to the aged. To spend one's declining years in contemplation, to prepare oneself for the imminent departure from this world by devoting oneself to the purification of the inner self and the worship of a God for whom one had perhaps too little time to spare in one's younger days, is regarded not only as a virtue in itself but also as the better part of wisdom as the time of reckoning draws near. Consistent with this ideal, we note that the religiosity of the elderly women in Rayāpur is markedly greater than that of their younger relatives and neighbours, if we measure this in terms of proportions of women at various stages of life and proportion of time spent in solitary and group worship. The majority of elderly women rise between four and five in the morning (often before their daughters-in-law awaken, contrary to the traditional rural pattern) and after going to the toilet and bathing spend one-half to one hour in prayer. Some go each morning to one of the village temples, others sit in front of their household shrine and 'take God's name', either alone or in the company of their husbands or other family members. Only after this do they take any refreshment.

The other major form of religious participation is group hymn (*bhajan*) singing. There are regular weekly sessions at one of the village temples, organised by a women's *satsang* group. The leader of this group is a Punjabi woman who lives outside the village, but almost all of the regular members are Rayā women and on any given occasion more than half of those in attendance are over 50 years of age. There is a regular active core of such older women with a few middle-aged and young women, most of the latter being women of nuclear households. The *bahūs* of the older women rarely if ever attend. In addition to this regular hymn meeting, there are others held irregularly in private homes in the village, usually to celebrate some happy family event such as a child's birthday. A woman who enjoys such gatherings can easily spend several afternoons a week singing religious songs with her peers and exchanging gossip in the intervals.

When queried, very few of the older women admit to having had a serious concern with religion in their youth, and in general they attribute their present preoccupation with such activities to their newly acquired leisure and to its appropriateness to their present stage of life. 'When did I have time for it before?' they say, or 'Now that it is my time of rest I can do this'. There are a number of older women who have attached themselves as disciples of a *guru* whose main *āshram* is in a city several hundred miles away, but who spends much of the year in Delhi. He comes for several weeks each year to the village itself, where he is hosted by one of the wealthiest local Rayā families.

Despite the popularity of religious pursuits among older Rayā women, there are a significant number in the sample who seldom or never gather to sing *bhajans* (except perhaps when they are invited to a private hymn singing in the home of a close relative or neighbour). One such woman put it this way: 'I don't have time for such things—I have to take care of my buffalo. Taking care of animals is a kind of worship (*pūjā*) too, you know'.

Sexual activity in old age

One manifestation of the perception of old age as a time of detachment from the concerns of early adulthood is the tendency among aging married persons to voluntarily and deliberately cease having an active sex life once their children—and particularly their sons—are married. While there are some exceptions, as a rule cohabitation is stopped when the first son's wife comes to live in the household, if not before. There are some cases of older couples maintaining an active sex life or at least sharing a sleeping room after this, but such is neither the ideal nor the statistical norm. Those who do continue to sleep together in old age typically have no married sons, or are couples in which the woman is a younger second wife and the son the offspring of the first wife. Actually, in such cases, a joint household is rarely maintained for long after the son's marriage.

The cessation of sexual relations between a couple may be gradual and unspoken, but often it is a decision discussed and deliberately entered upon. One woman, for example, described the way that her husband had come to her on the day of their eldest son's wedding saying: 'From now on we will live together as brother and sister'. Since that day they have not shared a bed. This practice is rationalised in terms of older people not 'needing' sex, and in terms of the 'shame' or 'embarrassment' (*sharam*) that would result if parents were to engage in sex while their son and his wife are also doing so in the same house: 'It is a matter of *shūram*. When the *bahū-beṭe* are doing that, how would it look for the *sās-sasur* to be doing it too'? Public opinion seems to be a significant factor in this sense of *sharam*, for without the custom of married couples having a private bedroom or a double bed (an innovative piece of furniture nowadays routinely included in the dowry but provocative of much amusement among the older generation), it rapidly becomes general family and later, neighbourhood knowledge if an older couple continues to sleep together: 'People would make all kinds of comments. They would say, "Imagine, their *bahū* has come and still they are carrying on like that". After all, we had our time, now it is the time of the *bahū-beṭe*'.

In earlier times, when the village had a farming economy, it was usual for the men of the family to sleep in an outbuilding (*gher*) and to spend most of their leisure time there as well, coming to the main house only for meals, and for occasional surreptitious visits to their wives at night. Even today many families maintain a separate *gher* where animals are tied and where the older men sit and entertain their guests and carry on interminable card games. Many of these older men also sleep in their *gher*—if they do not have one, they are generally assigned a downstairs sitting room, usually the front room of the house, which serves the same general function. The older woman will then sleep in another room with the children, while each young married couple, and sometimes young unmarried men, are given a bedroom to themselves.

It is interesting in this connection, particularly to observers of the aging process among women in Western societies, that awareness of the menopause as a period of physical or psychological stress seems to be quite absent among Rayā women. Considerable questioning on this subject from both pre- and post-menopausal women has failed to elicit any notion that the cessation of the menstrual cycle should cause distress in women or that it should be accompanied either by marked physical symptoms or temperamental and emotional difficulties. It is generally felt that if the menstrual periods stop when a woman is still relatively young (i.e., in her thirties) she may become weakened 'because of the heat that goes from there to the head at this time.' The chief problem otherwise is considered to be the danger to eyesight, which is observed to become poor at around the time of (normal) menopause, and again is attributed to 'heat' (*garmī*) rising to the head. However, cooling foods are recommended as a sufficient antidote.

Many women express relief at the cessation of menstruation, because it is 'messy' and a 'bother,' and (for those who have sufficient sons and daughters) because it means the end of child-bearing. Of course, for many women sexual relations have already ceased by this time, for the first son is often already married by the time the mother is forty-five. The emotional upheavals that are associated with menopause in West seem puzzling to my informants, as does the idea that a woman should feel at this time that she is 'no longer a woman', that she is no longer desirable to her husband, and so on. My inquiries on the latter point were met with hilarity: 'Well, he certainly isn't going to go off and get somebody else at this point, is he'? or, 'He's an old man too, after all, what would he expect'?

This is not to say that what in the West are recognised as menopausal symptoms are totally absent for these women as they experience the physiological changes that are taking place in their bodies. But whatever symptoms these women may have, they are not associated by them with the decline in their reproductive capacity and are not even regarded as forming a complex, as being related to one another. It would be difficult indeed to entangle 'menopausal' symptoms from others which flow directly from the social-structural circumstances in which women typically find themselves during this time of life. For example, the menopause would tend to coincide roughly for most women with the time during which her children are marrying and new wives are being incorporated into the family. A woman does not need to look for physiological explanations for the tensions and stresses of these years. And as for the physical symptoms, a person's health is expected to decline gradually as he gets older. Discomforts of the kind that a doctor would associate with menopause are probably taken in their stride as part of this general process of aging. Thus, whatever physical or emotional symptoms of the menopause may be present among these women, they are given no cultural elaboration nor considered unique or peculiar to the period we characterise as the 'change of life'.

I have tried in this paper to present some observations on the lives and self-perceptions on one group of aging women in an Indian city. These observations are based on data that were still in the process of being collected, and are meant to be tentative and suggestive of the directions their analysis will take rather than conclusive and definitive. The study of aging in India is in its infancy and whatever empirical research has been done has taken the form of sociological surveys with formal interview schedules probing for quantifiable facts about the living conditions and problems of the aged, their interests and activities, their needs and attitudes.[8] Such studies serve an important purpose and are necessary in order to gain one kind of perspective on the life and social roles of older persons in India. The aims of the present study have been somewhat different, however. Hopefully, what our sample lacks in size and representativeness may be made up by what it can reveal about the cultural and social framework without which no rounded picture of the aging woman in India would be complete.

8. See, for example, W.H. Harlan, 'Social Status of the Aged in Three Indian Villages', *Vita Humana*, 7 (1964), pp. 239-252; B. Raj and B.G. Prasad, 'A Study of Rural Aged Persons in Social Profile', *The Indian Journal of Social Work*, 32 (1971), pp. 155-162; K.S. Soodan, *Aging in India* (Calcutta: Minerva Associates, 1975); and the recently completed but still unpublished study by the Delhi School of Social Work on old persons in the greater Delhi area.

Select Bibliography

Agnew, Vijay. *Elite Women in Indian Politics.* New Delhi: Vikas Publishing House, 1979.

Ahmad, Imtiaz (ed.). *Kinship and Marriage Among Muslims in India.* New Delhi: Manohar Publications, 1976.

Ahmad, Karuna. 'Women's Higher Education: Recruitment and Relevance', im Amrik Singh and Philip G. Altbach (eds.), *The Higher Learning in India.* New Delhi: Vikas Publishing House, 1974.

Ahooja-Patel, Krishna. 'Self-Reliance: The Next Step for Women', *Marga*, 5 (n. 1, 1978), 1-13.

Andrea Menefee Singh. 'Rural Urban Migration of Women Among the Urban Poor in India: Causes and Consequences', *Social Action*, 28 (Oct-Dec 1978), 326-356.

—— and Alfred de Souza. *The Position of Women in Migrant Bastis in Delhi.* New Delhi: Indian Social Institute, 1976, mimeo.

—— and Alfred de Souza. *The Urban Poor: Slum and Pavement Dwellers in the Major Cities of India.* New Delhi: Manohar Publications, 1980.

Asthana, Pratima, *Women's Movement in India.* New Delhi: Vikas Publishing House, 1974.

Banerjee, Nirmala. 'Women Workers and Development', *Social Scientist*, 6 (n. 8, 1978), 3-15.

Bardhan, Pranab. 'Some Employment and Unemployment Characteristics of Rural Women: An Analysis of NSS Data for West Bengal, 1972-73', *Economic and Political Weekly*, 13 (n. 12, March 25, 1978), 421-26.

Barnabas, A.P. 'Population Growth and Social Change: A Note on Rural Society', *Social Action*, 24 (Jan-March 1974), 25-32.

Bernard, Jessie. *The Future of Marriage*. London: Souvenir Press, 1972.

Beteille, Andre. 'The Family and Social Change in India and Other South Asian Countries', *The Economic Weekly*, 16 (n. 5-7, 1964), 237-244.

Bhasin, Kamla (ed.). *The Position of Women in India*. Bombay: Leslie Sawhney Programme of Training in Democracy, 1973.

Boserup, E. *Women's Role in Economic Development*. London: George Allen and Unwin, 1970.

Bos-Kunst, Emmy. *Women of Azam Basti: A Social Study Among Women of A Slum Area in Karachi, Pakistan*. Karachi: National Planning Commission, 1970.

Buvinic, M., N. Youssef and B. von Elm. *Women Headed Households: The Ignored Factor in Development Planning*. Washington DC: International Centre for Research on Women, 1978.

Cain, Mead, Syeda Khanam and Shamsun Nahar. 'Class, Patriarchy and Women's Work in Bangladesh', *Population and Development Review*, 5 (n. 3 September, 1978), 405-438.

Chakravorty, Shanti. 'Farm Women Labour: Waste and Exploitation', *Social Change*, 5 (March-June 1975), 9-15.

Chandrasekhar, S. *Infant Mortality, Population Growth and Family Planning in India*. London: George Allen and Unwin, 1972.

Cooney, Rosemary S. 'Female Professional Work Opportunities: A Cross-National Study', *Demography*, 12 (February 1975), 107-120.

Cormack, Margaret. *She Who Rides a Peacock: Indian Students and Social Change.* Bombay: Asia Publishing House, 1961.

——. *The Hindu Woman.* Bombay: Asia Publishing House, 1961.

Dasgupta, Kalpana. *Women on the Indian Scene: Annotated Bibliography.* New Delhi: Abhinav Publishers, 1976.

Department of Social Welfare. *Women in India: A Statistical Profile.* New Delhi: Ministry of Education and Welfare, Government of India, 1978.

de Souza, Alfred (ed.). *The Indian City: Poverty, Ecology and Urban Development.* New Delhi: Manohar Publications, 1977.

Devadas, P. Rajammal. 'Women in Agricultural Productivity and Home Improvement', *Voluntary Action,* 20 (n. 6 June, 1978), 3-7.

D'Souza, Anthony A. and Alfred de Souza (eds.). *Population Growth and Human Development.* New Delhi: Indian Social Institute, 1974.

——Anthony A. 'The Indian Family in the Seventies: An Integrated Family Policy', *Social Action,* 22 (January-March 1972), 1-15.

D'Souza, Stan and S. Rahman. 'Estimates of Fertility in Bangladesh', *Social Action,* 28 (n. 4, 1978), 367-389.

D'Souza, Stan. 'Fertility Implications of Nuptiality Patterns in South Asia', *Social Action,* 29 (n. 4, October-December, 1979), 342-376.

Dube, Leela. 'Woman's Worlds: Three Encounters', in Andre Beteille and T.N. Madan (eds.), *Encounter and Experience.* New Delhi: Vikas Publishing House, 1975, 157-177.

Dube, S.C. 'Men's and Women's Roles in India: A Sociological Review', in Barbara Ward (ed.), *Women in the New Asia.* Paris: UNESCO, 1973.

Dumont, Louis. 'Marriage in India: The Present State of the Question—III: North India in Relation to South India', *Contributions to Indian Sociology,* 9 (1966).

——. 'Dowry in Hindu Marriage: As a Social Scientist Sees it', *The Economic Weekly,* 11 (n. 15, 1959), 519-521.

Epstein, Cynthia F. *Woman's Place: Options and Limits of Professional Careers.* Berkeley: University of California Press, 1970.

Gandhi, M.K. *Women and Social Justice.* Ahmedabad: Navajivan Publishing House, fourth ed., 1958.

Goldstein, Rhoda L. *Indian Women in Transition: A Bangalore Case Study.* Metuchen, N.J.: The Scarecrow Press, 1972.

———. 'Tradition and Change in the Roles of Educated Indian Women', in Dhirendra Narain (ed.), *Explorations in the Family and Other Essays.* Bombay: Thacker and Company, 1975, 268-287.

Gore, M.S. *Urbanisation and Family Change.* Bombay: Popular Prakashan, 1968.

Gulati, Leela. 'Female Work Participation: A Study of Inter-State Differences', *Economic and Political Weekly,* 10 (Jannary 11, 1975), 35-42.

Gupta, Giri Raj. *Marriage, Religion and Society: Pattern of Change in an Indian Village.* New Delhi: Vikas Publishing House, 1974.

Hate, Chandrakala. *Changing Status of Women.* Bombay: Allied Publishers, 1969.

Hunt, Pauline. 'Cash Transactions and Household Tasks: Domestic Behaviour in Relation to Industrial Employment', *Sociological Review,* 26 (n. 3, New Series, August 1978), 555-572.

Indian Social Institute. *The Indian Family in the Change and Challenge of the Seventies.* New Delhi: Sterling Publishers, 1972.

International Labour Office. *Women Workers in a Changing Society* (Employment of Women with Family Responsibilities). Geneva: International Labour Office, 1964.

———. *Women Workers and Society: International Perspectives.* Geneva: International Labour Office, 1976.

Israel, Ben Ruth. 'Housewives and Equality: The Social Security Aspects', *Labour and Society,* 4 (n. 4, October 1979), 373-383.

Jacobson, Doranne and S. Wadley. *Women in India: Two Perspectives.* New Delhi: Manohar Publications, 1977.
Jahan, Rounaq. 'Bangladesh: The Hidden Millions', *People* (International Women's Year issue), 2 (n. 2, 1975), 18-19.
Jain, Devaki. *Women's Quest for Power.* Sahibabad: Vikas Publishing House, 1980.
Kapadia, K.M. *Marriage and Family in India.* Bombay: Oxford University Press, 1958.
Kapur, Promilla. 'The Changing Role and Status of Women', in *The Indian Family in the Change and Challenge of the Seventies.* New Delhi: Sterling Publishers, 1972.
———. *Marriage and the Working Woman in India.* New Delhi: Vikas Publishing House, 1970.
———. *The Changing Status of the Working Woman in India.* New Delhi: Vikas Publishing House, 1974.
Kapur, Rama. 'Role Conflict among Employed Housewives', *Indian Journal of Industrial Relations*, 5 (July 1969), 39-76.
Karlekar, Malavika. 'Professionalisation of Women School Teachers', *Indian Journal of Industrial Relations*, 11 (n.1, July 1975), 53-64.
Katzenstein, Mary F. 'Towards Equality: Cause and Consequences of the Political Prominence of Women in India', *Asian Survey*, 18 (n. 5, May 1978), 473-86.
Khanna, Girija and Mariamma A. Varghese. *Indian Women Today.* New Delhi: Vikas Publishing House, 1978.
Khan, Saifullah V. 'Pakistani Women in Britain', *New Community* 5 (n. 1-2, 1976).
Kolenda, Pauline M. 'Region, Caste and Family Structure: A Comparative Study of the Indian Joint Family', in Milton Singer and Bernard Cohn (eds.), *Structure and Change in Indian Society.* Chicago: Aldine Publishing Company, 1968, 339-396.
———. 'Family Structure in Village Lonikand, India: 1819, 1958 and 1967', *Contributions to Indian Sociology*, 4 (1970), 50-72.

Korson, J. Henry. 'Career Constraints Among Women Graduate Students in a Developing Society', *Journal of Comparative Family Studies* (1970), 82-100.

Krauss, Wilma Rule. 'Political Implications of Gender Roles: A Review of the Literature', *American Political Science Review*, LXVIII (December 1974), 1706-1723.

Kumar, Siva Chitra. 'Social Behaviour of Students: A Women's College in Mysore City', *Economic and Political Weekly*, 10 (n. 22, May 1975), 859-866.

Madras School of Social Work. *Working Mothers in White Collar Occupations*. Madras: Madras School of Social Work, 1956.

Mamdani, Mahmood. *The Myth of Population Control: Family, Caste and Class in an Indian Village*. New York: Monthly Review Press, 1973.

Mandelbaum, David G. *Human Fertility in India*. Berkeley, Los Angeles: University of California Press, 1974.

Martha Darling. *The Role of Women in the Economy*. Paris: Organisation for Economic Cooperation and Development, 1975.

Mazumdar, Vina. 'Women Workers in a Changing Economy'. *Yojana*, 19 (May 1, 1975), 15-17.

——. *Role of Rural Women in Development*. New Delhi: Allied Publishers, 1978.

Mazumdar, Vina and Kumud Sharma. 'Women's Studies: New Perceptions and Challenges', *Economic and Political Weekly*, 14 (n. 3, Jaunary 20, 1979), 113-120.

Meher, M.R. 'Problems of Women's Employment', *The Indian Journal of Social Work*, 32 (July 1971), 129-135.

Mitra, Asok. 'Employment of Women', *Manpower Journal*, 14 (n. 1, April-June 1978), 1-29

——. *Implications of Declining Sex Ratio in India's Population*. New Delhi: Allied Publishers, 1979.

——. et al., *The Status of Women: Household and Non-household Economic Activity*. New Delhi: Allied Publishers, 1979.

———. *The Status of Wowen: Literacy and Employment.* New Delhi: Allied Publishers, 1979.

Mukherjee, B.N. 'Status of Women as Related to Family Planning', *Journal of Population Research*, 2 (January-June 1975), 5-33.

———. 'Status of Married Women in Haryana, Tamil Nadu and Meghalaya', *Social Change*, 4 (1974), 4-17.

Nanda, B.R. (ed.). *Indian Women: From Purdah to Modernity.* New Delhi: Vikas Publishing House, 1976.

Nandi, S.B. 'Status of Women in the Polyandrous Society', *Man in India*, 57 (n. 1, 1977). 137-151.

Nath, Kamla. 'Urban Women Workers: A Preliminary Study', *The Economic and Political Weekly.* 17 (Sept. 11, 1965), 1405-1412.

———. 'Women in the Working Force in India', *The Economic and Political Weekly*, 31 (1968), 1205-1215.

OECD. *Equal Opportunities for Women.* Paris: Organisation for Economic Cooperation and Development, 1979.

Omvedt, Gail. 'Women and Rural Revolt in India', *Social Scientist*, 61 (n.1, August 1977), 1-18.

Palmer, Ingrid. 'Rural Women and the Basic Needs Approach to Development', *International Labour Review*, 115 (n. 1, Jan-Feb 1977), 97-107.

Papanek, Hanna. 'Purdah in Pakistan: Seclusion and Modern Occupations for Women', *Journal of Marriage and the Family*, 33 (August 1971), 517-530.

———. 'Men, Women and Work: Reflections on the Two-Person Career', in Joan Huber (ed.), *Changing Women in a Changing Society.* Chicago: University of Chicago Press, 1973, 90-110.

———. 'Women in South and South-East Asia: Issues and Research', *Social Change*, 7 (March 77), 24-37.

Pastner, Carroll McC. 'Accommodations to Purdah: A Female Perspective', *Journal of Marriage and the Family*, 36 (n. 2, 1974).

Punekar, Vijaya. 'Fertility, Education and Social Change', *Sociological Bulletin*, 23 (March 1974), 99-111.

Ramanujam, B.K. 'The Indian Family in Transition: Changing Roles and Relationships', *Social Action*, 22 (Jan-March 1972), 16-25.

Ramu, G.N. *Family and Caste in Urban India*. New Delhi: Vikas Publishing House, 1977.

Reid, Elizabeth. 'Women at a Standstill: The Need for Radical Change', *International Labour Review*, 3 (n. 6, June 1975), 458-468.

Rittter, Kathleen V. and Lowell L. Hargens. 'Occupational Positions and Class Identifications of Married Working Women: A Test of the Asymmetry Hypothesis', *American Journal of Sociology*, 80 (January 1975), 934-948.

Rojas-Aleta, Isabel, Teresita L. Silva and Christine P. Eleazor. *A Profile of Filipino Women*. Manila: Philippine Business for Social Progress, 1977.

Rosi, Alice. 'A Biosocial Perspective on Parenting', *Daedalus*, 106 (n. 2, Spring 1977), 1-31.

Ross, Aileen D. *The Hindu Family in Its Urban Setting*. Bombay: Oxford University Press, 1961.

Rowbotham, T. *Women, Resistance and Revolution*. Harmondsworth: Penguin Books, 1974.

Ruether, Rosemary Radford (ed.). *Religion and Sexism: Images of Women in Jewish and Christian Trends*. New York: Simon and Schuster, 1974.

——. *New Woman: New Earth*. New York: Seabury, 1975.

Sachidananda. 'Social Structure, Status and Mobility Patterns: The Case of Tribal Women', *Man in India*, 58 (n. 1, Jan-March 1978), 1-12.

Schavern, Wassen-van Paula. 'Planning the Emancipation of Women', *Planning and Development in the Netherlands*, 8 (n. 1, 1976), 4-16.

Schoonenboom, I.J. and H.M. in't Veld-Largeneld. 'Values Affecting Women's Position in Society', *Planning and Development in The Netherlands*, 8 (n.1, 1976), 17-33.

Seear, B.N. *Re-entry of Women to the Labour Market After an Interruption in Employment*. Paris: Organisation for Economic Cooperation and Development, 1971.

Shah, A.M. *The Household Dimension of the Family in India.* New Delhi: Orient Longman, 1973.

Sharma, Ursula. 'The Problem of Village Hinduism: Fragmentation and Integration', *Contributions to Indian Sociology* (New Series), 4 (December 1970), 1-21.

Singh, K.P. *Status of Women and Population Growth in India.* New Delhi: Munshiram Manoharlal Publishers, 1979.

S.N.D.T. University. *Women in India.* Bombay, SNDT University, 1975.

Srinivas, M.N. *Changing Position of Indian Women.* New Delhi: Oxford University Press, 1978.

—— and E.A.Ramaswamy. *Culture and Human Fertility in India.* New Delhi: Oxford University Press, 1977.

Standing, Guy. 'Education and Female Participation in the Labour Force', *International Labour Review*, 114 (n. 3, Nov-Dec 1976), 281-297.

—— and Glen Sheehan (eds.). *Labour Force Participation in Low Income Countries.* Geneva: International Labour Office, 1978.

Status of Women. A Symposium on the Discriminated Section of Society. *Seminar*, 165 (May 1973).

Strober, Myra. 'Women Economists: Career Aspirations, Education and Training', *American Economic Review*, L15 (May 1975), 92-99.

Szalal, Alexander. 'The Situation of Women in the Light of Time-Budget Research'. World Conference of the International Women's Year. New York: United Nations, E/CON. 66/BP/6, April 15, 1975.

Takahashi, Nobuko. 'Women's Wages in Japan and the Question of Equal Pay'. *International Labour Review*, 3 (January 1975), 51-68.

Tellis-Nayak, J. and S. Costa-Pinto. *Towards Self-Reliance: Income Generation for Women.* New Delhi: Indian Social Institute, 1979.

Tinker, H. *The Banyan Tree: Overseas Emigrants from India, Pakistan and Bangladesh.* Oxford: Oxford University Press, 1977.

Vatuk, Sylvia. *Kinship and Urbanisation: White Collar Migrants in North India.* Berkeley, Los Angeles: University of California Press, 1972.

Vreede-De Stuers, Cora. *Parda: A Study of Muslim Women's Life in Northern India.* Assen: Van Gorcum and Company, 1968.

——. 'Attitudes of Jaipur Girl Students Towards Fami y Life', in Dhirendra Narain (ed.) *Explorations in the Family and Other Essays.* Bombay: Thacker and Company, 1975.

Wasi, Muriel (ed.). *The Educated Women in Indian Society Today.* New Delhi: Tata McGraw-Hill, 1971.

Watson, J.L. *Between Two Cultures: Migrants and Minorities in Britain.* Oxford: Blackwells, 1977.

Index

Abortion, 176-178; see Legislation
Adoption, 173-174; see Legislation
Age at marriage, 37, 42, 145, 150, 154, 259, 296; see Marriage
Ahmad, Imtiaz, 74
Ahmad, Shadbano, 203
Akram, M., 276
Ali, M. Ameer, 201
Altekar, A.S., 184, 185
Anand, Kulwant, 130, 131, 133, 134
Anandamayi, 187
Arya Samaj, 185

Ballard, C., 275
Banerjee, Nirmala, 89
Farot, A.J., 171
Bean, L.L., 100
Bean, S.S., 241
Belwinkel, Maren, 78
Beteille, Andre, 66
Bhatt, Ela, 63, 92
Bhatty, Zarina, 66, 200, 209
Blacker, J.G.C., 52
Bos-Kunst, Emmy, 70
Boserup, Ester, 50
Brass, W., 36
Bruce, Judith, 92

Brown, R., 242
Buddhism, 187, 188
Bujra, J., 214, 279
Buvinic, M., 38, 39

Caplan, P., 214, 279, 284
Caste, 76-79, 242, 245, 247, 251, 252, 254, 262, 288; Brahmins, 77, 217, 243, 245, 246, 247, 248, 249, 253, 257, 260, 261, 262; Divarus, 243, 245, 246, 249, 252, 257, 260, 261; dominant caste, 288; Girijans, 243, 245, 249, 252, 253; Harijans, 243, 248, 249, 251, 252; Lingayats, 243, 245, 249, 252; Nayars, 76; Potters, 243, 252, 255; Sudras, 243, 246, 247, 248, 249; Vokkaligas, 243, 245, 253; see Marriage, Women
Chandrasekhar, S., 177
Chatterjee, Mary, 89
Christianity, 182, 183, 187, 189-193; anti-feminism of, 191; model of womanhood, 192-193; see Religion
Cohn, Bernard, 67
Cormack, Margaret, 75

Dahya, B., 264
Dandekar, R.N., 186
Darling, Martha, 52
Daughter, 290, 291, 292, 300; attitude to, 46, 201
Daughter-in-law, 296, 298, 299, 300, 301, 302, 303, 304, 305, 306
Deere, C.D., 49
Denti, Ettore, 100
Derrett, J.D.M, 173
de Souza, Alfred, 74
D'Souza, Stan, 33, 36
D'Souza, Victor, 126, 127, 129, 131, 136
Dirasse, L., 45
Divorce, 76, 77, 143, 148, 155, 157, 166, 167, 168, 169, 170, 171, 203, 204, 261; alimony, 204; attitude to, 166, 171; divorced women, 38, 39, 40, 63, 101, 166; judicial separation, 170, 289; and remarriage, 77, 170, 203; *see* Legislation
Dixon, Ruth, 92
Dowry, 76, 85, 157, 167, 202; bride price, 76, 77, 85; *mehr*, 204; *see* Legislation, Marriage
Dube, Leela, 169
Durand, John D., 50, 51

Education, attitude to, 259; and employment, 125, 126, 128, 129, 133, 135, 136; and marriage, 84, 259; *see* Employment, Women
Employment, agricultural, 50, 87, 89, 110, 126, 260; asymmetry hypothesis, 132-135; and caste, 77, 78, 89, 81; constraints, 39, 44, 51, 88, 120, 142, 147, 149, 152, 161, 162; curvilinear relationship, 121, 128-129, 135-136; displacement of women workers 48, 49, 89; and education, 114, 121, 133, 135; equal opportunity, 43, 44, 45, 88, 149, 165; food-for-work programme, 141-164; in domestic service, 45, 107, 110, 119; in informal urban sector, 51, 57, 63, 65; measurement of economic activity, 32, 48-50, 51, 52, 56, 57, 97; occupational mobility, 79, 110; occupational prestige, 106, 126, 127, 131, 133; occupational range, 106, 107, 108,110,111, 119, 125, 279; occupational structure, 106-113, 126, 128-129, 130-131, 137; part-time, 48, 52, 53; primary family supporters, 63, 148, 158, 159; professional women, 107, 110, 120; and protective legislation, 90; and religion, 102; rural, 108-110, 111, 120; self-employment, 51, 63, 92, 111, 119, 148; turnover of women, 90; unpaid family workers, 50, 51, 57, 147; urban, 103, 106-108, 110, 111, 114, 119, 120, 127; *see* Legislation, Marriage, *Purdah*, Women
Enjen, Claude, 225
Etiquette, 24-262; *akka*, 249, 253, 254, 256; *amma*, 245, 246, 247, 249, 250, 252, 262; and changing relationship, 257-261; dimension of power, 246-250; forms of address, 241, 246 252, 256; *HuDugi*, 246, 247, 248, 255, 256, 262; kinship terms, 246-250, 253; plural forms, 251; use of husband's name, 261, 262; use of personal name, 246; *see* Caste
Ewing, Gulshan, 165, 178

Family, disposition of income, 89; egalitarian relations in, 203, 259; family life-cycle, 34, 39, 40, 60; family status consistency, 132, 133, 135; joint family, 40, 75, 79, 80, 81; nuclear, 40, 80, 138, 139; power relations in, 81, 82, 89, 208, 209, 248, 258; sharing child rearing, 81, 82; sharing household tasks, 81, 82, 301; structure

of, 40, 79-82, 91; see Caste, Marriage, Methodology
Farooq, Ghazi M., 100, 102, 121
Foote, Nelson M., 126
Francis, David R , 91

Geertz, Clifford, 241
Goldstein, Rhoda, 77, 81, 84
Gore, M.S., 80
Gough, Kathleen E., 67

Habib, Miriam, 34
Hackenberg, B., 68
Hargens, Lowell L., 137, 139
Harper, Edward B., 73
Hate, Chandrakala A , 73, 82, 83
Hill, K., 46, 47
Hinduism, 182, 186; *Bhakti* movement, 72, 185; see Religion
Hunt, S., 277
Husband, 38, 41, 53, 63, 64, 65, 67, 80, 82, 114, 120, 121, 126, 128, 129, 132, 135, 139, 147, 150, 154, 155, 159, 168, 169, 202, 228, 306, 30?; and power in family, 202, 259; relationship with wife, 63, 258, 259, 306; roles of, 145, 146, 205, 260; see Family, Wife

Ibbetson, D.C.T., 199
Islam, 166, 182, 183, 184, 238; attitude to women, 201, 206, 207; conversion to, 199; hypothesis of Islamism, 102; see Muslims, Religion

Jacobson, Doranne, 73, 74, 216, 218
Jain, M.K., 36
Jainism, 187
Jeffery, P., 264
Joshi, Heather, 88

Kapur, Promilla, 75, 83
Karlekar, Malavika, 64
Karve, Irawati, 70

Karwanski, R.A., 99, 122
Kassebaum, Gene, 79
Khan, V. Saifullah, 44, 264, 267, 269, 271, 272, 275, 276, 277, 280, 283, 284
Khare, R.S., 224
Kolenda, Pauline, 71, 74, 77, 79, 80, 81
Korson, J. Henry, 121, 204
Kutty, A.R., 168, 169

Legislation, and abortion, 176-178; and adoption, 173-174; customary law, 168; equality before law, 165, 168, 170; Hindu Code Bill, 200; inheritance, 171-173; personal laws, 166, 200, 211; protective labour legislation, 90, 174-176; see Divorce, Dowry, Employment, Marriage
Lomas, G.B. Gillian, 266
Lubell, Harold, 78
Lynch, Owen M., 208

Madan, T.N., 70
Majumdar, D.N., 188
Mankekar, Kamla, 175, 176
Marriage, 67, 82-86, 90, 166-168, 173, 194, 274, 289, 290; arranged marriage, 83, 84, 85, 202, 207, 260, 261, 274; and caste, 66, 76; ceremonies, 200; child marriage, 150, 166, 185; choice and consent of girl, 202, 261, 274; cousin marriage, 150, 166, 185; and education, 84, 86; and employment, 90; and kinship, 67, 76, 80, 82-86; matrimonial advertisements, 84; see Employment, Family, Women
Mehta, Rama, 216
Methodology, attitudinal studies, 65-67; caste factor, 69, 76-79; choice of enumerators, 53, 55, 57, 59, 65, 102, 108; social factor, 69-70; cultural factor, 38, 69-70; family structure, 79-82; in studies

of women, 32, 34, 35, 37, 40, 41, 47, 50-53, 61, 62-69, 71, 86; invisibility factor, 64, 65, 86, 91, 145-146, 164; participant observation, 59; research issues, 61, 62, 86-93; regional factor, 70-71; religious factor, 69, 71-76; selection of staff, 54, 55, 56, 58, 102; survey research, 59, 64, 68, 69, 96, 98, 103, 108, 112; time-use surveys, 35, 53-54; *see* Caste, Family, Marriage, Migrants

Mies, Maria, 197

Migrants, Bangladeshi, 265, 266, 270, 272, 274; colonial framework of migration, 269-272, 282; cultural factor, 263, 264, 267, 268, 273, 274, 277, 279, 283; housing of, 266, 267; Indian migrants, 265, 266, 267, 270, 271, 272, 279, 282, 283; isolation of, 269, 272, 277, 278, 281; life-styles of 263, 270, 272, 275, 276, 278; living conditions of, 266-269; mechanics of migration, 271, 272, 273, 282; motivation to migrate, 44, 63, 64, 67, 87, 88, 271, 281; Pakistani, 265, 266, 270, 272, 273, 274, 276, 279, 282; problems of adaptation, 263, 272, 276-281, 284; sex-ratio of, 87; women migrants, 43, 63, 64, 67, 86, 87, 88, 2 4, 268, 272-276, 278, 280; women migrant workers, 274, 278, 279, 284; *see* Marriage, Women

Minattur, J., 178

Muslims, 66, 199; Ashrafs, 200, 201, 203, 204, 205, 208; attitude to education, 206; concept of woman, 201; converts, 199; divorce among, 168-169; employment of women, 206, 207; non-Ashrafs, 200, 201, 203, 204, 205, 208; and personal law, 166, 200, 211; property rights of women, 204; Muslim women, 66, 75, 199-211, 219, 283; *see* Employment, Religion

Nath, Kamla, 126, 127

Old women, 287-309; concept of rest and service, 298-304; definition of, 288; life-stages, 288, 295-296, 303; menopausal symptoms, 307, 308; patterns of residence, 290-291; perception of, 288-289; preparation for old age, 291-295; religious participation, 304-305; sexual activity of, 306-308; work activities, 297, 301-304; *see* Family, Women

Omvedt, Gail, 67, 90
Oppenheimer, Valerie K., 138, 139

Papanek, Hanna, 106, 215, 219
Parsons, Talcott, 138, 139
Pastner, Carroll McC., 106
Premi, M.K., 63
Purdah, 117, 121, 185, 202, 203, 210, 213-239, 267, 274, 277; concept of, 202, 213; evaluation of social spa e, 220-228; Hindu *purdah*, 214; and married women, 228, 229; Muslim *purdah*, 214; negative effects of, 234-237; One's 'own place', 230 232; prestige symbol, 203, 208, 209; private space, 266-228; public space, 220, 221, 223, 224, 238; and relations with women, 232-234; and structure of social relations, 216; use of public space, 218-219; *see* Marriage, Methodology, Women

Rack, P., 277
Ramu, G.N., 79
Rao, M.S.A., 87
Rao, Seshagiri, 92
Religion, 69, 71-76, 179-197; attitudes to women, 188, 195-197; ascetical

ideals, 184, 187, 191-192; and caste, 74; and education, 75, 185; female deities, 73, 181; 'high' religion, 73, 179, 186; institutionalised roles, 182, 183; popular religion, 73; priestesses, 181; religious beliefs, 73, 74, 179; religious values, 72, 74; status of women in, 72, 179, 180, 183, 184, 187, 195-197, 204, 207; *see* Christianity, Islam, Ritual
Ritter, Kathleen V., 137, 139
Rituals, 73, 185, 249, 250; exclusion of women, 181, 183; life-crisis ceremonies, 261; ritual status of women, 181, 182, 183; *upanayana* rite, 185; *see* Religion
Rogers, S., 215
Ruether, Rosemary, 193
Russell, Letty M., 192

Saeed, Kishwar, 107
Safa, Helen, 90
Saiyed, A.R., 203
Saraswati, Swami Dayanand, 185
Segal, R., 270
Sex division of labour, 145, 146, 148, 163, 203, 301; sex based stereotypes, 32, 35, 49, 57, 59; sex biases, 35, 49; sex ratio, 36, 43, 47, 87, 88; sex roles, 203; sex segregation, 65; *see* Methodology, *Purdah*, Religion, Statistics
Shah, A.M., 40
Shah, Makhdoom, 56, 101
Shah, Nasra, 56, 101, 107, 117
Sharma, Ursula, 213, 214
Singer, Milton, 79
Singh, Andrea M., 45, 64, 66, 72, 74, 78, 80, 87, 89, 92
Smith, David J., 266, 268, 272
Smock, Audrey, 43, 43
Snow, Robert, 90
Son, 292, 294, 296, 300, 306
Soodan, K.S., 309
Srinivas, M.N., 76, 77, 209

Standing, G.M., 53
Statistics, 33, 34, 35, 43, 45, 46, 51, 52 56, 58, 59, 61, 86, 87; census data, 32, 35, 37, 38, 39, 40, 41, 52, 58, 60, 64, 67, 96, 97, 98, 103, 112; data 'producers' 34, 57, 59; data 'users', 34, 57, 59; microstudies, 40, 59, 64; on women, 33, 43, 44, 45, 46, 48, 51, 52, 57, 58, 60, 86; and national planning, 38, 48, 54, 60, 88; quality of d ta, 33, 35, 47, 48, 56, 59, 68, 97, 102, 108; and status of women, 33, 60; *see* Employment, Methodology

Tavard, G.H., 189, 190, 192
Tinker, Hugh, 271
Torrado, S., 40

Unni, K.R., 84

Vaid, K.N., 174
Vatuk, Sylvia, 82
Von Furer-Haimendorf, C., 72
Vreede-De Stuers, Cora, 77, 214

Wadley Susan, 73, 74
Walle, E. van de, 47
Watson, J.L., 264, 269, 281
Widow, 38, 39, 41, 63, 101, 145, 148, 151, 155, 168, 260, 261, 289; marriage of, 77, 85, 166, 203; situation of, 39; *see* Caste, Religion, Statistics
Wiebe, Paul, 79
Wife, 51, 273, 275, 289, 293, 296; education of, 127, 128, 133, 135, 136; occupational status of, 126, 128, 130, 132, 135, 138, 139; working wives, 114, 280; *see* Education, Family, Methodology
Wilson, A., 284
Women, basic services for, 90, 91; dependency assumption, 62, 64,

65, 88, 145, 152, 158; education of, 33, 40, 42-43, 125, 133, 135, 145, 157, 158, 259; fertility patterns of, 145; identity and self-image of, 51, 62, 68, 77, 193; invisibility of, 64, 145; labour force participation of, 33, 34, 44, 48, 49, 95-123, 125, 127, 128, 130, 133, 136, 138, 194; life expectancy of, 46, 48; motivation to work, 113, 118, 121, 128, 143, 149; policies regarding women, 62, 91; in religious traditions, 179-197, 204, 207; and social change, 194-195, 210-211; submission to male authority, 202; *see* Education Employment, Family, Methodology, Statistics

Yalman, Nur, 73, 73